D1429094

HISTORY

OF

THE COMMONWEALTH

AND

PROTECTORATE

Volume IV.—1655-1656

WINDRUSH
PRESS
GLOUCESTERSHIRE · ENGLAND

HISTORY

OF

THE COMMONWEALTH

AND

PROTECTORATE

1649—1656

BY

SAMUEL RAWSON GARDINER

HON. D.C.L. OXFORD ; LITT.D. CAMBRIDGE ; LL.D. EDINBURGH ; PH.D. GÜTTINGEN:
FELLOW OF MERTON COLLEGE ; HONORARY STUDENT OF CHRISTCHURCH ;
FELLOW OF KING'S COLLEGE, LONDON

IN FOUR VOLUMES

VOLUME IV.—1655-1656

THE WINDRUSH PRESS

GLOUCESTERSHIRE · ENGLAND

History of the Commonwealth and Protectorate
Volume Four
was first published by
Longmans, Green and Co.
in 1903

This edition first published by
The Windrush Press
Windrush House
Main Street, Adlestrop
Gloucestershire GL56 0YN
in 1989

ISBN 0 900075 95 3 (cased)
ISBN 0 900075 01 5 (paperback)

British Library Cataloguing in Publication Data

Gardiner, Samuel Rawson
History of the Commonwealth and Protectorate: 1649–
1656.
Vol. 4, 1655–1656
1. England, 1625–1660
I. Title
942.06'2

ISBN 0-900075-95-3 (cased)
ISBN 0-900075-01-5 (paperback)

The publishers regret that it has been impossible to include
the coloured pull-out maps of the original edition.

Printed and bound in Great Britain by
Biddles Ltd, Guildford and King's Lynn

CONTENTS

OF

THE FOURTH VOLUME

CHAPTER XLI

THE LIMITS OF TOLERATION

CHAPTER XLII

MORAL ORDER

CHAPTER XLIII

THE PROTECTORATE AND THE CORPORATIONS

CHAPTER XLIV

THE CROMWELLIAN SETTLEMENT OF IRELAND

CHAPTER XLV

HISPANIOLA AND JAMAICA

CHAPTER XLVI

THE BREACH WITH SPAIN

CHAPTER XLVII

THE PROTESTANT INTEREST

CHAPTER XLVIII

COLONISATION AND DIPLOMACY

CHAPTER XLIX

PARLIAMENTARY ELECTIONS

MAPS

THE COMMONWEALTH

AND

PROTECTORATE

CHAPTER XLI

THE LIMITS OF TOLERATION

THE Royalists, against whom the energy of the Major-Generals was directed, were far from being the only enemies of the Protector. As the strength of the partisans of the Stuarts lay in their appeal to 'the known laws,' the strength of the Republicans lay in their championship of the supremacy of Parliament, though they might differ as to the mode in which that assembly was to be chosen. Of those who adhered to the ancient methods, one of the most unbending was Ludlow, who had slipped away from Ireland in October in defiance of the Protector's orders. He had no sooner landed than he was arrested and placed in confinement in Beaumaris Castle, where he was offered liberty on the sole condition of signing a bond similar to that by which Royalists engaged themselves not to take part in any conspiracy against the Government. For some time he met this demand with a blank refusal, though in the end he was persuaded to sign an engagement to take no step against the Protector, at least till he had presented himself before him at Whitehall.

1655.
Royalists and Republicans.

Oct.
Ludlow's confinement in Beaumaris Castle.

When at last, on December 13, Ludlow made his appearance
before Oliver, he declared his readiness to submit to the
Government and his ignorance of any design at that
time formed against it. " But," he added, " if Providence open a way and give an opportunity of appearing on behalf of the people, I cannot consent to tie my hands
beforehand, and oblige myself not to lay hold of it." Oliver
appears to have thought that an enemy so outspoken could not
be really dangerous, and set him at liberty to do his worst.[1]

Dec. 13.
Ludlow at
Whitehall.

Long experience had shown that Lilburne's influence over
the crowd was more dangerous than Ludlow's doctrinaire
attachment to Parliamentarism. Yet, on giving
assurance that he would maintain a peaceable demeanour, he was relieved from exile in Jersey and
brought over to Dover Castle. He had not been long in his new
prison when he wrote to his wife that he was now one of ' those
preciousest, though most contemptible people called
Quakers,' and had consequently abandoned his
militant career for ever. The letter fell into the
hands of Fleetwood, who, ever on the alert to alleviate the lot
of sectaries, showed it to the Protector. Oliver was, however,
obdurate.[2] A Quaker Lilburne might indeed cease to stir up
the populace in defence of the outraged laws, but it was hardly
possible for anyone connected with Government to contemplate
with equanimity the idea of his heading bands of fanatics bent
on breaking up congregations and insulting preaching ministers
as hirelings and dead dogs. His confinement at
Dover was therefore prolonged, though his treatment
there was far more lenient than it had been in
Jersey.[3] Here he remained till in August 1657 the deputy

Oct.
Lilburne in
Dover
Castle.

He declares
himself a
Quaker.

His im-
prisonment
at Dover.

---

[1] Ludlow's *Memoirs*, ed. Firth, i. 427–36. On the date of the
interview, see Mr. Firth's note at p. 432 ; and compare Whiteley to
Nicholas, Jan. $\frac{10}{20}$, *S.P. Dom.* cxx. 27.

[2] The accepted story of Lilburne's liberation is derived from Wood's
Athenæ, iii. 353, but is contradicted by the evidence in *The Resurrection
of John Lilburne*, E, 880, 2.

[3] Council Order Book, *Interr.* I, 76, p. 544.

governor of the Castle allowed him liberty on parole that he might be present at his wife's confinement at Eltham. When the news of his temporary release reached Whitehall, a peremptory order was issued commanding his return to prison within ten days. On August 29,[1] however, just as the period of grace was about to expire, the turbulent agitator breathed his last. He was far in advance of his age in upholding the doctrine of popular sovereignty, but his repeated warnings against the danger of throwing aside respect for law were appropriate to the needs of his time, though given with unnecessary asperity, and with a complete ignorance of the political conditions which limit the activity of practical statesmen.

1657.
Aug. 29.
His death.

At the opposite end of the scale from Lilburne and the Levellers were the men of the Fifth Monarchy. If they had contented themselves with proclaiming the approaching reign of the saints, they would have been in no danger from the Protector. What stirred him to take action against them was that they were never weary of asserting that the reign of the saints was incompatible with the tyranny of that enemy of God, Oliver Cromwell—assertions greedily welcomed by ignorant men, steeped in the phraseology of the Scriptures, but having no real understanding of the conditions under which the exhortations and prophecies they adopted had been addressed to the Hebrew world. How difficult it was to silence men of this type was shown in the cases of Feake and Rogers, who were removed to the Isle of Wight in October.[2] Of the two, Feake gave the least trouble. It is true that he succeeded in making his escape to London; but when he was re-arrested, he was allowed to remain, under the guard of a single soldier, in a house rented by himself,[3] doubtless in consequence of an engagement to abstain from political allusions in his sermons. Rogers was less

Republicans
and Fifth
Monarchy
men.

Oct. 9.
Feake and
Rogers in
the Isle of
Wight.

---

[1] Petition of Lilburne's widow, Nov. 4, 1657, *S.P. Dom.* clvii. 73.

[2] Downing to Clarke, Nov. 8, 10, *Clarke Papers*, iii. 6, 11.

[3] Feake's Preface to *The Prophets Isaiah and Malachi* is dated from

easily controlled.   He was permitted to take up his abode in
a country house near Freshwater, till his persuasive tongue
attracted the peasants of the neighbourhood to drink in his
Rogers per- denunciations of the Protector.   As he positively
sists in de- refused to hold his peace, there was nothing for it
nouncing the
Protector. but to send him into closer confinement at Carisbrooke, where he found a sympathetic fellow-prisoner in
Harrison.   Even here crowds flocked to listen to the full-
flavoured denunciations of the tyrant which he delivered from
the window of his cell, the soldiers themselves often finding
pretexts for remaining within earshot.   The gaoler and his
subordinates, who were responsible for Rogers's
His ill-treat- silence, were not unnaturally furious, and revenged
ment at
Carisbrooke. themselves after the rough manner of their kind.
They dragged the bedding from beneath him, allowed his
provisions to run short, ill-treated his sickly wife, and flung
his maidservant out of doors, after stripping her clothes from
her back.[1]

It would be unreasonable to hold the Protector personally
responsible for the excesses of his officers.   On the other hand,
if his views on toleration did not quite reach the
Oliver's
practical standard of the nineteenth century, they were in
tolerance. advance of all but the choicest spirits of the day in
which he lived, whilst his practice time after time outran
his profession.   Again and again he had associated himself
with the opinion that blasphemy and atheism, whether they
were dangerous to the Government or not, were insufferable in
a Christian State.   Yet, when he was called on to put his
opinion in practice, his generosity of spirit proved too strong
for his theories, and he showed himself anxious to alleviate the
lot of the sufferers, if not to remit entirely the penalties imposed
on them by law.

The Protector's dealings with Biddle furnish a case in point.

his own hired house.   He does not say what was its locality, but as we
have no hint of his having been sent back to the Isle of Wight, it may be
presumed that it was somewhere in London.

[1] Rogers, *Jegar Sahadutha*, E, 919, 9.

In the summer of 1655, after his liberation on bail,[1] Biddle was

Biddle
again in
trouble. again in trouble, not altogether by his own fault. A Baptist named Griffin challenged him to defend his creed in public, and Biddle naturally, if imprudently, took up the glove. The disputation, opened in

June 28.
A disputa-
tion at
St. Paul's. St. Paul's on June 28, was adjourned to the following week ; but before the appointed day arrived Biddle was arrested by an order from the Council.[2] The Lord Mayor, in committing him for trial, hinted that he might be exposed to the monstrous penalties of the Presbyterian

July 27.
The Council
refuses to
release him. Blasphemy Ordinance of 1648.[3] On July 27 the Council, which was evidently set against him, passed over his petition for redress. In September, when

Sept.
An appeal
to the Pro-
tector, who
refuses to
intervene. the day of his trial was approaching, his supporters presented a petition to the Protector himself, in which they alleged that Biddle's case was covered by the articles of the Instrument which assured liberty of conscience to all who professed faith in God by Jesus Christ. To this allegation Oliver sternly replied 'that the liberty of conscience provided for in those articles should never, while he hath any interest in the Government, be stretched so far as to countenance them who deny the divinity of our Saviour, or to bolster up any blasphemous opinions contrary to the fundamental verities of religion.'[4] A week later, exasperated at the discovery that the wording of the petition had been altered after some of the signatures had been appended, he used even

---

[1] See vol. iii. p. 258.

[2] Council Order Book, *Interr.* I, 76, p. 155. There is nothing in *A True State of the Case* (E, 848, 12), an account of the matter drawn up by Biddle's followers, to show that Griffin appealed to the secular arm. It is said that the informer was a Mr. Brookbank, but the fact that a public disputation had been held must have been notorious.

[3] There is, however, nothing to show that the trial would have been held under the Presbyterian Blasphemy Ordinance, or that, if an attempt had been made so to hold it, the Court would not have ruled that the ordinance was superseded by the later Blasphemy Act. The Lord Mayor's *obiter dictum* could not possibly settle a question of law.

[4] *Merc. Pol.*, E, 854, 1.

stronger language. If Biddle, he declared, were in the right he himself and all other Christians were no better than idolaters. No countenance should be given to the avowal of such opinions. Yet, firm as this declaration was, it was not

Oct. 5. Biddle removed to the Scilly Isles. followed by corresponding acts. On October 5 the Council, with the full concurrence of the Protector, ordered the removal of Biddle to the Scilly Isles.[1] The act of the Protector may have been illegal, but it was undoubtedly one of kindness to the sufferer, who would have had harder measure at the hands of a court of law.

The unpopularity of Socinians, however, was slight in comparison with the unpopularity of ' Quakers.' Magistrates

Unpopularity of the ' Quakers.' detested them for their insolence in refusing to acknowledge the dignity of local authority by bowing or removing their hats, whilst they alienated the masses by condemning their revelries. Religious people of fixed opinions were irritated not only by the pertinacity of their arguments, but by the unseemly interruption of their favourite preachers. Behind all this was a widely-spread conviction that the doctrine of the inner light was a blasphemous assumption of the personal inspiration of the Almighty. In the summer of 1655, in the course of a missionary tour in the West, Fox

Fox at Kingsbridge, arrived at Kingsbridge. Seeking a lodging at an inn, he addressed the tipplers, warning them that it was time to receive light from Christ. At once the innkeeper, fearing a diminution of his custom, stepped up to the promulgator of a doctrine so dangerous to his interests. "Come," he said, holding a candle in his hand, " here is a light

and at Menheniot. for you to go into your chamber." At Menheniot Fox, according to his own account, succeeded in making a ' priest confess he was a minister made and maintained by the State.' At St. Ives he and his companions were

---

[1] *Merc. Pol.*, E, 854, 1. Council Order Book, *Interr.* I, 76, pp. 326, 328. On Oct. 24 there was a petition to the Council from two stationers, asking that steps might be taken against a book with the title of *Præadamitæ*, on the ground that it cast a slur on the Biblical account of the Creation.

hustled in the street and brought before one Peter Ceely, a

He is
arrested at
St. Ives, and
sent to
Launceston
gaol.

justice of the peace, who sent them off as prisoners to Launceston gaol, apparently on suspicion that they were Roman Catholic missionaries in disguise.[1] On the way they met Desborough, on his first visit to his district as Major-General, and reproved him for speaking against the light of Christ, with the result that he refused to interfere in their favour.

After many sufferings the imprisoned 'Quakers' were brought at the spring assizes before Chief Justice Glyn, who

1656.
Fox before
Glyn.

rebuked them for refusing to remove their hats. On this Fox asked where there was any mention in Scripture of a magistrate ordering that hats should be taken off. "If," he added, "the law of England doth command any such thing, show me that law, either written or printed." "I do not carry my law books on my back," replied Glyn sharply, and ordered the gaoler to remove the prisoners. Soon afterwards, however, Glyn, imagining that he had found a satisfactory repartee, directed that they should again be placed at the bar. "Come," said the judge, "where had they hats from Moses to Daniel? Come, answer me! I have you fast now."

It was ill discussing points of Scripture with Fox. "Thou mayest read in the third of Daniel," was the prompt reply, "that the three children were cast into the fiery furnace with their coats, their hose, and their hats on." "Take them away, gaoler!" cried the discomfited judge. Yet in the end he

Fox fined for
contempt of
Court and
sent back to
prison.

mastered his annoyance, and taking no heed of the accusation brought against the prisoners—whatever it may have been—contented himself with fining them twenty marks apiece for contempt of court, and

---

[1] In his *Journal* Fox says that Ceely 'tendered the oath of abjuration to us, whereupon I put my hand in my pocket and drew forth an answer to it which had been given to the Protector.' The oath referred to was probably the one required from Roman Catholics, and may be connected with the delusion that the 'Quakers' were Roman Catholics in disguise. Fox's objection was not to its substance, but to its being an oath.

ordering that they should remain in prison till that sum had been paid. Glyn probably did not count on the obduracy with which Fox was likely to stand out against the admission that he had committed a fault where he could see no fault at all, and, noisome as was the atmosphere of a gaol in those days, the imprisoned 'Quakers' preferred to endure every hardship rather than acknowledge that they could justly be required to uncover their heads in the presence of a fellow-mortal, however exalted his worldly rank might be. An attempt to induce Glyn to reconsider his sentence, on the ground that it was unsupported by law, having naturally failed, one of Fox's devoted followers, Humphrey Norton, sought out the Protector, offering to give himself up to imprisonment in Doomsdale—the filthiest dungeon in the filthy gaol—if his teacher might be liberated in his stead. Such devotion roused Oliver's astonished admiration. "Which of you," he asked, turning to the Councillors who stood around him, "would do so much for me if I were in the same condition?" To Norton he could but reply that it would be a breach of the law to imprison him with no charge hanging over his head.[1]

*1656.
An appeal to the Protector.*

Yet, though the Protector refused to commit an innocent man, the right of pardon was in his hands, and he transmitted orders to Desborough to let the imprisoned 'Quakers' go free.[2] Desborough accordingly informed them that the gaol-doors were open to them if they would promise to go home and preach no more. On their raising objections, he asked them to give an engagement to comply with his wishes 'if the Lord permitted.' This compromise was, however, swept aside by the indomitable 'Quakers,' who told the Major-General that they knew it to be the will of God that they should 'go to speak at some other place.' Desborough upon this refused to have anything more to do with them ; but a month later Colonel Bennet, the master

*Aug.
Desborough ordered to liberate the 'Quakers.'*

---

[1] Fox's *Journal* (ed. 1891), i. 265–318. Mr. Hodgkin gives Norton's name from a MS. of the *Journal*. *George Fox*, 137.

[2] Desborough was at Launceston on Aug. 12, *Thurloe*, v. 302. Fox's letter to him is dated Aug. 13.

of the gaol, informed them that he would detain them no longer, on the sole condition that they would pay his fees.

Sept. 13.
who are set
free.
Fox characteristically replied that no fees were due from innocent prisoners. Fox attributed his liberation without payment to the power of the Lord softening the evil heart of the Colonel. More worldly observers might suspect that the gaoler was to some extent influenced by strict orders from Whitehall.[1]

As in Rogers's case, the Protector's instruments had outrun their master's wishes in their persecuting zeal. In their eyes

Fox de-
nounces
amusements.
Fox was guilty of the fault which seldom admits of pardon—the fault of exaggerating their own extravagances. If they denounced the amusements of others which might possibly tend to the nurture of immorality, he denounced their amusements even when they were obviously innocent. Fox had condemned Desborough to his face when he found the Major-General seeking relaxation in a game of bowls, using language which would have been appropriate if Desborough had been a drunkard. Even the Protector must have felt it impossible to secure mildness of treatment for men who set at defiance both the popular sentiment and the feelings of influential classes. In this respect he could not count on

Major-
Generals
complain of
the
'Quakers.'
the willing co-operation of the Major-Generals. "We are extremely troubled in these parts with Quakers," wrote Worsley from Cheshire. When he reached Lancashire he told the same tale : "We are much troubled with them that are called Quakers. They trouble the markets, and get into private houses up and down in every town, and draw people after them." Goffe in Hampshire was even more disquieted. Writing before Fox's proceedings in Cornwall had landed him in Launceston Gaol, he unbosomed himself to Thurloe in such terms as these : " Fox and two more eminent Northern quakers have been in Sussex, and are now in this county, doing much work for the devil, and delude many simple souls. . . . I have some thoughts to lay Fox and

[1] Fox's *Journal*, 318–22.

his companions by the heels if I see a good opportunity." [1]   It

Nine
'Quakers'
liberated at
Evesham. may at least be conjectured that the liberation of nine 'Quakers' imprisoned in Evesham gaol, apparently for non-payment of fines imposed for contempt of court, was owing to the intercession of the kindly Berry.[2]   Even the Protector probably wavered between his dislike of infringing the principles of religious liberty and his dislike of the disorder which almost invariably resulted from the indiscretion of the new sectaries.   He can have been little moved by Fox's appeal : " You say the Quakers come to disturb you in your churches—as you call them.   Was it not the practice of the Apostles to go into the synagogues and temples to witness against the priesthood that took tithes ? " [3]   There was little similarity between the sober argument of a Paul in an avowed discussion and the exasperating taunts of a ' Quaker ' fanatic.

So far as disturbances of public congregations were concerned the Protector had already made his mind known by his

Apr. 13.
The
Protector
orders the
arrest of a
'Quaker.' proclamation of February 1655,[4] and about a year later he personally interfered to carry out his principles in practice.   A ' Quaker' having stood up in the chapel at Whitehall to argue in support of his creed, Oliver, being himself present, directed that the offender should be taken before the nearest justice of the peace.[5]   As for the punishments inflicted by magistrates and judges for contempt of court or for supposed contravention of the Blasphemy Act, the Protector could only interfere by exercising his right of pardon, and this right he may not in such cases have been inclined to use.

Whilst the ' Quakers' irritated the popular sentiment by the arrogance with which they defied the social habits of the

Jews in
England. country, and by their determination to thrust themselves forward in public congregations, the little colony of the Spanish and Portuguese Jews who had for some years been stealing into London, either to escape the terrors of

[1] Worsley to Thurloe, Dec. 14, 21 ; Goffe to Thurloe, Jan. 10, *Thurloe,* iv. 315, 333, 408.

[2] Berry to Thurloe, March 14, *ib.* iv. 613.   [3] Fox's *Journal,* i. 305.

[4] See vol. iii. p. 260.   [5] *The Public Intelligencer,* E, 493, 7.

the Inquisition or in pursuit of gain, was doing its utmost to escape observation.   It was formed, for the most part, of men of wealth and position, with wide commercial alliances on the Continent and in the Spanish and Portuguese colonies.   Their numbers were now sufficient to suggest the establishment of a

A synagogue established. synagogue in Creechurch Lane, access to which was jealously guarded against intruders, lest they should call down the action of the authorities upon the worshippers.[1] Yet it could not fail to occur to other Jews who had not yet visited England, and who were consequently out of touch with English prejudice, that the Puritan reverence for the heroes of the Old Testament, together with the growth of the spirit of toleration, might open the doors to a large immigration, and that permission might be given to the newcomers to worship more openly the God of their fathers in the long-established fashion.   The first to make the attempt was Manuel Martinez

1654. Dormido's petition Dormido, an Andalusian, who had spent five years in the prisons of the Inquisition, and after carrying on his trade in Amsterdam since 1640, had found himself ruined in 1654 by losses sustained in consequence of the Portuguese reconquest of Pernambuco from the Dutch.

Dec. 5. rejected by the Council. He accordingly made his way to England, where the Protector received him with favour, and recommended his petition to the Council, which, however, refused to make any order upon it.

Naturally, the existing colony, fearing to endanger the

[1] A statement in *Perfect Proceedings* (E, 842, 6) that 'this day,' *i.e.* June 2, 1655, 'some Jews were seen to meet in Hackney—it being their Sabbath day—at their devotion, all very clean and neat, in the corner of a garden by a house, all of them with their faces towards the East, their minister foremost, and the rest all behind him,' may safely be rejected. This worship in the garden is not in accordance with Jewish usage, and everything we know of the history of the early Jewish community precludes the notion that there was a second synagogue at Hackney. Mr. Lucien Wolf has suggested to me that the congregation was one of some sect of Judaising Christians.   For the customs of the Jewish colony see especially Mr. Lucien Wolf's *Resettlement of the Jews, Cromwell's Jewish Intelligencers*, and *Crypto-Jews under the Commonwealth.*

tacit connivance under which it lived, abstained from taking

Manasseh
Ben Israel part in Dormido's enterprise, and the further prosecution of the suit fell upon Manasseh Ben Israel,
an enthusiastic but somewhat dreamy Amsterdam rabbi and
physician, who took the cause of all Judaism upon his shoulders,
and imagined that he could prevail on England to become the
refuge of the poor and persecuted of his race.[1]   When he

1655.
Oct.
arrives in
London. arrived in London in October, circumstances had
occurred which made a more favourable decision
probable.   As war with Spain loomed in the near
future, the services of the Spanish Jews in England became

Aug. 17.
Carvajal
made a
denizen. more valuable.   On August 17 the leading man
amongst them, Antonio Fernandez Carvajal, who
had resided in England twenty years, received letters
of denization from the Protector,[2] and then, or possibly at an
earlier date, offered to the Government the services of his
correspondents on the Continent to gather intelligence of
Spanish preparations and Stuart plots.   In September another

Sept.
Services of
Caceres. wealthy Jewish merchant, Simon de Caceres, laid a
plan before Thurloe for an expedition against Chili,
and another for the fortification of Jamaica.[3]   Even
the Council must have perceived that it was unwise to discourage such men.

On November 5 Manasseh published his *Humble Addresses*
to the Protector, defending Jews from calumnies raised against

Nov. 5.
Humble
Addresses. them, and arguing, with some defect of worldly
wisdom, that as England was the only country re-

Demands of
Manasseh. jecting them, their re-establishment would, according to the prophecies, be the signal for the coming
of the Messiah.[4]   A few days later he prepared a request for

---

[1] [See Mr. Lucien Wolf's *Menasseh Ben Israel's Mission to Oliver
Cromwell*, 1901, which contains a detailed account of the proceedings of
Manasseh in London, and of the discussions relating to the readmission
of the Jews.   Mr. Wolf also reprints 'The Humble Address' and two
other pamphlets by Manasseh.]

[2] *Patent Rolls*, 1655, Part iv. No. 12.   [3] *Thurloe*, iv. 61, 62.

[4] *The Humble Address of Manasseh Ben Israel*, E, 490, 1.

the admission of his race on an equality with the natives of England. He also asked that Jews might be permitted to open public synagogues, to possess a cemetery of their own, to carry on trade without hindrance, to erect a judicature which might decide disputes between members of their community, reserving an appeal to the courts of the land, and also that all laws enacted to their disadvantage might be repealed.[1] The Council, to which these demands were referred by the Protector, passed them on to a committee chosen from amongst its own members.[2]

Nov. 13.
Reference to a committee.

The committee, feeling itself incompetent to decide the question without further enlightenment, asked permission to associate with itself a number of ministers and merchants, together with Chief Justice Glyn and Chief Baron Steele.[3]

Nov. 15.
A conference summoned,
Dec. 4-18.
but separates without any direct result.

The conference thus summoned met at Whitehall two or three times a week between December 4 and 18, with no direct practical result, though the Protector was present on each occasion and showed himself favourable to Manasseh's request. Opinion was divided amongst the ministers and in the Council itself, and the only evidence of an attempt to arrive at a common conclusion is to be found in an unsigned paper, which probably gave the opinion of the Committee of Council, though it does not seem ever to have been presented to the Council itself.[4]

[1] Wolf, *Resettlement*, 15.

[2] Reference by the Council, *S.P. Dom*. ci. 117.

[3] Chief Justice St. John was also summoned, but for some reason or another he did not take part in the proceedings.

[4] The paper is printed from the original (*S.P. Dom*. ci. 118), with the title ' Report of the Council of State on Manasseh's Petition,' by Mr. Wolf (*Resettlement*, 16). The absence of any notice of it in the Council Order Book shows that this is not a correct description. Mrs. Everett Green does not commit herself to the authorship of the paper, but dates it on Nov. 13, which is obviously a mere guess. There are none of the erasures which would show it to be a draft, and I am therefore inclined to take it to be a resolution agreed on by the committee, but never presented. It is not improbable that Oliver hindered its presentation, fearing an adverse decision if it came before the Council. The endorse-

Whoever the compilers may have been, their conclusion was merely hypothetical. They declared it to be necessary to suspend their judgment on the propriety of admitting Jews to England till certain safeguards had been provided.[1] All claims to maintain a private judicatory must be forbidden, Jews must be prohibited from defaming the Christian religion, from working on the Lord's Day, from employing Christian servants, from bearing office in the Commonwealth, and even from printing in the English language anything opposed to Christianity. Nor were they to throw obstacles in the way of the conversion of any members of the community ; whilst a severe penalty was to be imposed on any Christian converted to Judaism. All this was followed by a strong condemnation of Jewish practices in general, and of Manasseh's plausible addresses in particular.

A committee report.

Whether the members of the conference were inclined to go even so far as this may be doubted. The divines were for the most part hostile ; the objections of the London citizens on the score of danger to their trade interests were insuperable.[2] Manasseh's sanguine expectation of a vast influx of Jewish paupers was by no means likely to conciliate opposition. The Protector, therefore, put an end to the conference, intimating that he would take the question into

The conference hostile.

ment is partly illegible, but the following words can still be read : ' Concerning admitting the Jews with limitations . . .'

[1] The wording of the paper is somewhat ambiguous. "That the Jews desiring it may be admitted into this nation, to trade and traffic and dwell amongst us as Providence shall give occasion.

"This as to point of conscience we judge lawful for the magistrate to admit in case such material and weighty considerations as hereafter follow be provided for ; about which till we are satisfied we cannot but in conscience suspend our resolutions in this case." I think, however, that the first paragraph is merely to be taken as the thesis with which the report is about to deal, not as a substantive proposition. [Mr. Wolf accepts this view. *Menasseh Ben Israel*, p. lxxxiv.]

[2] The Dutch ambassador understood that the refusal of the latter to concur with the proposals was the main cause of the Protector's dropping the affair. Nieupoort to the States General, Jan. $\frac{11}{21}$, *Add. MSS.* 17,677 W, fol. 208.

his own consideration. That consideration, however, was of no personal benefit to Manasseh. An answer to his petition was refused, and though the Protector solaced him with a pension, he was forced to cross the sea discomfited, together with a number of Jews who had accompanied him and had shared his hopes.[1]

Nevertheless, the abortive conference had accomplished much. In the course of the discussion an opinion had been elicited from the two judges who had taken part in the proceedings that there was no law forbidding Jews to return into England.[2] After this the Protector's strength was to sit still.[3] Unless a successful action were brought against a Jew for mere residence in England, no executive interference was needed to confirm him in rights which he had never lost. As no such action was ever brought, it may be held that the legal re-settlement of the Jews dates from this extra-judicial opinion of Glyn and Steele, though the exact day on which that opinion was given is no longer ascertainable.

It did not, however, follow that because Jews were admitted to live in England they would be allowed to practise A verbal their religion. The benefits of the Act passed in promise. 1650 to repeal all clauses in statutes imposing penalties for not attending church were limited to those who resorted on the Lord's Day to some place of prayer or preaching,[4] a condition which no Jew could be expected to fulfil. Oliver, however, might be trusted to see that the spirit rather than the letter of the Act was carried into practice, and he gave to the 1656. Jews a verbal assurance that the recusancy laws should March 24. not be enforced against them. A petition asking for a A written engagement written confirmation of this engagement was referred refused. by the Protector to the Council in the following March,

[1] *A Narrative of the Late Proceedings* [by H. Jessey].

[2] *Ib.* p. 9.

[3] "The Jews, though the generality of the divines oppose, yet we hear they will be admitted by way of connivancy." Robinson to Williamson, Dec. 31, *S.P. Dom.* cii. 77a.

[4] *Scobell*, ii. 131.

but, as might have been expected, it met with no response.[1] Even if that body had been more favourably disposed towards the Jews than was the case, it was hardly likely to commit itself by a formal order to the effect that the existing law should not be carried into effect. That there was no intention of interfering with the quiet exercise of the Jewish worship is shown not merely by the uninterrupted continuance of the synagogue in Creechurch Lane, but also by the purchase of a Jewish cemetery in February 1657.[2] By that time Manasseh Ben Israel had left England, and the Government was able to feel that in conferring favours on the old Jewish colony it had to deal with men who, unlike Manasseh, were sensitive to the danger of challenging public opinion by undue demonstrativeness.

1657.
A Jewish
cemetery.

How furtive was the concealment which these Spanish and Portuguese Jews had long practised was brought to light by a case which resulted in the withdrawal of any claim on the part of the Government to interfere with the trade of Jews in England. A certain Antonio Rodrigues Robles, who had large commercial undertakings on foot, was denounced as a Spaniard, a demand being made for the confiscation of his goods, on the ground that he was the subject of a prince at war with England.[3] In a petition referred by the Protector to the Council [4] he made answer that he was a Portuguese 'of the Hebrew nation,' whose father and other relations had been burnt or tortured in Spain by the Inquisition. Inquiry was ordered, and in the main the evidence supported his contention ; but not only was some support given to the assertion of his Spanish birth, but it came out that he had been in the habit—and the practice was one common to others of his race—of attending Mass in the chapel of the Spanish ambas-

1656.
March 24.
Case of
Robles.

[1] Petition of Seven Jews, March 24, *S. P. Dom.* cxxv. 58.

[2] Account by Mr. Israel Davis in the *Jewish Chronicle*, Nov. 26, 1880.

[3] War having by that time been declared.

[4] On March 24, the day of the reference to the Council of the petition for a written confirmation of religious toleration.

sador, a practice of which the only conceivable motive was a desire to obtain the support of Spain if any commercial difficulty should arise with the English authorities. What had hitherto been helpful had become dangerous, and the members of the Jewish community were now as anxious to disclaim all con-

May 14.
Report by
the
Admiralty
Commis-
sioners.

May 16.
Its conse-
quences.

nection with Spain as they had formerly been desirous of establishing it. On May 14 a report by the Admiralty Commissioners, to whom the investigation had been referred, professed inability to decide whether Robles was a Spaniard or a Portuguese, but two days later the Council, giving no reason for its decision, ordered the liberation of his goods.[1]

The direct consequence of this order may easily be exaggerated. It merely decided that Robles was not to be treated as a Spaniard. His legal status, and that of all his coreligionists of full age, with the exception of Carvajal and his son, was that of an alien,[2] though as such he would be allowed to trade in England under comparatively disadvantageous circumstances. In the eye of the law the Hebrew nation, to which Robles claimed to belong, was non-existent. Nevertheless, as had been the case with the conference, the indirect result of the Robles case was considerable. The Jews in England shook themselves loose from the Spanish connection, and thereby shielded themselves from the unpopularity which could not fail to accrue to them if they remained attached to the enemies of the State. Practically, if not legally, even those who had been born in Spain would be thought of, not as Spaniards, but as Jews ; whilst, after all, as children of aliens born in England were legally recognised as Englishmen, their disqualifications would not outlast a single generation. There might be difficulties still in their way, but they would be difficulties attaching to their religion rather than to their

---

[1] Wolf's *Crypto-Jews*, 7–10, where references to the State Papers are given.

[2] An alien was defined in the judgment in Calvin's case to be a person not born within the King's allegiance, or, as it would be put in 1656, not born in the dominions of the Commonwealth.

race. In the meanwhile they knew that they were able to render themselves serviceable to the existing Government as intelligencers, and that the Protector's favour was secured to them not merely by his tolerant instincts, but by his interests as well.

All that was required for the toleration of Jews was the laying aside of ill-founded prejudices. Between the English people and the toleration of Roman Catholics lay the memory of persecutions inflicted and endured, and the consciousness of the existence of a compact ecclesiastical organisation which might easily be brought to bear upon the political as well as upon the religious development of the country. They were in consequence excepted from toleration by *The Instrument of Government* itself, and though recusancy fines were no longer levied under that name, they continued to be demanded from those who refused to take the oath of abjuration, which contained engagements— such as the renunciation of the Papal authority and the doctrine of transubstantiation—which no Roman Catholic could be expected honestly to take. In April 1655, after the explosion of the Royalist insurrection, a proclamation was issued announcing that the law would be enforced, not only against laymen who refused this oath, but also against priests and Jesuits.[1] Yet with the passing away of the alarm there appeared an increased desire to abstain from direct interference with religion.[2] In October Sagredo, who had recently arrived as the first ambassador sent by Venice to England since the hopelessness of the resistance of Charles I. had been manifested, described the policy of the Government as a resolution 'to deprive the Catholics of their possessions, but to let them hear as many Masses as they would.' At all events, when Cardenas left London twenty priests

1654.
The case of the Roman Catholics.

1655.
April 26.
Proclamation against them.

Oct.
Policy of the Government.

Mass at the Venetian Ambassador's.

---

[1] *Proclamation*, April 26, 1655, B.M. press-mark, 669, f. 19, No. 74.

[2] If there had been any recrudescence of persecution during this year it would surely have left its mark on the correspondence of the Nuncio at Cologne, whose business it was to forward English news to Rome.

migrated to the Venetian Embassy, where the large hall was insufficient to contain the crowds flocking to attend Mass. The wrath of the Protestant clergy was increased by the knowledge that English priests were allowed to preach sermons in their own language.[1]   Representations were accordingly made to the Council on the subject; and the Council suggested that Sagredo might be warned.   To this, however the Protector demurred, saying that the Venetian had done no

1656.
Arrest of
Englishmen
attending it. more than the ambassadors of other nations.   Yet, on the following Sunday, guards were placed round the Embassy, and the worshippers arrested as they passed out into the street.[2]   More than four hundred were conveyed to prison.   Many of these were compelled to enter into recognizances to appear at the next Middlesex Sessions;[3] but as neither Sagredo nor his secretary, Giavarina—who after the ambassador's departure acted as resident on behalf of the Venetian Republic—took any further notice of the affair, it is to be presumed that all escaped with a warning not to

Sept. 25.
The
Catholics
virtually
tolerated
in their
religion. repeat their offence.[4]   At all events, Bordeaux, writing eight months later, declared that though the laws against the Catholics had not been modified, the connivance shown to them, the number of priests remaining at large in London, and the freedom with which the chapels of foreign ambassadors were frequented, were sufficient evidence that his co-religionists received better treatment under the Protector than had been accorded to them by any former Government, whether Royal or Parliamentary.[5]   There was, on the other hand, no disposition

[1] Schlezer to the Elector of Brandenburg, *Urkunden und Actenstücke*, vii. 733.

[2] Sagredo to the Doge, Oct. $\frac{19}{29}$, *Venetian Transcripts, R.O.* For Sagredo's mission see *infra*, chap. xlviii.

[3] *Middlesex County Records*, iii. 244, 245.

[4] This presumption is strengthened by a remark of the editor, Mr. Cordy Jeaffreson (*ib.* 244) in the cases of other persons against whom a true bill was found for hearing Mass, that 'these true bills exhibit no minute touching arraignment or the consequences thereof.'

[5] Bordeaux to Brienne, $\frac{\text{Sept. 25}}{\text{Oct. 5}}$, *French Transcripts, R.O.*

C 2

to relieve them of recusancy fines. Their purses, in short, were to continue to suffer. Their religious worship—so long as it was not too ostentatious—was left unmolested.

Little less may be said of those whose standard was the Book of Common Prayer, and who were politically far more dangerous. To join in worship at St. Gregory's was, indeed, no longer permitted them, but, for the most part, they were not denied the shelter of a private roof. In August 1656, Evelyn tells us that he 'went to London to receive the Blessed Sacrament, the first time the Church of England was reduced to a chamber and conventicle, so sharp was the persecution. . . . Dr. Wilde preached in a private house in Fleet Street, where we had a great meeting of zealous Christians, who were generally much more devout and religious than in our greatest prosperity.' At Christmas in the same year he again visited London 'to receive the Blessed Communion this holy festival at Dr. Wilde's lodgings, where I rejoiced to find so full an assembly of devout and sober Christians.' At Christmas in 1657 he had a more unpleasant experience. This time he was in the chapel of Exeter House, where, whilst Gunning was administering the Communion, soldiers burst in, pointed their muskets at the members of the congregation, and stopped the service, on the plea that those who attended it had broken the ordinance against the keeping of Christmas Day. No personal injury, however, was done to the worshippers, who after a short detention were allowed to return to their homes.[1] Other evidence leads to the conclusion that there was little real persecution. It is not recorded that the congregation which met at Oxford in the house of Dr. Willis, the physician, opposite Merton College, was interfered with in a single instance.[2] Faringdon, an able and attractive preacher, who had been adopted as the regular pastor of a church in Milk

Evelyn's experience.

A congregation at Oxford.

Faringdon's preaching tolerated.

----

[1] Evelyn's *Diary and Correspondence*, i. 316, 317, 323. For further interference at the same time, see *Clarke Papers*, iii. 130.

[2] Wood's *Athenæ*, iii. 1059.

Street, was silenced for a while, but appears to have been
permitted before long to return to his ministrations.[1]
John Hales, indeed, upon the issue of the Protector's
Declaration of November 24,[2] voluntarily left the
refuge which, upon his expulsion from Eton, he had found as
tutor to Mrs. Salter's son, lest he should bring harm on his
patroness ; but his death, occurring not long after the
time when the rigour of that Declaration began to be
relaxed, makes it impossible to say whether, if his life had been
prolonged, he would have found it necessary permanently to
forsake that haven of rest.

Case of John Hales.

May 19. His death.

The measure dealt out to those scholars and gentlemen who
never failed in their attachment to the services of the Church
as they had been developed in the days of Laud was
certainly very far from religious liberty. Old association of their doctrine and discipline with the harshness
of episcopal rule before its overthrow by the long Parliament,
and still more a present fear lest its revival should lead the way
to political revolution, stood in the way of that. There was,
however, a connivance, seldom violated so long as the congregations did not obtrude their worship on public notice, and
granted all the more readily because that worship was in no
sense popular. It was, moreover, well understood that if the
Royalists were to regain their hold on the general feeling, they
would owe it to other causes than their attachment to the
Church which had recently dominated the land.

Partial conniv- ance.

Whether the Anglican formularies were to recover their
place of honour or not, there were signs that if Puritanism was
to stand, it would be a Puritanism very different
from the Puritanism which had fed the fires of the
opposition against Charles and Laud. The strict
Calvinistic dogmatism which still furnished material for most
of the sermons of the day had not only been rejected by George

A reaction against dogmatic Puritanism.

---

[1] Walker's *Sufferings of the Clergy*, ii. 96.   Wood (*Athenæ*, iii. 457)
gives no account of Faringdon's dismissal.

[2] See vol. iii. p. 334.

Fox and the Society of Friends, but was beginning to relax its hold upon deeper thinkers on the Puritan side. Such men, indeed, were unlikely to approve of the opinion of Sanderson, who, retaining his parish at Boothby Pagnell, where he was in the habit of reciting to his congregation the petitions of the Prayer Book from memory, told Izaak Walton that the 'Holy Ghost seemed to assist' its 'composers, and that the effect of a constant use of it would be to melt and form the soul into holy thoughts and desires and beget habits of devotion';[1] but they would feel some sympathy with Evelyn's complaint, that 'there was nothing practical preached or that pressed reformation of life, but high and speculative points and strains that few understood, which left people very ignorant and of no steady principles : the source of all our sects and divisions, for there was much envy and uncharity in the world : God of his mercy amend it.'[2]

Sanderson at Boothby Pagnell.

Evelyn's complaint of speculative preaching.

The reaction against Calvinism which had arisen in the early part of the century in the University of Oxford, but had received a check from the unwise attempt of Charles and Laud to force it prematurely on the world, was now doing its work in a more modest but no less serious fashion in the University of Cambridge. Oxford, reformed by the Independents, was content with the vigorous Vice-Chancellorship of Owen, and though making no inconsiderable progress in discipline and learning, developed at this time no special school of religious thought. With Cambridge it was otherwise. Reformed by the Presbyterian Manchester whilst Oxford was still garrisoned for the King, that University was now giving birth to ideas which could not fail to influence the coming generation.

A Cambridge movement.

The leader of the Presbyterian party at Cambridge was Anthony Tuckney, successively Master of Emmanuel and St. John's. Tuckney was by no means a sour or gloomy fanatic. He had done his best to save Sancroft, the

Anthony Tuckney.

---

[1] Walton's *Lives* (ed. 1817), ii. 253.   [2] Evelyn's *Diary*, i. 317.

future Archbishop, from ejection in consequence of his refusal to take the engagement.[1] He had, however, been a leading member of the Westminster Assembly of Divines, and though he refused to vote for the election to fellowships at St. John's of candidates represented to be godly, on the ground that they might deceive him in their godliness, but could not deceive him in their scholarship, he was none the less disinclined to countenance any open attack upon the Calvinistic teaching which he had adopted as his own.

In 1651 Tuckney fell into a controversy with his old pupil, Benjamin Whichcote, now Provost of King's and Vice-Chancellor of the University, in which he upheld the importance of maintaining the received dogmas. Whichcote's favourite quotation from the Book of Proverbs : "The spirit of man is the candle of the Lord," reminds us at first sight of Fox's teaching on the inner light. In truth the only agreement of the two was in their determined opposition to the reigning Calvinism. Whilst Fox held firmly to a supernatural indwelling of God's light in the heart and conscience, Whichcote believed that reason was given by God to enable men to appropriate Divine truth. "What," he demands, "doth God speak to but my reason? and should not that which is spoken to hear? Should it not judge, discern, conceive what is God's meaning?"[2] Unlike Chillingworth and Hales, who had striven to impose limits on dogmatism, Whichcote cut at the root of dogmatism itself. Though he founded no theological school, he shed round him an influence more powerful than any school, an influence dissolvent of the systems —Laudian or Calvinistic—which confronted him on either hand. The Latitudinarians, who contributed so much to break up the narrowness of English ecclesiasticism, were his spiritual descendants. Whichcote's view of religious life was far from implying a return to the Anglicanism beloved by Hammond

Benjamin Whichcote.

[1] Sancroft to Brownrigg, May 24, 1651, D'Oyly's *Life of Sancroft*, i. 59. This would be quite in unison with Tuckney's wish that no one might be forced to sign the Westminster Confession.

[2] *Eight Letters of Dr. A. Tuckney and Dr. B. Whichcote*, 48.

and Sanderson. His protest was made, not against the wider Puritanism which held individual religion to be above all Church organisation, but against the cramping hold of Puritan orthodoxy on the human mind. Yet in his appeal to reason as the judge of truth he was undoubtedly in harmony with that spirit of the Renaissance which for more than a century had played so large a part in the evolution of the English Church.[1]

Equally decisive was the reaction against ecclesiastical chaos indicated by the spread of Baxter's system of voluntary associations.[2] By the beginning of 1657 it had been adopted in fourteen counties.[3] These associations provided, in the first place, for the ordination of ministers, and, in the second place, for the establishment, by a mutual understanding between the clergy and their congregations, of a discipline which would enable the former to repel persons of scandalous life from participation in the Lord's Supper. Those who took part in these meetings were Presbyterians and Independents, though all Presbyterians and all Independents did not submit to their decisions. From the point of view of the historical development of religious systems, this temporary expedient is mainly interesting as showing that the tide was turning against sectarian organisation as well as against sectarian theology.

1653-57. Spread of voluntary associations.

So long as Oliver lived and ruled there was no likelihood that either of these movements would go to strengthen the opposition to his Government. Resistance to the enforcement of dogmatic belief or of organised systems of discipline was near to his heart, and if the Protector's life had been prolonged beyond the ordinary span of humanity, it is likely enough that those very elements which strengthened the Church of the Restoration might simply have given endurance to the ecclesiastical system of the Protectorate by ridding it of its harsher elements.

Oliver's relations with these movements.

---

[1] On Whichcote see an appreciation by Bishop Westcott in *Masters of English Theology*, 147. Compare Tulloch's *Rational Theology*, ii. 45.

[2] See vol. iii. p. 26.

[3] Shaw's *Church under the Commonwealth*, ii. 152-165.

A still more powerful solvent of Puritan exclusiveness lay in the devotion of a little group of men, mostly Oxonians by education or adoption, to the study of natural science. This society, in which Wilkins, the warden of Wadham, who was married to the Protector's sister, was officially pre-eminent, included such men as Robert Boyle, John Wallis, Christopher Wren, and Seth Ward. Its members met occasionally in London, but more usually at Oxford, ultimately gaining a sanction for their labours on the creation of the Royal Society after the Restoration. It does not, indeed, appear that Oliver showed any special protection—which, indeed, was never asked of him—to studies so alien from his own habit of mind ; but he assuredly threw no difficulties in their way. Intellectual activity as such was certain of his favour, so long as it did not attempt to thwart him on the political stage. Cleveland, the satirist, had, as has been seen,[1] escaped persecution through his goodwill. Hobbes was left undisturbed in his most unpuritanical lucubrations. Cowley, who preferred to dedicate himself to the muses in England instead of intriguing against the Commonwealth as secretary to Jermyn and the Queen-Mother, was left unquestioned ; whilst Davenant, formerly threatened with death by Parliament,[2] was not only living without danger in London, but before the end of 1656 started at Rutland House, without molestation, an entertainment in which declamation alternated with music—which may justly be regarded as the dawn of the revival of the drama in England.

Students of natural science.

The future Royal Society.

Protection to intellectual activity.

[1] See vol. iii. p. 344.

[2] See vol. i. 309 ; and art. ' Davenant ' in the *Dict. of Nat. Biography*. The cases of Brian Walton and Pocock, often referred to in this connection, seem hardly to the point. The former simply received from the Protector a continuation of the favour, originally granted by the Council of State, of receiving the paper for his polyglot Bible Customs free. The preface, in which this statement is made, is in a copy of the edition of 1657 in the B.M. (press-mark 675, c. 1). As for the latter, the ejectors received such testimonies in his favour from Oxford that they refused to eject him from his living. The Protector had nothing to do with the matter,

CHAPTER XLII

MORAL ORDER

ON August 28, 1655, at a time when the appointment of the Major-Generals was still in contemplation, the Council—probably in consequence of a statement in a pamphlet[1] that the Protector in reducing the army had taken care to disband as many Anabaptists as possible— ordered the appointment of commissioners to put in force the law against unlicensed printing, and at the same time directed that no newspaper should be allowed to appear without a license from the Secretary of State.[2] The Protector waited for twenty-four days before giving his approval to the first order, and for forty-two days before giving his approval to the second ; but this delay on his part was probably owing less to any dissatisfaction with these repressive measures than to a perception that they would require the strong hand of the Major-Generals to enforce them.[3]

1655.
Aug. 28.
Orders
against
unlicensed
printing.

Of the nine weekly newspapers still in existence, one — *Mercurius Politicus*—was the organ of the Government ; another —*Mercurius Fumigosus*—was a retailer of dull indecencies. Of the remaining seven, five took care never to venture on dangerous ground ; whereas the other two—*The Faithful Scout* and *The Perfect Diurnal*—occasionally permitted themselves the use of closely veiled innuen-

Character of
the news-
paper press.

---

[1] *A Short Discovery of His Highness's Intentions*, E, 852, 3.

[2] Council Order Book, *Interr.* I, 76, p. 252.

[3] Sept. 21 and Oct. 9, when the two orders were respectively approved, were notable dates in the development of the new system. See vol. iii. pp. 321, 325.

does directed against the men in authority. If the Protector had contented himself with the suppression of these two and of *Mercurius Fumigosus,* his action would have gone no further than might have been expected from him in the circumstances in which he was placed. What he did was to decree that thenceforward only two newspapers should appear—*Mercurius Politicus* and *The Public Intelligencer*—both edited by the same man, Marchamont Needham, in the interests of the Government, and appearing respectively on Thursdays and Mondays.[1] The last independent newspaper appeared on October 3.

Only two newspapers to appear.

Oct. 3. Appearance of the last independent newspaper.

The character of these official newspapers was not such as to compensate for the loss of unofficial criticism, faint as that criticism was at the time of its extinction. It is true that they dealt very fully with the transactions on the Continent, and that Englishmen were permitted to discuss with some knowledge of 'what the Swede intends and what the French,' and to amuse themselves with accounts of the latest festivities at the Court of Louis XIV., or of the latest pranks of Queen Christina. So far as home affairs were concerned the information doled out was of the meagrest. There was, no doubt, some readiness to interest the reader in naval affairs, in the orders and declarations which from time to time emanated from the Government, or in loyal addresses presented to His Highness. Other news was admitted sparingly or not at all. It was only to be expected that criticisms of the policy of the Government, which found free expression in men's mouths, should be excluded, but it is strange that no care was taken to utilise the press in justification of the policy of the Protectorate, in the way that had been familiar to Englishmen when Milton wielded the pen in defence of the Government of the Commonwealth when the Scots threatened invasion in the days preceding Dunbar. It is, at all events, easily to be understood that the

---

[1] It is incorrect to speak of the two as practically one newspaper appearing twice a week. They often contain the same news repeated in the same words, and must therefore have been intended for two different sets of readers.

author of *Areopagitica*, however staunch was his support of the Protectorate, would refuse to demean himself by writing in its defence under such conditions.

To what extent—if at all—Milton approved of the institution of the Major-Generals we have no means of knowing.

The Major-Generals to raise the standard of morals.

For Oliver's tolerationist policy and for his energy in keeping down the Royalists he had, doubtless, the warmest admiration, and probably he was not averse to his determination to use the authority of the Major-Generals to raise the standard of morals. Whether that determination, which could hardly fail to rouse more widely spread opposition than bonds and decimations imposed on a single class, had sprung from Oliver's own brain or from that of some other member of the Council, it is beyond question that the Protector threw himself with characteristic energy into the struggle. The City of London had been, to some extent, an obstacle in the way of the equal working of

Skippon Major-General of London.

the action of the Major-Generals. Skippon, whose personality was acceptable in the City, had been named as its Major-General ; but, either in consequence of the infirmities of age, or through his own averseness to the high-handed duties required of the holder of the post, he appears to have been disinclined to carry out the functions

Barkstead appointed to act as his substitute.

of the office ; and Barkstead, the Major-General for the remainder of the County of Middlesex, was directed to act as his substitute in the City. Yet the Government hesitated long before authorising the Major-General to make use of his powers in the midst of a community accustomed to self-government for many generations ; and nothing was done till it was found that the Royalists of other districts flocked surreptitiously to London in order to escape notice in their own homes, though by so doing they incurred the penalties denounced in the Proclamation which forbade them to come within a radius of twenty miles of the capital and which had been renewed after its expiry in the autumn.

At last, on March 5 the Protector summoned to Whitehall

the Lord Mayor, together with the Aldermen and other citizens,

in order that he might present his resolution to them in the fairest colours. Assuring them that he had no thought of encroaching on their rights, privileges, or liberties, he represented his position as an enforcer of the law on those who had hitherto been on the side of disorder. " We had, indeed," he said, " many good laws, yet . . . we have lived rather under the name and notion of law than under the thing ; so that 'tis now resolved to regulate the same—God willing—oppose who will." Idle and loose persons, he added, were pouring into the City in flight from the Major-Generals, and some provision must be made against the dangers they brought with them. " The sole end of this way of procedure," he significantly added, " was the security of the peace of the nation, the suppressing of vice, and the encouragement of virtue." [1]

The whole activity of the Major-Generals was summed up in these words. It is, indeed, possible that if they had been
allowed to restrain their actions to that of a police force employed to keep the peace, by the suppression or discouragement of active Royalism, posterity would have heard little of the illegality of their commissions.

It was as discouragers of vice and encouragers of virtue that they roused the most virulent opposition. Yet the duty imposed upon them in this respect had long · been traditionally expected from sovereign power, and though the procedure against the Royalists was undoubtedly not warranted by any existing law, it was by no means necessary to make use of extra-legal powers to countenance actions which would stir up a hornet's nest in every county in England. In
putting in force the laws in this respect the Major-Generals had at their disposal the services of the justices of the peace, through whom it was easy to act without placing themselves too clearly in evidence. [2] In

[1] *Clarke Papers*, iii. 65.

[2] In the eyes of the legal purist the ordinances and Acts of Parliament, not having received Royal assent, and the ordinances of the Pro-

every district, indeed, the justices of the peace were backed by
the authority and impelled forward by the energy of the Major-
Generals, who had under their orders a militia
numbering in all 6,220 horse and 200 foot.[1] In
London not a single militiaman was quartered,
except those raised by the civic authorities,[2] and
Major-General Barkstead was therefore unable to put in
motion a man of them without the voluntary co-operation of
those authorities.[3]

The numbers of the militia.

No militia in London.

In all parts the Major-Generals found it necessary to impart
vigour to the Boards of Ejectors, which had been appointed to
carry out the ordinance of 1654 for the ejection of
scandalous or inefficient ministers who might have
crept into cures during the times of anarchy.[4]
Unfortunately, proceedings taken in this direction have only
reached us in detail in the case of a certain Bushnell,
ejected from the vicarage of Box. Though the
evidence handed down is insufficient to enable a modern
inquirer to speak positively on his deserts, there is enough to
show that he was to some extent the victim of the ill-natured
gossip of the neighbourhood, and that with grave charges of
immorality were mingled accusations of having used in his
ministrations the forms of the Prayer Book, of having played
with cards and dice, and of having been disaffected to the
Government.[5]

Enforcement of the ejection ordinance.

Bushnell's case.

tector issued before the meeting of his first Parliament, were invalid.
In considering the Protector's intention it is necessary to assume the
contrary.

[1] Including non-commissioned officers, but excluding commissioned
officers.

[2] See vol. iii. p. 318. The London militia is not reckoned among the
6,220.

[3] On the other hand, he disposed of his own Tower garrison of regulars.

[4] Worsley to Thurloe, Nov. 9, 13, Jan. 23, April 29, *Thurloe*, iv.
179, 189, 473, 746 ; Whalley to Thurloe, Nov. 17, Dec. 1, *ib*. iv. 211,
472 ; Desborough to the Protector, Jan. 4 ; Desborough to Thurloe,
Jan. 4, *ib*. iv. 391.

[5] *A Narrative of the Proceedings . . . in the case of Walter Bushnell*,

The ejection of scandalous clergymen was an easy task compared with that of rectifying disorders amongst the lay **Regulation of markets.** population. In Lancashire, Worsley had much to say against the practice of holding markets on Saturday or Monday, as occasioning 'the Lord's Day to be much violated.'[1] In other matters different Major-Generals did not always see with the same eye. Whalley showed unusual liberality in giving **Horse-races.** permission to the Earl of Exeter to run horses for a cup at Lincoln, on the ground that the intention of His Highness was not ' to abridge gentlemen of that sport, but to prevent the great confluences of irreconcilable enemies ' ; though Worsley had already absolutely prohibited **Bear-baitings.** such races in Cheshire.[2] The Bear Garden at Bankside had long been an object of Puritan dislike, and orders had been given for its suppression by the Long Parliament in 1642, and by the Council of the Provisional Dictatorship in 1653.[3] Powerful as had been the Governments which had launched these decrees, their prohibitions still remained without effect. It is possible, indeed, that an incident occurring in the autumn of 1655 may have influenced public opinion in another direction. Not only was a child inadvertently locked in among the bears by the keeper and incontinently devoured, but the bearwards, after offering to console the mother with half the profits of the next baiting, put her off with 3*l.* out of 60*l.* which had come in on that occasion.[4] However this may have been, the

---

E, 1837. This was the only case that Walker found to suit his purpose amongst the ejections under the Major-Generals, so that it may be gathered that most, if not all, of the remainder dealt with mere scandalous living. There was a reply to Bushnell's *Narrative* in *An Answer of Humphrey Chambers*, E, 187, 4. Chambers, however, only replies to so much of Bushnell's book as personally affected his own character, but what he says leaves the impression that Bushnell's statements were often very inaccurate.

[1] Worsley to Thurloe, Dec. 3, *Thurloe*, iv. 277–78.

[2] Worsley to Thurloe, Dec. 4 ; Whalley to the Protector, March 12, *ib.* iv. 315, 607.

[3] *Great Civil War*, i. 75 ; *Commonwealth and Protectorate*, ii. 234.

[4] *Perfect Proceedings*, E, 854, 2.

appointment of the Major-Generals was the doom of the bears.

Pride kills
the bears. By Barkstead's order Pride took with him a company of soldiers; after slaying the bears with his own hand, he employed his men to wring the necks of the game-cocks in other parts of the town.[1]

It soon became evident that there was much to be done before vice could be defeated and virtue triumph. "One great evil I find here, which I know not how to remedy," reported Berry from Brecon, "and that is the want of able preachers. Certainly, if some course be not taken these people will some of them become heathens."[2] From Carmarthen he wrote somewhat more cheerfully: "I had a very good appearance of the gentlemen in these parts, and they act very cordially; and I am persuaded that not only the tax, but something of reformation, will be carried on in poor Wales, whom I seriously profess my heart pities and loves. They are a poor people and have suffered much." At Winchester, reported Goffe, 'the justices do all seem desirous to endeavour after the reformation of open profanes.'

It was, however, easier to inflict punishment on 'profanes' than to reform them. The order for the imprisonment of Imprison-
ment of idle,
debauched
and profane
persons. Cavaliers with no visible means of support suggested the idea of ridding the country of all—whether Cavaliers or not—whose lives made them burdensome to the neighbourhood. "The commissioners," wrote Worsley from Cheshire, "some of them this day expressed that they could find near sixty gentlemen in this county—many of them younger sons—that were fit to be sent out of this Commonwealth; which done would much tend to the security thereof and terrify others."[3] To purge the wheat from the chaff by the banishment of evil-doers was the fixed idea of the Major-Generals and the commissioners. Though

[1] *Clarke Papers*, iii. 64; Letter of Feb. 28 in Carte's *Original Letters*, ii. 82.

[2] Berry to Thurloe, Jan. 12, Feb. 28, March 6, *Thurloe*, iv. 413, 565, 582.

[3] Worsley to Thurloe, Feb. 23, *ib.* iv. 534.

the prisons were filled to overflowing, it was difficult to keep abreast of the tide of roguery. "This," boasted Whalley, " I may truly say, you may ride over all Nottinghamshire, and not see a beggar or a wandering rogue." "I hope," he was in conscience compelled to add, "suddenly [1] to have it so in all the counties under my charge, if it be not already; but I much fear it." Part of the blame, at least, he put on the shoulders of the Government. "When I was last in London," he had written a fortnight earlier, " I told you the not taking rogues, such as our instructions ordered to be sent beyond the seas, off our hands, makes us neglect the imprisoning of them; a better work for the safety and satisfying the country cannot be. I wonder it should be so much neglected. . . . Sir, I beseech you, let it not be forgotten, but consider how the gaols may be delivered for the ease and safety of the countries." Three months later he repeats the same demand: " Horse-stealers, robbers, and other condemned rogues lie in the gaols. To continue them there is a charge to the country; to give them liberty there is to make more; and your this long forbearing them without sending them beyond the seas, I fear hath increased their number, to the dissatisfaction of the country. When you expect great things from them,[2] you shall do well to gratify them with as many small things as you can. The clearing of gaols and countries of rogues would be very pleasing to them." [3] Butler wrote from Oundle in much the same strain: " The other humble motion is that you would please to help me to a vent for those idle vile rogues that I have secured for the present . . . being not able to provide security for their peaceable demeanour, nor fit to live on this side some or other of our plantations. I could help you to two or three hundred at twenty-four hours' warning, and the countries would think themselves well rid of them." [4]

If, indeed, the two or three hundred at all resembled the

---

[1] *I.e.* 'soon.'   [2] *I.e.* 'from the people of the country.'

[3] Whalley to Thurloe, April 21, April 9, July 14, *Thurloe*, iv. 718, 686, v. 211.

[4] Butler to Thurloe, April 14, *ib.* iv. 696.

sixteen whose names were set down on a list sent up by the
same Major-General, it would be easy to agree with
him that the country would be the better for their
absence; though, on the other hand, it can hardly
be doubted that the advantage would be more than counterbalanced by the evil consequences of the introduction of a
system of administrative punishment to the exclusion of all
judicial or legal procedure. Of the sixteen persons named,
the first three had no employment or profession, were 'very
drunken fellows and quarrelsome, and are all single men, fit
for the service beyond the seas'; the fourth 'hath a wife in
London, hath wandered up and down this twelvemonth, pre-
tending himself to be a farrier, hath gone a wooing to two
maids in this country, and got monies of them to the value of
10*l.* upon promise of marriage, and hath been formerly in the
King's army.' The next three and the twelfth were of the same
quality as the first three; the eighth and ninth were 'suspected
to live only upon the highway, keeping each a good horse and
pistols and having no estate at all, nor following any calling';
the tenth had 'brewed these nineteen years without a license, . . .
kept a lewd house, and is suspected for the highway, at least to
harbour highwaymen'; the eleventh was 'a mad ranting blade
who had paid 6*d.* for swearing, and had run two countrymen
through the arms without provocation'; the thirteenth was
strongly suspected to be a highwayman, and had 'in a few
years made away with a good estate, abused his wife by words
and blows to her utter distraction,' having also in his business
as a bailiff committed 'the greatest abuses imaginable, forging
writs and frightening men, and forcing them, where no debt is,
to confess judgments'; the fourteenth was 'a pitiful drunken
wretch, every way as profane as the devil can make him'—was
believed to have no estate and to live 'upon the snatch altogether, and being a profane jester to some gentlemen of the
country.' Of the fifteenth, a certain Goddard Pemberton,
Butler professes it to be unnecessary to say anything, as 'he is
so notorious.' Of the last, Paine Clarke, he avers that 'he is
almost as scandalous in point of filthiness as the other, and

hath spoken most scandalous words of the Protector, as hath
been proved before me.' [1]

Yet, in spite of the urgency of the Major-Generals, the
Protector and Council were slow to move in this matter. It
was not till July 22 that an order was given to hand over
persons reprieved or discharged at the last assizes to the Major-
General of the district for transportation or banishment, and
that, too, only in the single county of Surrey; [2] whilst it was
not till August 14 that the Major-Generals in all districts were
directed to send in lists of such dangerous persons, rogues and
vagabonds as they had apprehended or might apprehend at any
future time, with a view of their being conveyed to some sea-
port and conveyed beyond the sea. [3]   As the earliest of these
dates was subsequent to the announcement that a Parliament
was to meet, it looks as if Whalley and Butler were in the right
in holding that the transportation of these vagabonds would be
a means of securing popularity.

In other directions, Whalley, at least, hesitated to step outside his legal powers.   He was, indeed, able to enforce the law
Enforce-   against inclosures, which ordered that two parts of
ment of the   three of arable land should be kept under tillage;
law against
inclosures.   but he restricted himself to forwarding to the Government a suggestion that a proclamation might be issued com-
Grievances   manding the officials in market-towns to open their
about   markets at ten or eleven in the morning instead of at
markets,   one in the afternoon—a delay which told against
the countryman, who, especially in the short winter days, was
forced to sell his corn at low rates if he was to sell it at all
and inn-   before darkness supervened.   The tricks of inn-
keepers,   keepers were for the same reason hard to reach.
Some of them sold oats at Stamford at six pecks the strike

[1] A list of the names of several persons committed to the gaol by
Major-General Butler within his association, *Thurloe*, iv. 632.   They
were in gaol at Northampton, Huntingdon, Oakham, and Bedford, thus
coming from four counties.
[2] Council Order Book, *Interr.* I, 77, p. 270.
[3] Lawrence to the Major-Generals, *ib.* p. 330.

D 2

instead of five, and that, too, at what was regarded as the insufferable price of 8*d*. the peck.[1] The more practical difficulty, that the law which condemned the offence of using false weights and measures had allowed no reward to the informer, stood in the way of the infliction of punishment on the offender.

and weights and measures.

Whalley's disinclination to carry out reforms on which his heart was set indicates plainly his reluctance, and no less the reluctance of the Government, to usurp the functions of the local magistrates, except in cases of absolute political necessity. There could be no doubt that laws against drunkenness, swearing and immorality existed in plenty. But their execution fell within the attributes of the justices of the peace. It was the attempt to override their jurisdiction which had provoked the storm which had swept away Mitchell and Mompesson in 1621, and, though Oliver had committed these matters to the Major-Generals, he was too wise to persist in a course which would have alienated the gentry—not too numerous—of his own party by attempting to act without them. Justices of the peace left to themselves had, indeed, been sluggish, and un-willing to bring down on themselves the hatred of their neigh-bours. When the Major-General of their district became a justice of the peace himself, and took part in their resolutions with all the authority of the Protector, by whose favour alone they retained their position and dignity, they might be ex-pected to move in accordance with the wishes of the Govern-ment.

The repression of drunkenness and immorality.

So far as our information reaches, this latter method proved effective. Worsley had scarcely reached the scene of his labours when he reported himself as urging mayors and aldermen to execute the 'laws against drunkenness, swearing, profaning the Lord's Day, and other wickednesses.'[2] On January 4 he ordered an inquiry to be made not only into the doings of Royalists, but also into the

Worsley's activity.

---

[1] Whalley to Thurloe, April 9, *Thurloe*, iv. 686.
[2] Worsley to Thurloe, Nov. 12, *ib.* iv. 187.

number and condition of alehouses, and the persons guilty of drunkenness and other sins.[1] On the 24th he reported that after a meeting between himself, the commissioners, and the justices of the peace for the hundred of Blackburn, in Lancashire, it had been resolved to suppress no less than two hundred alehouses in that hundred alone. Worsley, indeed, wished that these stringent measures could be taken without diminishing the revenue from the Excise, but no one could be more firmly convinced of the righteousness of the deed. The alehouses, he wrote, were 'the very bane of the county,' bringing forth 'all manner of wickedness.'[2] A fortnight later he proceeded to Chester, where near upon two hundred alehouses were shut up, either because they were kept by Royalists or persons too well off to need the profit, or as standing in dark corners, or as being of bad repute. "These," wrote the commissioners, "were the places of receipt of wickedness, drunkenness, sabbath-breaking, and other impieties." Nor did these energetic reformers stop here. "We . . . have also," they reported, "suppressed the excessive number of malsters, and restrained them and the beer-brewers from selling malt or beer to any suppressed or unlicensed alehouse-keeper, other than for his own private use ; and have also inflicted deserved punishment upon several persons unduly and pretendedly married, contrary to the law, and the persons that married them;[3] as also upon several persons which, by a strict enquiry, were found to be loose and idle persons that live without calling, and upon common tiplers, drunkards, and sabbath-breakers, and others ; and we are resolved—with our said Major-General— unanimously to make it our business, not only to take care of the performance of what is already ordered, but also to use our utmost endeavours . . . to punish offenders, discourage such

---

[1] Declaration by Major-General Worsley, Jan. 4, *Merc. Pol.*, E, 91, 19.

[2] Worsley to Thurloe, Jan. 24, *Thurloe*, iv. 449.

[3] This would mean persons married not by a justice of the peace, as the law directed, but by a minister of religion, presumably an Episcopalian clergyman.

as are loose and idle, and to free ourselves of discontented
spirits that bear ill-will to the so dearly purchased peace." [1]

The course taken by Whalley was very similar. In Warwick-
shire, for instance, the justices decreed that one-third of the ale-
Whalley
and Berry. houses, and also the whole of those 'in by-corners,'
should be put down. [2]   At Shrewsbury the justices,
amongst whom Berry was reckoned, forbade anyone to keep an
inn or alehouse who was not of honest conversation or well-
affected to the present Government.   Nor was anyone to receive
a license for the sale of ale or beer who could not entertain at
least two soldiers or travellers with their horses; while all
licenses to houses standing alone and out of the town were to
be suppressed.   A list of licensed houses was to be publicly
read at the Shropshire quarter sessions, in order that those who
heard it might be ready to inform against unlicensed houses.
The preamble of this order shows how inextricably the desire
to safeguard the Government was entwined with the desire to
safeguard morality.   " The justices of the peace of this county,"
it begins, " being very sensible of the great mischiefs and
inconveniences which do daily happen to this Commonwealth
by the multitude of inns and alehouses, especially where those
that keep them are persons of lewd life and conversation, and
considering that the end of the law in licensing inns was not to
set up houses to tipple in but to make provision for entertainment of strangers and travellers, where officers and soldiers of
the army are by the discipline of the war also ordered to
quarter, and nowhere else ;—and finding by sad experience that,
where persons of dissolute life and disaffected to the Govern-

---

[1] Worsley to Thurloe, Feb. 9; the Commissioners for Cheshire to
Thurloe, Feb. 9, *Thurloe*, iv. 522, 523.   There is no mention in either
of these letters of justices of the peace, but the latter bears only six
signatures, the first being that of the Mayor of Chester.   The number
shows that all the commissioners for the county cannot have signed, and
the reference at the end to His Highness's encouragement to ' what else
our city shall stand in need of ' seems to imply that they belonged to the
corporation, and probably included amongst themselves the justices of the
city.

[2] *Merc. Pol.*, E, 492.

ment are licensed to sell ale or beer, those houses are the cages of all uncleanness and wickedness, and that in them the late secret plots and conspiracies against His Highness and this Commonwealth have been promoted and carried on, do jointly agree and resolve to put the laws that concern the regulating of inns and alehouses, and correcting the evils therein committed, in effectual execution, whereby they may discharge the trust reposed in them, be faithful to their country, and deliver their own souls from the guilt of those many abominations that are daily committed in such places." [1]   If such orders as these were observed, wrote Berry exultingly to Thurloe,[2] ' I am persuaded it would suppress one half of the deboistness and profane practices of this nation.'

In February the Middlesex Justices in quarter sessions issued an order even more drastic than that which had delighted

The Middlesex Justices at work.

Berry.   All alehouse-keepers were to be suppressed who might be convicted ' for the profanation of the Lord's Day by receiving into' the 'house any company, or for swearing, drunkenness, suffering disorderly tippling, gaming or playing games of skill or chance, or of permitting anyone who might be in the house on Sunday morning to leave it before Monday, except with the object of repairing to divine worship, without the approbation of a justice of the peace.'[3]   A few weeks later the soldiers took possession

March 16. Seizure of horses.

in London of a considerable number of horses taken out by their grooms for exercise on Sunday, and their masters were only allowed to recover them on Monday morning by paying a fine of 10s. for each.[4]   Harsh as these proceedings were, they at least emanated from the authorities known to the law, and in no single particular did

[1] Order of the Justices for Shropshire, *The Public Intelligencer*, E, 491, 16.

[2] Berry to Thurloe, Jan. 12, *Thurloe*, iv. 413.

[3] Order of Quarter Sessions, Feb. 19, *The Public Intelligencer*, E, 492, 11.   See also the form of recognisances drawn up in June by the Westminster Justices, *Merc. Pol.*, E, 494 4.

[4] Letter from London, March 21, Carte's *Original Letters*, ii. 93.

they deviate from the line traced out by two ordinances of the Long Parliament.[1]   The same may be said, so far as the observance of ordinances is concerned, of the suppression of bear-baiting and other popular amusements.

The fact was that Puritan legislation had hitherto been very imperfectly carried out.   Its thoroughgoing enforcement under the impulsion of the Major-Generals must have contributed, far more than such of their actions as overstepped the legal pale, to spread the notion that Puritanism in authority was no better than a canting hypocrisy. The Royalist Opposition, it can hardly be doubted, was reinforced not merely by the roysterers and drunkards, but by that widespread class of good fellows who care more for the ease and enjoyment of life than for its stricter duties, who form a vast and inert mass when spirited action is called for, but who offer a stubborn resistance to a Government which calls on them for a forward step towards a purer and a nobler life.   The strong measures of the Protectorate were too far in advance of the average morality of the age to be otherwise than generally offensive.   In strict theory, no doubt, the Englishman's alehouse was closed and his Sunday liberty curtailed by constitutional justices of the peace, but he knew perfectly well that if there had been no Major-Generals the justices of the peace would not have been roused from their habitual inertness.   It was, therefore, only to be expected that the wrath of the aggrieved tippler would flare up, not against the magistrates under whose direct authority he suffered, but against the Major-General who inspired them, and still more fiercely against the Major-General's master.

Streams of opposition have a tendency to combine in one channel, and the dislike of interference with formed habits of life could not but add weight to the demand for a restoration of some sort of Parliamentary authority whereby Englishmen might secure themselves against the forcible interruption of

The Opposition strengthened.

---

[1] Passed respectively on April 6, 1644, and April 19, 1650, *Scobell*, i. 68, ii. 119.

those habits. Strangely enough, the outcry for Parliamentary
Opposition
of the
extreme
Baptists. government was re-echoed by the extreme Baptists,
whose only ostensible difference with the Protectorate
arose from its recognition of an endowed Church.
1655.
Nov. ?
Vavasor
Powell's
petition. To make known the sentiments of these men Vavasor
Powell, who in the autumn of 1655 was diligently
preaching in North Wales, drew up a petition to the
A political
manifesto. Protector to which he obtained the signatures of 323
of his followers. It was less a petition than a hostile
manifesto accusing Oliver of having deserted the blessed cause
supported by the old Parliament—the cause of true religion.
The Protector, it was urged, had ceased to take thought for
'the advancement of Christ's kingdom, the extirpation of
Popery, the privileges of Parliament, and the liberty of the
subject.' According to Powell, by the terms of the Instrument
he had engaged to draw the sword against those who conscientiously objected to the establishment of a tithe-receiving
minister in each parish. Yet he was now raising taxes, not only
without the consent of the people, but in defiance of the very
Instrument on which his power was based. Oliver was next
charged with exalting his sons, his favourites, and his servants,
though some of these were wicked men. Moreover, soldiers
were maintained in pomp and luxury, whilst the poor were
impoverished by taxation, and treasure wasted in the late secret
design in the Indies, whereby the Commonwealth had been
thrown open to invasion and rendered 'a scorn and snuff to
the nations round about.'[1] The conclusion was still more
trenchant. "We," the subscribers testified, "disclaim all ad-
herence to, owning of, or joining with these men in their ways ;
and do withdraw and desire all the Lord's people to withdraw
from these men, as those who are guilty of the sins of the
latter days, and that have left following the Lord,—and that
God's people should avoid their sin, lest they partake with them
in their plagues."[2]

[1] The same complaint appears in Feake's Preface to *The Prophets
Isaiah and Malachi*. By this time the failure of the expedition was
known in England.   [2] *A Word for God*, E, 861, 5.

Such a declaration was incoherent enough, but was none the less acceptable to an easily excited people, and Powell was

Nov. 28.
Powell
brought be-
fore Berry. accordingly arrested and brought before Berry at Worcester. Berry, who joined to kindliness of heart a spice of humour, a quality for the most part lacking amongst the Cromwellian officers, was the very man to deal with an honest enthusiast. He listened with friendly attention to Powell's protestation that he had no thought of raising disturbances in the country, and that he intended nothing more than to work on the Protector's heart by the petition, without any other thought than to discharge his own conscience. Then, with sympathetic tact, the Major-General soothed the perfervid Welshman, allowing him to preach four sermons on one day in four several churches ; after which he invited him

Powell
dismissed. to dinner, and sent him home in a calmer frame of mind, having simply bound him over to appear whenever he was summoned.[1]

Powell's wish to maintain a peaceable attitude was no doubt sincere, but amongst his admirers there were some less discreet

Dec. 3.
His mani-
festo read in
London. than himself. On December 3 the Welsh manifesto was in print, a copy of it having been conveyed to the Protector.[2] On the same day a certain Cornet

It is read by
Cornet Day
and ampli-
fied by Simp-
son. Day read it at Allhallows, and was followed by Simpson, the Fifth Monarchy preacher, who stigmatised all who took part in the Government as thieves and robbers, and the Protector himself as a thief,

Day's arrest.
Simpson in
hiding. tyrant, and usurper. Day was at once arrested and thrown into prison, whilst Simpson found means of concealment, from which he emerged from time to time to hurl bitter words against the occupants at Whitehall. After a while, however, he changed his tone, announced his belief that the expectation of the Fifth Monarchy was a delusion, and repudiated any desire to forward an insurrection against the Protectorate.[3]

[1] Berry to Thurloe, Nov. 17, 21, *Thurloe*, iv. 211, 228.

[2] The date of publication (E, 861, 5) is given by Thomason.

[3] Thurloe to H. Cromwell, Dec. 17, 25, Jan. 1, Feb. 19, *Thurloe*, iv. 321, 343, 373, 545 Newsletter, Dec. 22, *Clarke Papers*, iii. 62,

His motives in this sudden change of front have not been ascertained.

At Whitehall the situation was regarded more seriously than might have been supposed, perhaps on the suspicion that Cornet Day had found sympathisers in the army. "It is certain," wrote Thurloe, "that the Fifth Monarchy men—or some of them, I mean—have designs of putting us in blood." The danger appeared the greater as pamphlets hostile to the Protectorate were being surreptitiously circulated through the country.[1] This knowledge of the existence of latent hostility amongst those who in the eyes of the Government ought to have been its close allies in the conflict it was waging against Royalism found expression in two remarkable pamphlets which appeared in defence of the policy of the Protectorate against the aspersions of the men who had bound themselves—as it were—to assail it in the rear.

Alarm at Whitehall.

The first of these, entitled *Plain Dealing*, was the work of Samuel Richardson, himself a Baptist, who, like Fleetwood, had given his support to the Protectorate. Arguing that the Government was not, as Powell had asserted, centred in a single person, but in a Protector and Council, he declared it to have been owned by God, and to have made itself notable by asserting 'the noble principle' of denying to 'the civil magistrate a coercive power in matters merely religious.' Such a benefit, continued Richardson, could be conferred by the Protectorate alone. "There is no ground," he urged, "to believe that the people of this nation would ever have given us this freedom, or that any Parliament chosen by them would ever give us this freedom, seeing the ministers and magistrates cannot see that the bond between magistrate and people is essentially civil."[2]

1656. Jan. 23. Richardson's Plain Dealing.

Merc. Pol., E, 491, 7. The last-named speaks of Powell as in custody concerning the paper. He may have been re-arrested but, if so, as we hear no more of him in this connection, he was probably released soon afterwards.

[1] *Merc. Pol.*, E, 491, 7 ; Thurloe to H. Cromwell, Feb. 5, *Thurloe*, iv. 505.   [2] *Plain Dealing*, E, 865, 3.

Richardson's idea was developed at greater length and with more force in a direct answer to Powell's manifesto, attributed to William Sedgwick of Ely.[1] The writer, whoever he was, saw clearly that, for the time at least, the Protectorate rested on the army. "Now," he wrote, "the General of these forces hath an unlimited power to enlarge his militia, to take in all honest men if he please, and to give them what pay he judges reasonable, and, in order to it, to raise what money he pleases in the three nations ; to restrain and secure what persons he suspects to be disturbers of his army and command, to inflict what punishment he pleases upon his enemies, to make what constitutions he will for the security of these forces, and to repeal all laws that are against their safety and quiet ; these things are natural and essential to a General in and with his army, which will be accounted absurd for either King or Protector of England to do. So royal and absolute authority in the hands of an honest General entrusted for and in fellowship with the whole party in a capacity distinct from the nation's is a thing worth remembering." Evidently the writer's model is pure Cæsarism, but it is Cæsarism directed not against a corrupt oligarchy, but against popular folly and presumption. The army, at all events, is to be the basis of the State. "Were it not," proceeds this author, "for the strength, honour, and success of the army, that which we call Parliament, Government and Commonwealth would have been made conspiracy [2] and rebellion." Then, turning on Powell—and his arguments strike the Levellers as directly as they strike Powell—he argues that it is mere folly to look to any Parliament, however chosen, to take thought for the interest of the Commonwealth. If, on the one hand, it is elected only by honest men, it will represent so many hostile opinions that the result will be mere distraction. A free

Jan. 28. Animadversions on a Letter.

---

[1] The attribution rests on Wood's assertion (*Athenæ*, iii. 894). There are passages which would be appropriate to Sedgwick. The main difficulty lies in the strength of the argument, for which none of Sedgwick's other writings prepare us.

[2] Misprinted 'confederacy.'

Parliament, on the other hand, would be destructive of all the aims which men like Powell had set before them, the majority of the nation being 'either malignant and opposing Reformation, or lately offended at it, or neutral and sottishly mindless of anything but their profit.'[1]

The dangers attending military despotism had no terrors for this champion of the Protectorate. "'Tis a thing," he continues, "that the Protector hath seemed a long time to design and that good people have talked of,—that honest men should only have place and power ; and yet now we have it we either mind it not or know not which way to settle it : I do heartily wish that we understood what a prize we have in our hand, and had light and judgment either to keep it justly or resign it wisely."[2]

To the historian, at least, no utterance has such a value as that proceeding from the mouths of those who, like children

Drift of the argument. blurting out things which their parents would fain conceal, display before the eyes of all men that hard skeleton of fact which the actors round into softness by covering it with the fair flesh of ideal hopes. The existing Government was but a Puritan oligarchy—and that, too, counted hostile by large numbers, perhaps by a majority, of Puritans— resting on the pikes and guns of an armed force. With this state of things Sedgwick—if Sedgwick was indeed the author of the pamphlet—was well content. It is to Oliver's credit that he knew better than his outspoken defender, and that he strove, though always in vain, to rest the Government on a civil basis, hoping that the time would arrive, and that speedily, when, as he expressed himself to the Nominated Parliament, all the Lord's people would be prophets—or, in other words, when all Puritan men would come to accept his policy, as alone capable of maintaining their cause. No wonder Thurloe, in

Thurloe's perplexity. forwarding this perplexing pamphlet to Henry Cromwell, shook his head dubiously over its arguments,

---

[1] The three classes are the Cavaliers, the Presbyterian Royalists, and those who stand outside party altogether.

[2] *Animadversions upon a Letter and Paper*, &c., E, 865, 5.

as being ' of a very strange and extraordinary nature.' " It is hard," he complained, " to judge whether they be for us or against us. This book stole out into the world, and now it is abroad I know not whether it be fit or convenient to stifle it." [1] It was soon, however, rumoured that the Protector had read it more than once, and the circulation of this rumour was attributed, probably without foundation, to Oliver himself.[2] It is more likely that it arose among those who wished him ill.

However this may have been, the mere inability to have recourse to Parliament for the purpose of legitimatising measures required by the circumstances of the hour had led the Protector into unexpected results. Starting, whilst the Parliament of 1654 was still in session, from the sound principle that the country must not be left to the irresponsible vagaries of a single House, he had attempted, after the dissolution of that Parliament, to rule England by the help of his Council alone, for the most part in accordance with the fixed Constitution set forth in the Instrument ; just as Charles I., after the dissolution of 1629, had attempted to rule England, in accordance with the practice of former sovereigns in times when Parliament was not in session. Like Charles I. he had been baffled by the fact that emergencies arising from time to time require to be dealt with either with the assistance of fresh legislation, or, if that is not to be had, with the tacit support of the nation itself. Neither of these conditions being present, Charles I. in 1629, having the judges on his side, was driven to have recourse to external legality, thus setting at naught the spirit of the law whilst preserving his loyalty to its literal meaning. Oliver, a stronger and more daring character, broke through the meshes of the law, whilst preserving his loyalty to the spirit, if not always to the letter, of the new Constitution. Unfortunately for him, that Constitution had never been ratified by the expressed or tacit approbation of the country. It had, moreover, been

(marginal note:) Oliver's Government compared with that of Charles I.

[1] Thurloe to Henry Cromwell, Feb. 5, *Thurloe,* iv. 505.
[2] Schlezer to —— ? *Actenstücke und Urkunden zur Geschichte des Kurfürsten Friedrich Wilhelm,* vii. 738.

launched with the expectation that it would be put in action as a whole, and was based on the belief that a way had been discovered in which Protector and Parliament might healthily react on one another, to the advantage of the whole nation. With Parliament silenced, each action of the executive, even when fulfilling no more than its constitutional functions, took an unexpected shape. Having no thought of rendering account for his actions, the Protector grew more and more careless whether they were in accordance with the law ; suiting them to his own sense of what was just and fitting, and thinking less and less of the impression created in the minds of the multitude outside his own sphere of influence.

That Oliver should elect to accompany the author of *Animadversions on a Letter*, at least part of the way, was the
Oliver's more probable as, in a less crude form, the advice
danger. given him was that he had already chosen. Yet, whilst the pamphleteer had been satisfied to acclaim the existing state of things as satisfactory in itself, Oliver could not but look further in advance. Some day or other, in accordance with his views, all the Lord's people must be prophets. It was because this was not so—at least in the sense in which he understood the phrase—that his efforts were doomed to failure. He was not wrong in holding that the Government must be in the hands of a minority—every Government, as a matter of fact, is in the hands of a minority—but in holding that the governing minority can defy the habits and beliefs of the majority for longer than the undefinable length of time which enables it—if that prove possible—to draw over the majority to its side. It was because the Protectorate undertook too much that it dug deep the pit into which it was to fall. Royalism was not in itself a danger, still less was an ecclesiastical reaction. The enemies of the Protectorate were many, and the day might come when they might find a rallying-point in the Crown and the Prayer Book ; but in 1656 that day had not yet arrived.

CHAPTER XLIII

THE PROTECTORATE AND THE CORPORATIONS

WITH whatever limitations it may have been restricted, the principle laid down in the replies to Powell's manifesto—

1656.
Jan.
The prin-
ciples of the
Government. that Government must be controlled not by the nation at large, but by a sober and trustworthy minority, was the basis, for the time being, of Oliver's constitutional views. So far as the country districts

Town and
country. were concerned, the right to appoint and dismiss the justices of the peace had placed local government in the hands of the Protector, whilst the curtailment of the franchise had gone at least some way to secure him a hold over Parliament. It was otherwise with the towns, the homes of self-government, where the magistrates were named without any reference to Protector or Council. It would, indeed, be absurd, except in a very few instances, to speak of the town corporations as in

The corpora-
tions. any sense popular bodies. Though the rule prevailing in the various municipalities was far from uniform, citizenship was for the most part confined to the free burgesses, who owed their position to apprenticeship, to descent from former burgesses, or to marriage with the daughter of a burgess. Authority, however, was invariably in the hands of a smaller governing body, for the most part known as the common council, and of certain executive officials, usually styled the mayor and aldermen, a certain number of whom acted within the borough as justices of the peace. The relations between these governing bodies or corporations and the free burgesses varied in different towns, and is to be regarded as the resultant of a long struggle carried on in past centuries between the general body of freemen and the smaller body entrusted with the conduct of affairs.

Whatever might be the exact constitution of each corporation, its characteristic feature was that the choice of its members [1]

Relations between the corporations and the Government. did not emanate from the central Government. The existence of a civil war, however, had unavoidably led to some interference, and the Long Parliament had—notably in the case of London—laid down restrictive rules for the conduct of municipal elections. A sweeping measure, passed as an Act on October 8, 1652,

1652. Oct. 8. Act regulating elections excluded from office, and also from the right of voting in municipal or parliamentary elections, not only all delinquents whose estates had been sequestered or their persons imprisoned, as adherents of the Royalist cause in the first Civil War, but also those who had adhered to that cause in the second war.[2] This Act, however, was to expire on September 28, 1655, and it was, therefore, only by stretching his constitutional powers beyond the bounds of strict legality that on September 21—the day on

1655. Sept. 21. enforced by proclamation. which the commissions of the Major-Generals were made out—the Protector issued a proclamation directing that this Act should continue in force. In so doing he defended himself on the ground that the Commonwealth had been endangered by 'the late horrid treason and rebellion,' carried on by a party which had made it its object 'to involve these nations in blood and confusion,' and which had openly professed its end to be 'to set up that power and interest which Almighty God hath so eminently appeared against.' So far the proclamation, like the Act on which it was based, was directed against Royalists alone; but a clause ordering that 'all magistrates, officers and ministers of justice elected and chosen within the several places of this Commonwealth shall be such as are of pious and good con-

---

[1] Except that when a new charter was granted the first members of the corporation were usually named in it.

[2] *Act of Parliament*, B.M. press mark, 506, d. 9, No. 146.

versation, and well qualified with discretion, fitness, and ability to discharge the trust committed to them,' left the door open to the exclusion of some who had never taken part in a Royalist movement.[1]

At the time when this proclamation was issued the Major-Generals were intended to act against Royalists alone, the instructions to them to support moral order being of a later date.[2] Yet when, two or three months later, the Major-Generals reported on the conduct of magistrates in the towns, they complained less of their Royalism than of their slackness in the suppression of vice.

Complaints of the Major-Generals.

The first note was struck by Whalley. " It hath been a general complaint to me," he wrote, " in Lincoln and Coventry especially, that wicked magistrates, by reason of their numbers, overpower the godly magistrates. They [3] no sooner suppress alehouses but they are set up again. They comfort themselves at present, as they tell me, with the hopes of my assistance, which they should presently have, were I in commission of peace in their corporations. However, they imagine I am. I shall at present declare to them what His Highness expects from them—that, as they are called to be magistrates, so they should answer the end of their magistracy, viz., suppress sin and wickedness, and encourage godliness. I shall give them in charge to put down as many alehouses as shall be judged necessary."[4] At Coventry Whalley's special attention had been drawn to Alderman Chambers, one of the justices of the peace, who was charged by the city constables with encouraging a man whom he had been obliged to convict of swearing to bring an action against the informer. He was also charged with abating the penalties required by law, and with threatening the constables for attempting to recover fines which he had himself imposed on the bench. It was also said that, under his protection, at

Dec. 1. Whalley at Lincoln and Coventry.

Alderman Chambers at Coventry,

---

[1] The proclamation is printed in the *Hist. Rev.* (Oct. 1900) p. 655, note 58.

[2] See vol. iii. p. 325.   [3] *I.e.* the godly magistrates.

[4] Whalley to Thurloe, Dec. 1, *Thurloe,* iv. 272.

least fifty unlicensed alehouses drove a traffic in the city.[1] Such
conduct, if it could be proved, would be severely dealt with
under any Government.   Convented before the mayor and four
or five aldermen, in accordance with the regulations in the city
charter, though in the presence of the Major-General, Chambers
was not only deprived of his office as alderman, but was
deprived of office. removed from the common council, and declared
incapable of holding any municipal office for the
future. "This," reported Whalley, "hath struck the worser
sort with fear and amazement, but exceedingly rejoices the
hearts of the godly.   Many have been with me, and bless God
for His Highness's care of them, it being a mercy beyond what
they expected." [2]

In other places recourse was had to the method which had
proved successful at Coventry. "I . . . shall take the bold-
ness at present," wrote Desborough, "to acquaint
1656. Jan. Resignation of aldermen and coun-cillors at Bristol. your Highness that at Bristol intimation was given
me by some honest people that sundry of the
aldermen and justices were enemies to the public
interest, retaining their old malignant principles, dis-
countenancing the godly and upholding the loose and profane,
which indeed is a disease predominating in most corporations.
Now I adjudged it my duty to declare against such wheresoever
I find them, but resolved to do it with as little noise as I could ;
and in order thereunto I made my repair to Mr. Mayor, and
acquainted him that such of his brethren, I understood, were
so and so ; and desired him from me to advise them tacitly to
resign, otherwise I should be necessitated to make them public
examples.   Whereupon Mr. Mayor engaged to deal faithfully
with them, and, as I understand, they have taken my advice,
which will make way for honester men." [3]   It is impossible to
come to any definite conclusion as to the political opinions of
the three aldermen who resigned under compulsion, Knight,
Locke, and Sherman.   They may be taken as having been

---

[1] Petition of certain constables of Coventry, *Thurloe*, iv. 273.
[2] Whalley to Thurloe, Dec. 5, *ib.* iv. 284.
[3] Desborough to the Protector, Jan. 7, *ib.* iv. 396.

Puritan Parliamentarians in October 1645, when the corporation was purged by ordinance after the capture of the city by Fairfax, as they were then allowed to retain their official positions.   On the other hand, two of them—the third, Knight, died before the Restoration—were replaced in their seats when Charles II. was established on the throne.[1]   The most probable conclusion from Desborough's language is that they had shrunk from associating themselves with the sanctimonious morality of their colleagues, who fined young men for walking in the fields on Sunday, and even ordered that the conduits which supplied water to the houses should stop running on the sacred day.[2] Bristol was a city in which the Royalist spirit which had welcomed Rupert in 1643 was still widely prevalent—as indeed might be expected—and had even gained strength as a recoil from the Sabbatarian action of the magistrates.   In December 1654 there had been fierce riots, directed against the ' Quakers,' which the aldermen were unable, and perhaps unwilling, to control, though shouts for King Charles had been raised by prominent sharers in the disturbance.[3]   Whether the three aldermen were led into Royalism by their dissatisfaction with the extreme pursuit of morality at the expense of others, or were thought by Desborough to be Royalists because they did not rise to the official standard of morality, is of little moment. The significant point is that not being Royalists before, they took the part of the King at the Restoration, passing through a period in which they held aloof from the moral coercion which was carried out under the shield of the Major-Generals.   What took place at Bristol is likely to have taken place elsewhere.

[1] Information derived from the municipal records, furnished me by Mr. John Latimer.

[2] Garrard's *Edward Colston*, 171–75.

[3] *The Cry of Blood*, E, 884, 3.   Nothing in their relation with the ' Quaker' troubles throws any light on the position of the three aldermen as bringing down Desborough's displeasure on their heads.   Sherman's name does not appear.   Knight and Locke were strongly against the ' Quakers'; but so were many others, against whom Desborough had no charge to bring.

As Desborough had intimated in his letter to the Protector concerning Bristol, he was prepared to proceed by direct
Dismissals   executive action wherever appearances could not be
at Tewkes-   saved by a seemingly voluntary resignation.   " There
bury and
Gloucester.   were also," he continued in the same letter, " articles
of delinquency proved against nine of the magistrates of
Tewkesbury, and particularly against Hill, their town clerk.   I
have also dismissed them, and four of the common council
of Gloucester, for adhering to the Scots King's interest." [1]
According to the authorities at Whitehall, the legal basis for
this action was the view that the Protector was justified in
putting in force the expired law against the presence of
Royalists in corporations. [2]   It was on a hint from Thurloe that
Butler allowed the Mayor of Bedford and four common
councilmen to resign office rather than meet the charges
brought against them. [3]   Yet that there was some shrinking
from putting in force the proclamation of September 21 appears
July 5.   from a letter written in July by Packer, Fleetwood's
A demand   deputy in Hertfordshire, asking ' to know His High-
from Herts.   ness's pleasure,' whether he might not proceed in
virtue of that proclamation to get rid of ' some very bad men
in corporations ' in the county who had ' been decimated and
under bond, and ' of ' others that are drunkards and profane
swearers.' [4]

Even when the interference of the Government was of a
more sweeping character, care was taken to act—at least
ostensibly—on the initiative of a party within the
1655.   borough.   On November 14 a petition from the
Nov. 14.
Case of   burgesses of Chipping Wycombe, complaining that
Chipping
Wycombe.   the mayor, the justices of the peace, and the majority
of the common council had combined to exclude fit persons

---

[1] Desborough to the Protector, Jan. 7, *Thurloe*, iv. 396.

[2] See vol. iii. p. 324.

[3] Butler to Thurloe, Feb. 16, March 20, *Thurloe*, iv. 540, 632.   The
new mayor, as appears by the Bedford Corporation records, was John
Grew, a leading member of Bunyan's congregation.

[4] Packer to Thurloe, July 5, *ib.* v. 187.

from the corporation, and to admit others who were unfit, was referred to Colonel Bridge for inquiry, together with another petition which charged them with fraudulent ill-treatment of the poor.[1]   Bridge, before entering on the inquiry, obtained from

Jan. 31.
Award by
Bridge

the persons concerned an engagement to submit to his award. When that award appeared, it was found to contain not merely a detailed opinion on the charges of malfeasance, but also a recommendation that three aldermen, together with Bradshaw, the mayor, should be struck off the burgess-roll ; and further, that the charter of the corporation should be surrendered for renewal, and eight new members added to the common council, to remain in it till the new charter had been granted.   This award was, on Lambert's

Feb. 20.
confirmed
by the
Council.

report, confirmed by the Council.[2]   Ultimately a new charter was granted to the borough,[3] the provisions being doubtless in accordance with Bridge's suggestions.   In these proceedings no allusion was made to political distractions, yet it is difficult to suppose that they were altogether absent.   At all events, it is noticeable that the borough which, in 1654, had returned its recorder, Thomas Scot, one of the most determined enemies of the Protectorate, chose Bridge as its member in 1656.   It may at least be affirmed with safety that a place which in the space of two years returned a regicide and a Cromwellian officer can have had no strong leaning towards the cause of the Stuarts.[4]

[1] Petition.   Council Order Book, *Interr.* I, 76, p. 378.   *S. P. Dom.* cxxiii. 482.

[2] Bridge's award, Jan. 31, *S. P. Dom.* cxxiv. 80, ii.

[3] The only evidence of the grant of the charter is a note over a page in the municipal records relating to a levy of money for the payment of expenses incurred in its procurement :—" This is to gain a charter from Oliver, in the Rumpers' time, which charter was burnt on the day our most gracious King Charles II. was crowned, whom I pray God to send long to reign."   *Hist. MSS. Com. Rep.* v. 556.

[4] On Oct. 9, 1650, Parliament resolved that ' for the better settling of the peace of Wycombe, and the promoting of the Parliament's interest there, . . . Stephen Bate, a discreet, religious person, nominated by the well-affected of that town, be appointed mayor.'   It was now proposed to

Whatever interest may be attached to the changes enforced at Chipping Wycombe is outweighed by the dealings of the Government with Colchester, partly because far more is known about them, but still more because political feeling had a more considerable share in the development of the case. During the greater part of the later Middle Ages the corporation had consisted of two bailiffs and a commonalty of free burgesses. By the time of Edward IV., however, we hear of an elected common council, which eventually claimed the right of returning members to Parliament, and was permitted to do so, at least from the accession of Mary to the third Parliament of Charles I. In 1628, however, a resolution of the House of Commons restored the franchise to the free burgesses ;[1] and in 1635 Charles settled the question, as he hoped for ever, by granting a new charter to the town. By this charter the place was to be governed by a mayor, nine aldermen, sixteen assistants, and sixteen ordinary common councillors. Of these the mayor was to be elected annually by the free burgesses, whilst the remaining forty-one were to be chosen for life, aldermen by the aldermen, assistants by the assistants, common councillors by the common council, though in each case the choice was restricted to one of two persons nominated by the burgesses. The first members

The case of Colchester.

Changes in the franchise.

1628. A resolution of the Commons.

1635. Charter of Charles I.

restore Bate to his aldermanship, of which he had been deprived in favour of Bradshaw, who was now in turn expelled. Bradshaw was described by Lambert as 'an unquiet and disaffected spirit, . . . a very contentious person, . . . and the original cause of the long and tedious suits in the said borough, . . . appearing always in opposition to the rights of the poor, the well-government of the said corporation, and, by stirring up factions and making parties, to the intent to carry on his own design, according to his own arbitrary will, contrary both to law and equity, and the charter and peace of the said corporation, to the great grief and sorrow of the sober and well-affected people thereof,' S. P. Dom. cxxiv. 80. Before the election of 1656 Bridge had been removed to the North to act as Major-General in succession to Worsley, so that there can have been no question of undue influence exercised by himself.

[1] Report to Parliament, March 22, 1659, C.J. vii. 617.

of the new corporation were, according to a usual practice, nominated in the charter by the King.[1]   In consequence of the adoption of this system variations in the temper of the free burgesses were indicated by the character and aims of the mayor, who was annually replaced, and not by those of the aldermen and other members of the corporation, who retained their places till death or some misdemeanour ensured their removal.[2]

In ordinary times such a system might have worked well, but it was hardly suited to the rapid changes of sentiment which arise in the midst of revolutionary excitement.   In 1647 and 1648 the Presbyterian opposition due to the interference of the army in politics, if not even more to the increase of taxation which the mere existence of that army rendered necessary, raised its head even higher in Essex than in other parts of the country.   A petition for a personal treaty with the King, presented to the House of Commons on May 4, 1648, is said to have received 30,000 signatures in the county, out of which 1,300 were contributed by Colchester alone.[3]   There can be no question that many of the townsmen who had stood for Parliament in the first Civil War welcomed the Royalist com-

1648.
Reaction in Essex,

and in Colchester.

---

[1] 11 Pat. Charles I., Part 9, No. 3.

[2] This is remarked by Mr. Round in an article on Colchester and the Commonwealth in the *Hist. Rev.* (Oct. 1900), xv.   The local knowledge of the writer has enabled him to throw light on some difficult points, and I have to a considerable extent modified my opinion in consequence.   As there are still some few points on which our agreement is not complete, I shall have frequently to refer to this article.   I shall for brevity's sake quote merely from the *Review* by volume and page.

[3] *C.J.* v. 551 ; *The Kingdom's Weekly Intelligencer*, E, 441, 19 ; Haynes to Fleetwood, Dec. 20, 1655, *Thurloe*, iv. 330.   It would be convenient if we could find a shorter description of these men than Presbyterian Royalists, but I cannot bring myself to call them, as Mr. Round does, Loyalists, partly because it seems to imply that one can be loyal only to a king ; but, still more, because there was in them no element of the personal devotion which we usually connect with loyalty. They wanted to use Charles for their own purposes, and were too dull to see that they could not do so.   If the term ' Loyalist ' is to be used at all, I would apply it to the old Cavaliers.

manders in the second, and even took arms on their behalf in the defence of the besieged town.[1] The almost inevitable result was that when victory declared itself on the side of Parliament in 1648, those who had adhered to the Parliamentary cause resolved that the town should not be left in the hands of men whom they regarded as traitors to the cause. As they had a majority of the free burgesses on their side, they were able to carry their wishes into effect in accordance with their charter—at least on the probably ill-founded assumption that the misdemeanour or other reasonable cause which that charter allowed as a sufficient reason for ejection from offices tenable for life were terms applicable to men guilty of taking the King's part in the late war.[2]

On September 4—the day fixed for the election of the mayor, the justices of the peace, and other officials—the majority took advantage of the opportunity to get rid of the obnoxious life members of the corporation. Amidst the wildest excitement[3] three aldermen, four assistants, and six common councillors were expelled, and their places filled by others whose principles were more in accordance with those of the victorious party. The number of new members was swollen to sixteen, as there were some death vacancies to be filled.[4]

Sept. 4. A municipal coup d'état.

[1] *Hist. Rev.* xv. 645.

[2] In an order by the new council, printed by Mr. Round (*ib.* xv. 646), the 'words of the Charter' are given as 'ill-behaviour or *scandalum magnatum.*' As a matter of fact the Charter allows expulsion 'pro malè se gerendo in officio suo . . . aut aliâ justâ et rationabili de causâ'— language loose enough to cover almost anything.

[3] "The tumultuous scene," writes Mr. Round, "that must have been witnessed on this occasion at the moot hall is reflected on the leaf of the assembly book that records its results. It was headed by the clerk 'fourth day of August, it being election day'; and although 'August' is erased, September has not been substituted. The list of the council, as it stood till then, was first set out by the town clerk, and then altered and cut about, as the Loyalist members were expelled and others elected in their places. Thus defaced it is unintelligible until we can compare the corporation lists before and after the purge." *Ib.* xv. 645.

[4] *Ib.* xv. 6;7.

The mayor elected on the same occasion was Henry Barrington, the leader of the successful party. He was a wealthy townsman, who appears to have made his fortune as a brewer.[1] His selection as a member of the Nominated Parliament in 1653 gives a clue to his religious position; and the same result is obtained from the charge subsequently brought against him, that he had refused to pay over any part of the money subscribed in London for the sufferers by the siege, except to the 'poor of the separate congregations.'[2] His name, indeed, is marked in a contemporary list as one of those who were against ministry and magistracy;[3] but as he at once rallied to the Protectorate, he must have been a most unscrupulous turncoat, unless either the mark was inserted in error or, what is more probable, he was one of those who voted with the extreme party in the last division without entirely concurring with their views.[4]

Henry Barrington.

At all events, this violent purge of the corporation was a source of weakness rather than of strength. Even in the hour of triumph one of the aldermen, one of the assistants, and three of the common councillors selected by the victorious party refused to take the oath required on entering upon office, thereby dissociating themselves from the party which had put them forward. In 1652 opinion had so veered

A reaction sets in.

---

[1] He is distinctly called a brewer in *Merc. Rusticus*, E, 103, 3, but as he was named mayor in the charter of 1635, which prohibited brewers from becoming members of the corporation, either the exclusion must have been mere verbiage or, as is more likely, he had by that time ceased to be actively employed in the trade. As other trades, not susceptible to Puritan objection, also disqualified from seats in the corporation, the probability is that the objection to those who exercised these trades was that if elected they would have to enforce rules for the regulation of a trade in which they themselves shared. In a grant of the mastership of a hospital in the suburbs made to him on Feb. 1, 1650, Barrington is described as esquire, which would hardly be the case if he carried on business as a brewer. See the *Patent Rolls* for that year.

[2] *Hist. Rev.* xv. 663.   [3] See vol. ii. 308.

[4] That there were members of this kind appears from a passage in *An Exact Relation*. See vol. ii. 324.

round amongst the free burgesses as to carry the election to

1652.
Growth of
the oppo-
sition.
the mayoralty of John Radhams an opponent, though not a thoroughgoing opponent, of Barrington's party; and in 1653 to give him as a successor Thomas Peeke,

1653.
Peeke
elected
Mayor.
whose antagonism to Barrington was of a more unbending character. So far as the general political situation may be supposed to have influenced the development of municipal parties, with which the personal element is often of preponderating influence, it would appear that at least one of the causes in the reaction was the growth of a party which, without being distinctly Royalist, was nevertheless shocked at the increasing weight of the soldiery in public affairs. The years which intervened between Barrington's election in September 1648, and Peeke's in September 1653, witnessed Pride's purge, the King's execution, the expulsion of the Long Parliament, and the setting up of the Nominees, Barrington himself being amongst those who, at the last-named date, were sitting and voting at Westminster. Men who had been revolted by these proceedings would naturally coalesce with their old opponents, the Presbyterian Royalists of 1648.[1] Peeke's name, however, seems to indicate that the party was not entirely composed of these materials, as he was one of those who, in 1662, refused to conform to the requirements of the Corporation Act.[2] The evidence becomes still more clear

1654.
A Parlia-
mentary
election.
when, in the Parliamentary elections in July 1654, Colonel Goffe was put forward by Barrington's opponents, and succeeded in securing 98 votes against 102 given to Maidstone, the treasurer of the Protector's household.[3]

---

[1] *Hist. Rev.* xv. 648.   [2] *Ib.* xv. 662.

[3] "As the names of the voters," writes Mr. Round, "are fortunately preserved, we can see that the voting went on strict party lines, except that Mr. Shaw voted for Maidstone, and Alderman Cooke for Goffe. The latter's supporters were headed by Peeke, then mayor, followed by Radhams, Gale, Reynolds, Rayner, and Milbanke; while Maidstone's list is headed by Barrington, who is followed by Greene, Vickers, the Furleys, and the other members of his party. My own explanation of this voting would be simply that, as Goffe was the only candidate in the

The mere number of Goffe's supporters proves nothing as to the political principles of the very large minority by which he was supported. Candidates have neither the will nor the power to reject votes given by those whose opinions do not entirely square with their own. The remarkable thing is not that Goffe was nearly elected, but that it occurred to anyone in Colchester to invite him to be a candidate, or to assure him of support if the overture proceeded from himself. In many elections the point at issue was the acceptance or rejection of the schemes of the Nominated Parliament, and those who wished to show their animosity to that Parliament had an excellent candidate in Maidstone, an official of the Government on terms of close intimacy with the Protector himself. If the Presbyterian opponents of Barrington's party were on the look-out for a candidate of their own, they would have no difficulty in finding one who, like Maidstone, but unlike Goffe, had a local connection with the county of Essex. On the other hand, if they were anxious to catch votes amongst a class which had little in common with themselves, and which comprised members of extreme sects, religious and political— Baptists, Fifth Monarchy men, Levellers, and thorough-paced Parliamentarians—Goffe was the very man to bind together so loose a coalition. As an officer in the army he was not only as attached to Oliver as Maidstone himself, but had actually taken part in expelling from the House those members of the extreme party who clung to their seats after their colleagues had gone

Character of Goffe's candidature.

---

field whose election could be deemed embarrassing to Cromwell, the anti-Cromwellians, even if Presbyterians, agreed to vote for him *en masse.* Their support of him in that case would not of necessity imply their own predilections " (*Hist. Rev.* xv. 663). It is only fair to give Mr. Round's words, as they appear to point to a solution which may reconcile the differences between us. That the Presbyterians were not the whole of the party is acknowledged in the words just quoted. My suggestion is that it included members of the advanced sects as well as a few Royalists of the original stamp. At first I laid less stress on the Presbyterian side of the party than I ought to have done, but I still think that he lays too great stress on the Royalist or semi-Royalist element.

to lay their authority at the feet of the Lord-General.[1] Yet, if such a record may have commended him to the lovers of order, his fervent religion was likely to secure him a favourable verdict from those who held that the Protectorate was too conservative, and who were ready, if power came into their hands, to sever the still existing connection between Church and State.[2]

Defeated in the Parliamentary election in July, the coalition had its revenge in the municipal elections in September, when

Sept.
The municipal elections.

its leader, Thomas Reynolds, who ultimately rallied to the Restoration, was chosen mayor.[3] His success encouraged his party to the strongest measures. Unlike the occupant of the mayoralty, aldermen, assistants and common councillors could only be removed by death or malfeasance, and some years, therefore, must pass before the majority amongst the burgesses could secure a majority in the corporation. To get over the difficulty Reynolds, taking example by the purge of 1648, assembled a meeting of the burgesses and persuaded them to expel from the corporation

Barrington and his partisans expelled.

not only Barrington himself, but also his son, Abraham Barrington, as well as to deprive Arthur Barnardiston of the recordership. The charges brought against these three were that they had neglected their duty, and had otherwise misconducted themselves. Against such violence

---

[1] See vol. ii. 327.

[2] This view of the case derives support from other arguments which will be adduced further on (see *infra*, pp. 70, 71). It does not militate against this view that Barrington's party included a Baptist, Samuel Crisp, amongst its adherents. The Baptists were split politically into two parties—those who accepted the Protectorate, and those who opposed it.

[3] It is not desirable to lay too great stress on party statements, but it is remarkable that Barrington and his party should have charged Reynolds with having been 'a very good friend to Mr. Alderman Barrington until he endeavoured to procure an Act of Parliament for maintenance of ministers in the said town, saying that that Act would enslave them and their posterities.'—*S. P. Dom.* xcviii. 22. If this is true it makes Reynolds, and not Barrington, an extremist.

Barrington was certain to protest, and his protest took the form of an application to the Upper Bench to restore himself and the recorder—Abraham Barrington was, for some unknown reason, not included in the case —to the posts they had formerly occupied.   Chief Justice Rolle, in giving judgment, took the reasonable ground that it was unjust to an official to deprive him of his office on certain charges without giving him an opportunity to disprove them, and ordered the restitution of the claimants, unless their opponents could show cause to the contrary.[1]

Whilst the case was still pending both sides were doing their best to secure the goodwill of the Protector, a statement of Barrington's case having been drawn up about the beginning or the middle of April.[2]   It may, however, be concluded, with some probability, that Oliver held

1655.
May.
Barrington
supported by
the Upper
Bench.

April.
An appeal to
the Pro-
tector.

[1] Only the case of the recorder is reported in Styles's *Narrationes Modernæ*, 446, 452 ; but we learn from the articles of Barrington's party (*S. P. Dom.* xcviii. 22) that both gained their case, and the Protector's letter of June 28, cited in the reply of Reynolds's party (*ib.* xcviii. 23), shows that the recorder and one alderman were concerned.   Rolle's judgment must have been delivered on or before May 28, the last day of Easter Term, as he resigned before Trinity Term commenced.

[2] There is a reference in it (*S. P. Dom.* xcviii. 20) to a commission of gaol delivery to be executed ' the 23rd of this instant April.'   The dates given in the *Calendar of State Papers* are hopelessly misleading, most of these documents being placed under the date of June 9, without any hint that this is merely the day on which the Council referred the statements and counter-statements to a Committee.   This incorrect date is also assigned to other papers evidently written much later.   The answer of the Reynolds party (*ib.* xcviii. 21) is one of those dated in the margin of the Calendar June 9, whilst in the text it is said to have been referred to the Council on April 3.   As a matter of fact the date of the reference is given, in Thurloe's hand, in the original, as April 31, which might be a mistake for April 30 or May 1 ; though it is more likely to have been May 31, a supposition which would be favoured by the likelihood that the Protector would have waited, before consulting the Council, for Rolle's judgment, and also by the fact that the papers on both sides were referred by the Council to the Committee on June 9 ; it being improbable that the Council should have waited for some forty days if the Protector had requested its opinion on April 30 or May 1.

back the papers presented to him on both sides till the end of

May 31.
The complaints on both sides referred to the Council. May; and it is at all events certain that it was not till June 9 [1] that the Council appointed the Committee which it empowered to examine the allegations of the two parties. Before, however, this Committee

June 9.
A Committee empowered to examine the case. had time to wade far into the business the case came again before Glyn, the new Chief Justice, who had stepped into Rolle's place,[2] and who now pronounced as strongly as his predecessor in favour

June.
Glyn's judgment. of the ejected officials. It is true that Glyn, before his elevation to the Bench, had acted as counsel for Barnardiston; but the judgment delivered by Rolle was so evidently just that it is useless to inquire whether this fact

Proceedings at Colchester. weighed to any extent with the new judge. Decisive as was the ruling of the court, the first news which reached London from Colchester was that the majority of the corporation—now composed of Barrington's opponents—had resolved to put themselves in order by passing a fresh vote of expulsion, doubtless—though nothing has come down to us to that effect—after giving a formal hearing to the aggrieved parties.[3] It was more than Oliver could endure, and

June 28.
Interference of the Protector. on June 28 he sent a sharp order to the corporation, commanding them to reinstate the ejected persons in accordance with the direction of the court, and prohibiting them, at the same time, from making any further

---

[1] The date given in the Calendar (June 7) is a misprint. Council Order Book, *Interr.* I, 76, p. 129.

[2] See vol. iii. p. 301.

[3] The report in Styles's *Narrationes Modernæ*, 452, ends: "Therefore let him be restored *nisi* and to-morrow." This judgment of Glyn's must have been delivered after June 15. The following passage in a later set of articles by Barrington's party (*S. P. Dom.* xcviii. 22) shows that the rule was afterwards made absolute, and was understood to cover the case of the younger Barrington. They say 'that the three persons as above turned out were by due course of law restored to their places. The said Mayor'—*i.e.* Reynolds—'and Mr. Thomas Peeke threatened to turn them out again; but His Highness, being acquainted with their design, sent an order to the Mayor.'

changes till the complaints of both parties had been fully investigated by the Council.[1]

When the petitions and declarations were laid before the Council there could be little doubt which side represented popular feeling in Colchester. The Barrington memorial was signed by four aldermen, six assistants, nine common councillors, 121 burgesses, and 122 other inhabitants, the signatures on the whole amounting to 262. The Reynolds petition was signed by no less than 971 persons, of whom eight were members of the corporation, whilst no distinction was drawn between the burgesses and other inhabitants who made up the remaining 963. It was easy enough to count the signatures. It was far harder at Whitehall to get to the bottom of the charges and counter-charges preferred on either side on matters of local notoriety.

The Committee of inquiry at work.

What, for instance, was the Committee to do with an allegation that Peeke, the mayor chosen under the influence of the Reynolds party in 1653, had sold defective cloth to the Corporation for distribution amongst the poor ; or that Reynolds himself, at the opening of his mayoralty, had summoned a meeting of the burgesses only to inform them that he invited them to drink at the house of Mr. Shaw, one of his own prominent supporters ; or, again, that he and Radhams, who had followed Peeke as mayor, had shown countenance to John Rayner, in spite of his having been convicted of swearing, whilst he himself had licensed a multitude of alehouses and had winked at the existence of many that were not licensed at all ? Peeke, too, it was alleged, had said at the time when he held the office of mayor that it was no matter how many alehouses

[1] The order is given in full in the reply of the Reynolds party : " Oliver P.,—Being informed that writs from our Upper Bench are issued out for restoring of the recorder and one of the aldermen lately by you ejected, our will and pleasure is that, after the execution of the said writs, you do forbear the displacing of the said persons, or making any alteration in the magistracy or common council of this town, until the business be determined by our Council, to whom the petitions of our town are referred.   Whitehall, June 28."— *S. P. Dom.* xcviii. 22.

The Reynolds party the more numerous.

were opened, as 'if they were let alone one alehouse would break another.' The latter charge was explained away by Peeke as merely indicative of his desire to see as many ale-houses as possible reduced to bankruptcy, whilst he absolutely denied the suggestion that the cloth supplied by him was of inferior quality. Rayner, on his part, averred that he had only once given vent to a profane oath, and that only under circum-stances of the greatest provocation, so that he could not be held guilty under the charter of 1635, which referred only to frequent swearers. Reynolds then carried the war into the enemy's quarters, charging them with neglect of duty and mis-appropriation of the property of the town.[1]

If it was hard for the Committee to discover the truth amidst these revelations, it was still harder to pacify the excited factions. It was something gained that on August 10 the expelled members of the corporation were restored to their seats.[2] Time, however, was flowing rapidly by, and on September 3 the municipal elections to the mayoralty and other executive offices must be held in accordance with the charter. As the result was certain to give another triumph to Reynolds and his associates, the Council, seeing no prospect of a report from their Committee before that date, consulted the Commissioners of the Treasury whether the elections could not be avoided on the highly technical ground that the charter having been removed from the custody of the town might be regarded as no longer in force, and that the Protector would therefore be acting within his rights if he appointed the new mayor—presumably only for the time being—a step which Barrington and his allies had asked him to take as long ago as the preceding April.[3] The Treasury Commissioners replied in the negative, though they thought that the Protector, whilst leaving the town to choose its own magistrates, might request that the names of those so chosen should be submitted to him

Marginal notes:

Aug. 10. The expelled members of the corporation restored.

The Council anxious to postpone the elections.

The Treasury Commissioners consulted.

---

[1] These charges are scattered over the petitions and declarations of the two parties.

[2] *Hist. Rev.* xv. 652.   [3] *Ib.* 650.

for his approval.[1]   Acting on this hint, the Council at once
passed an order on August 30 that a letter should be
written to this effect ;[2] and there can be no doubt
that it was actually written, and was, in all probability,
signed by the Protector on the following day.   At the
last moment, however, its despatch appears to have
been countermanded.[3]   The explanation of this apparent
vacillation may be that Reynolds, meeting with Colonel Jones,
a member of the Council, gave some assurance that the election
would fall on candidates who had not committed themselves
strongly to either of the factions.   Jones, at all events, in parting
with Reynolds recommended him to 'go home and cause an
honest mayor to be chosen.'

Either Reynolds's notions of honesty differed from those
prevailing at Whitehall or he found himself unable to control
his followers.   The elections on September 3 were
carried on strict party lines.   Radhams was chosen
mayor, Peeke and Milbanke—the latter having been
one of the signatories of the Essex petition—were named
justices of the peace, whilst Rayner, who had acknowledged
himself guilty of having once sworn a profane oath, was elected
chamberlain.

The result was a fresh petition from the leaders of the
Barrington party, declaring that the Protector's order of June 28

[1] Report of the Treasury Commissioners, Aug. 30, *S. P. Dom.* c. 70,
I.   It is difficult to say why the Treasury Commissioners were consulted,
unless it were on account of the legal eminence of two of them—Whitelocke and Widdrington.

[2] Council Order Book, *Interr.* I, 76, p. 260.

[3] The letter is given in *Thurloe*, iii. 753, dated Aug. 31, but unsigned.
It is, however, entered in the Council Order Book, *Interr.* I, 76, p. 262,
with the letters O. P. at the head.   That it was not sent is shown by the
fact that no reference was ever made to it by either side, even under
circumstances which would almost have compelled its mention.   The
explanation in the text, that the Protector heard of Jones's conversation
with Reynolds after he had signed the letter, does not profess to be more
than a probable hypothesis.   For the conversation with Jones, see the
' Reply of Reynolds and others,' *S. P. Dom.* xcviii. 23.

—by which, as they alleged, elections had been prohibited till
An appeal the questions in dispute had been settled—had been
from the
Barrington set at naught by the late proceedings at Colchester,
party. on which ground they recurred to their former
suggestion, asking that the Protector should himself 'appoint a
mayor or some other person to govern the said town till the
consideration of the charter . . . may receive such an issue as
may be an effectual remedy to the aforesaid grievances.' [1]

A question Whether the order in question could fairly be made to
of interpre- bear this interpretation or not—and its wording was
tation.
undeniably ambiguous [2]—it was as open to Barrington
to argue that a prohibition 'to make any alteration in the
magistracy or common council' forbade the holding of ordinary
elections, as it was to Reynolds to argue that it merely forbade
a repetition of the revolutionary measures by which the two
Barringtons and the recorder had been thrust out of office.
The Council prudently refused to involve themselves in the
meshes of an academical discussion, and were no less unwilling
Sept. 26. to advise the Protector to appoint a mayor by his own
Local com- authority. On September 26, doubtless feeling the
missioners
empowered impossibility of threshing out the points in dispute
to conduct
an inquiry. without more local knowledge than they possessed,
they named seven commissioners to conduct the inquiry, most
of them being Essex men, and all of them East Anglians. In
Reynolds the meanwhile they directed that the newly elected
to retain
office, mayor was to forbear to act, and that his predecessor,
Oct. 11. Reynolds, was to retain office till further orders. On
as well as
other ma- October 11 this order was extended to the mainten-
gistrates. ance in office of the other magistrates, who would

---

[1] This petition is printed by Mr. Round, *Hist. Rev.* xv. 653.

[2] For the order see *supra*, p. 64, note 1. It may be argued that the
letter of Aug. 31, by making, as Mr. Round shows, ' no mention of the
alleged order of June 28 forbidding any further election,' shows that the
Protector did not intend in June to prohibit ordinary elections. Barring·
ton, however, so far as we know, had not seen the suppressed letter of
Aug. 31, and it was open to him to draw inferences from the actual word·
ing of the order of June 28.

in due course have been superseded by those recently elected in their room.[1]

Up to this point it is hardly possible to speak of the conduct of the Government otherwise than in terms of commendation, except on the general ground that it ought not to meddle at all in municipal disputes—a view of the case which was not put forward at the time, and which could hardly be urged by those who, like Barrington and Reynolds, had voluntarily submitted to the Protector's judgment. How fairly and reasonably the Council had acted may be gathered from the fact that, instead of responding to Barrington's proposal that the mayoralty should be filled by the Protector himself, it had left that office in the possession of the leader of the party most distasteful at Whitehall. It may have hoped that the relegation of the case to local commissioners would expedite a settlement.

The action of the Government fair and reasonable.

Towards the end of November, however, the death of Barnardiston brought matters to a crisis, as it became necessary either to force upon the town a successor in the recordership, or to submit to having a Royalist like Shaw[2] established as a life-holder of that important office. Moreover, by this time the Major-Generals were at work in their districts, and the minds both of the Protector and of the Councillors were turned in the direction of more authoritative action than they would have countenanced in the summer. On December 4 Oliver no longer hesitated, but, assuming that Barrington's interpretation of his letter was the right one, proceeded to order Haynes, the deputy Major-General of the district, to visit Colchester, and to give directions to the mayor not merely to hold the election of a new recorder, but also to carry out the elections of other office bearers in place of those chosen on September 3 ; Haynes himself being required to remain in the town till this order had been executed. Yet, unless the mere

Nov. Death of the recorder.

Dec. 4. Haynes to be present at the elections.

---

[1] Order in Council, Sept. 26, *S. P. Dom.* c. 153.

[2] Shaw had been chosen recorder when Barnardiston was turned out. Petition of the mayor and others, *ib.* xcviii. 21.

presence of Haynes were sufficient to cow the hitherto determined opponents of the Barrington party, little would have
been gained by this measure, if it had stood alone.   Oliver,
accordingly, put a weapon into Haynes's hands which could
hardly fail in procuring submission.   Care, he informed his subordinate, was to be taken ' that the
electors and elected be qualified according to our
late proclamation '—the one, that is to say, of September 21, ordering the execution of an Act of Parliament
which expired on September 28, and which consequently had
no legal validity at the time when these instructions were given.[1]
In this case, as in so many others, the Protector departed as slightly
from strict legality as was possible if he was to gain his ends.[2]

*The pro-
clamation
of Sept. 21
to be en-
forced.*

Haynes perfectly understood the intentions of his master.
The proclamation in question, reciting the words of the expired
Act, declared ' that no person or persons whatsoever that had
his estate sequestered, or his person imprisoned for delinquency,
or did subscribe, or abet the treasonable engagement in the
year 1647, or had been aiding or assisting the late King, or
any other enemies of the Parliament, should be capable to elect
or be elected to any office or place of trust or power within
this Commonwealth, or to hold or execute any office or place of
trust or power within the same.'[3]   Such a definition included not
only the old Cavalier party, which had openly sided with Charles I.
in the first Civil War, as well as those Presbyterian Royalists who

[1] The Protector to Haynes, Dec. 4, Morant's *Hist. of Essex*, I,
Colchester, 74.   For the Proclamation, see vol. iii. p. 324.

[2] It might, indeed, be argued that the deviation from the law was
even slighter than is expressed above.   When the Act was passed Parliament had fixed its own dissolution for Nov. 3, 1654, and expected to be
succeeded by another which would be in session in Sept. 1655.   It might
therefore be argued that the intention of the Legislature was merely that
the Act was then to be reviewed in the light of a situation existing at the
time named.   As no Parliament happened to be in existence at the time
the intention of the makers of the Act would be best carried out by its
prolongation.   Such an argument, however, would hardly commend
itself to a court of law.

[3] *Hist. Rev.* xv. 655.

had thrown in their lot with Capel and Norwich in the siege of 1648, but also those who, without taking any active part on that occasion, had given their signatures—as it is said that no less than 1,300 had done—to the Essex petition, in which what was now styled the treasonable engagement had received support.[1]

The elections having been fixed for December 19, Haynes, who had arrived in the town some days before that date, went carefully over the burgess roll, marking for exclusion the names of all who fell under one or other of the heads set forth in the proclamation. Yet, after all his efforts, there still remained so many of the opposition on the roll that when the day of election arrived the majority for Barrington's party was no more than 74 to 66 ; showing that so far as the numbers voting at the Parliamentary election of 1654 can be taken as a standard, some 70 burgesses must have been struck off the list.[2] Small as the majority was, it was sufficient. A Barringtonian, Thomas Lawrence, was chosen mayor ; and the other officers were elected from the same party, except that Peeke, either as a matter of personal favour or in order to show some semblance of comprehensiveness, was placed in the unimportant office of coroner.[3]

Another purge at Colchester.

Dec. 19. The Government nominees elected.

It is impossible to speak with certainty on the interesting question of the composition of what before this last purge had been a majority amongst the burgesses, and had been also—upon the evidence of the far greater number of signatures to Reynolds's first reply than could be secured for Barrington's original petition[4] —a considerable majority amongst the inhabitants who were

What was the composition of the two parties?

---

[1] See *supra*, p. 56.

[2] Haynes to Fleetwood, Dec. 20, *Thurloe*, iv. 330. The voters in 1654 were 200, which would give 60 as the number of the exclusions ; but as some voters must have been absent from the poll from illness or other causes, the probable number of the excluded may be set at 70 or thereabouts.

[3] List of officers, *ib.*   [4] 971 to 262. See *supra*, p. 64.

not burgesses. One thing, however, is clearly shown by the evidence before us, namely, that Barrington's supporters were not merely a minority, but also a diminishing minority. At the Parliamentary election of 1654 they mustered 102 ; at the municipal election of 1655 they were reduced to 74. Of the majority, those now struck off the burgess roll can only, in accordance with the terms of the Proclamation, have been those who had shown themselves hostile to Parliament before the end of 1648 ; and the nucleus of the new party, which in 1654 supported Goffe, and which supported Reynolds in 1655, may therefore be looked for amongst the well-to-do and more or less conservative burgesses, who are vaguely credited with the style of Presbyterians, and who, whether or not they had any conscious tendency to Royalism, were at least alienated by the existing Government. The increase of the majority hostile to Barrington since the summer of 1654 may fairly, though only conjecturally, be set down to dissatisfaction with the dismissal of the first Protectorate Parliament, and, still more recently, with the establishment of the Major-Generals.[1]

Yet, after all is said, it may be presumed that the party led by Reynolds did not entirely consist of sober-minded Puritans dissatisfied on political grounds with the Government of the day. The choice of Goffe as a candidate in 1654 points, as has been already shown,

The opposition probably a composite one.

---

[1] As will be seen, I accept Mr. Round's argument as conclusive so far as the main body of Reynolds's party amongst the burgesses is concerned. He says of the signatories of the Barrington petition : "When their names are examined they do not appear to me, with the exception of the first three, to be those of men of any account, so far as the social history of the town at this time is known. When, on the other hand, we turn to the petition of the Reynolds party, one recognises name after name of the substantial men in the town. Mr. Thurston, for instance, had himself paid no less than 500*l.* of the 6,000*l.* extorted by Fairfax and his troops from the non-Dutch inhabitants after the siege. Several of the other signatories are known to me, as is their good commercial position. The petition was also signed by many of the Dutch congregation, whose wealth was such that 6,000*l.* was exacted from them alone " (*Hist. Rev.* xv. 651).

to the necessity of conciliating burgesses whose religious fervour was of a quality very different from that of men content with the ministrations of a Presbyterian clergy, and such men were likely to be found in the ranks of the Baptist extremists, or even of the Fifth Monarchy men and Levellers. Barrington's party, on the other hand, according to this view of the case, would mainly consist of the Independents and of such of the Baptists as had, like Fleetwood and the bulk of the London ministers, ranged themselves on the side of the Government. That the wilder elements of Puritanism were fully represented in Colchester is known from Evelyn's remark, made after a visit in the summer of 1656, that it was ' a rugged and factious town now swarming with sectaries ' ; whilst it is also significant that out of the 971 who signed Reynolds's petition, no fewer than 277, or more than a fourth of the whole number, were unable to sign their names except with a mark.[1] How many illiterates there were amongst the 122 inhabitants, not being

[1] I have taken it for granted that all the burgesses would be able to write. The charges brought by the Barringtonians against the other party indicate, if they do no more, that the latter was to some extent of a composite character. On the one hand they charge them with ' designing to introduce notorious and grand malignants to be magistrates . . . as appeareth by their propounding Mr. John Meridale and Mr. Henry Lamb to be elected ; ' whilst, on the other hand, they speak of them as ' threatening utter ruin to the interest of religion and sobriety,' language which would be inappropriate to a party composed entirely, or almost entirely, of Conservative Presbyterians or the like. Again, one of the declarations of Reynolds's party thanks the Protector for having brought with him ' that which is the greatest of all mercies, a just freedom and liberty in the worship of Jesus Christ.' *S. P. Dom.* xcviii. 19, 21, 24. I quite acknowledge that we must not look too closely into the arguments put forward on the spur of the moment by partisans, but there is, nevertheless, some conclusion to be drawn from the nature of the arguments chosen, and still more from the omission of other arguments. There were so many things which Barrington might have said of a purely Conservative and Presbyterian opposition which, nevertheless, he did not say. It may be remarked that the subsequent petition for a new charter proceeding from the triumphant Barringtonians claims support on the ground that they countenanced ' religion and sobriety.' They can hardly have meant that Presbyterians were deficient in these qualities.

burgesses, whose names are to be found at the foot of the Barrington petition we cannot say, as all the names are written in a single hand.

Such considerations, however, it must be admitted, cannot be stretched to cover the whole ground. In municipal, even more than in national disputes, personal questions range themselves side by side with political ones, which they not infrequently overtop. It is by no means unlikely that Barrington had given offence by some peculiarity of his character or demeanour, and that he had shown himself overbearing and contemptuous in his dealings with his fellow-citizens. Nor can there be much doubt that the opposition to his authority was reinforced, not only by those who conscientiously differed from him in politics or religion, but also by a large number of the easy-going and self-indulgent, to whom the Puritan strictness of his rule was abhorrent. On the whole, it may be concluded that the growth of Reynolds's party up to the summer of 1654 is best explained on the supposition that Presbyterians who were not Royalists tended to coalesce, on the one hand, with the Presbyterian Royalists of 1648, and, on the other hand, with the more fanatical sects, but that the great increase in the numbers of the combined party in 1655 must be set down to the dissatisfaction arising in the minds of the non-political class with the growing tendency of those in power to enforce the strict observance of Puritan legislation.[1]

Personal questions involved.

The majority thus secured by Haynes was too slight to be depended on after his own minatory presence had been withdrawn, and it was the Major-General himself, who pointed out that further measures were required if the municipal situation was to be saved.

Dec. 20. Haynes calls for further restrictions.

[1] This is brought out in many of the charges against Reynolds's party. In one he is said to have been asked why he had connected himself with the wicked party, and to have answered that it had stood by him when the others forsook him. Whether the conversation was distorted or not, this report of it points to its being understood that some at least of his followers did not reach the standard of Puritan morality.

" How great need," he wrote to Thurloe, " these few and weak hands and hearts have to be strengthened I submit to your Honour's consideration, especially considering the populousness of the place, and that here were 1,300 hands set to the personal treaty and petition. I humbly offered this as a consideration to His Highness that, unless some speedy change be made in such malignant corporations, it's not for such honest men that would serve you to abide in their present stations ; for no longer than such a severe hand as there was in this election be held over them will any good magistracy be countenanced ; which, if it may by any means provoke to the doing something effectual in the charters of corporations, I have my end, and I am sure the hearts of most that fear God will be rejoiced." [1]

Haynes's hint was soon taken.   Early in the spring a Committee of Council was appointed to consider the renewal of charters in which changes were demanded [2] by the corporations themselves.   So far as Colchester was concerned, it was easy to procure a petition from the purged corporation laying blame for the past distractions on the defective constitution of the borough, by which 'in many particulars too great power is given to the people to slight the magistracy of the . . . town, and render them useless in their places, whereby wickedness and profanity is much increased, to the great discouragement of honest men.'   The conclusion to which all this tended was that a new charter should be granted which would give better support to the magistracy than the old one had hitherto done. [3]   The Committee, as might have been expected, pronounced in favour of the proposal, and in the course of the summer a new charter was pre-

1656
A Committee for the renewal of charters.

March 10.
A petition from Colchester.

The new charter.

---

[1] Haynes to Fleetwood, Dec. 20, *Thurloe,* iv. 330.

[2] The date of its appointment is unknown, but the first notice of it is on April 4, though it must have been in working order before that. Council Order Book, *Interr.* I, 77, p. 29.

[3] Petition to the Protector.   Account of the proceedings, March 10, *S. P. Dom.* cxxvi. 14, 14, I.

pared, transferring the right of nomination to offices and to the common council from the burgesses to the common council itself.[1] Henceforward, the burgesses being excluded from the new corporation, were to preserve no other right than that of exclusive eligibility to office. The new corporation, moreover, was to choose the Parliamentary members, the free burgesses being excluded from the franchise in political as well as in municipal elections. In other respects the amendments were distinctly for the better. The high steward, recorder, aldermen and common councillors, were to hold office for life, and to be liable to removal for misdemeanour as before, but the vague authority to remove them 'for any reasonable cause' was omitted, and it was specified that the charges made against accused persons, together with the answers given in reply, should in future be delivered in writing. Alehouses were to be licensed only at quarter sessions, and then by the mayor and two justices. To secure the permanency of this system the first mayor, aldermen and common council were named in the charter,[2] as Charles had named them in his charter of 1635. It is, however, one thing to secure the temporary predominance of certain persons at a time when party divisions are comparatively undeveloped, and another thing to stereotype the victory of a minority which would never have secured power without the employment of overwhelming force. Something of this kind appears to have been present to the mind of the Protector and his advisers, as, though they took good care to

Aug. 21.
The new
corpora-
tion nomi-
nated.

place in the new corporation a considerable majority of the Barrington party, they allowed some of their opponents to take part in the affairs of the borough,

[1] As before, after the nomination of two persons to each vacancy had taken place, the final choice was vested in different bodies, according to the nature of the position or office. See p. 55.

[2] The charter itself has not been preserved, but we have notes of alterations proposed by Desborough and Sydenham to the Council, and an Order of Council of June 12 recommending that the charter be presented to the Protector, as amended, for renewal. As nothing is heard of the Protector's dissent, it may be taken that we have in these notes the charter as it finally passed the seal. *S. P. Dom.* cxxviii. 59, 60, 60, 1.

at least as critics. Radhams and Gale, though belonging to the now depressed party, retained their seats as aldermen, whilst two of their allies were placed in the common council. These latter, however, forfeited their seats by refusing to take the oath of office.[1]

Charters were renewed in several places besides Colchester, but the only trace of a political object is to be found in Carlisle, from which city a complaint reached the Council in January that a Royalist mayor had been elected, who opposed the reformation of alehouses, favoured the election of disaffected aldermen, besides being guilty of other misdemeanours.[2] The result was a sharp order for the execution of the proclamation of September 21, though at the request of the Major-General of the district four Royalist common councillors were allowed to retain office for the benefit of the town.[3]

Jan. 17.
The business
of Carlisle.

In the remaining cases there is nothing to lead us to suppose that any other than a local object was served by the remodelling of the corporations. At Salisbury, for instance, the corporation itself petitioned for a new charter, mainly, it would seem, to obtain thereby a confirmation of the purchase by the city of property formerly belonging to the dean and chapter; though they at the same time asked for a diminution of their numbers, on the ground that the trade of the place having decayed—perhaps because the cathedral dignitaries were no longer purchasers from the tradesmen of the place—a sufficient number of qualified citizens were no longer available for service in the common council.[4] A petition from Leeds, too, reveals no more than

Cases of
Salisbury
and Leeds.

---

[1] *Hist. Rev.* xv. 658. Council Order Book, *Interr.* I, 77.

[2] Petition read in Council, Jan. 17, *S. P. Dom.* cxxiii. 42.

[3] Lawrence to the Mayor, &c., of Carlisle, Jan. 18 ; Lawrence to the Major-General for Cumberland, Jan. 18, Council Order Book, *Interr.* I, 76, p. 484 ; 77, p. 484.

[4] Petition of the Corporation of Salisbury. A copy of the Protector's charter is amongst the Municipal Records, as is also the Journal of the Common Council.

dissatisfaction with local conditions ; [1] and it is probable that the other demands for the renewal of charters which were brought before the Committee bore the same complexion.

The troubles at Colchester, therefore, were from one point of view exceptional, as nowhere else were parties arrayed against one another in a struggle so decided and pro-

The case of Colchester exceptional from one point of view, and of general importance from another.

longed. From a different point of view they furnish a sample of the conflict which was disturbing the nation itself. In Colchester, as in England at large, the opposition to the Protectorate showed no sign of crystallising into a distinctly Royalist movement.

One party asserts that its opponents are tainted with malignancy, a charge which those opponents promptly disclaim. There is no hint of that kind of talk about bringing back the King which might be prudently kept from observation in quieter times, but would be sure to spring to light when divisions ran as high as they did in the Essex borough. In Colchester again, as in England at large, a heterogeneous majority was arrayed against the Protectorate. Wherever this phenomenon met his eye, Oliver's remedy for the mischief was the upholding in power of a determined minority, capable of keeping at arm's length alike the political opposition of the Royalists, the religious opposition of the sects, and the social opposition of the worldly and profane. So long as he lived he was resolved that the ill-informed and evil-minded multitude should not bear sway in England. The 'honest party' alone was to be placed and maintained in power. That the 'honest party' owed its pre-eminence to the sword that he wielded was to him an unfortunate accident, which he strove to mitigate, but which, in the nature of things, it was impossible for him to shake off. Unfortunately for the permanence of the Protectorate, the increasing prominence which the doctrine that the supremacy of the 'honest party' must at all hazards be maintained had assumed in Oliver's mind had seriously affected his chance—never very great—of reconciling the nation to his

[1] Petition of the inhabitants of Leeds, Dec. 2, 1656, *S. P. Dom.* cxxxi. 7.

Government.   Starting after the dissolution of his first Parliament with the notion that he was justified in disregarding the law whenever it came in conflict with the duty of maintaining the Constitution, he found himself towards the end of 1655 in possession of the military organisation of the Major-Generals, which he had established as a weapon against the enemies of the Constitution, but which readily lent itself to other services.   The sword drew on the man ; and he sought to use that organisation, not merely to combat the partisans of the exiled claimant of the throne, or the partisans of the sovereignty of a single House, but the elements of society in which the moral and religious standard was lower than his own.   In such a struggle he found himself necessitated to trespass beyond the limitations of the law even more frequently and more decisively that when his efforts had been directed to the maintenance of a political claim which was in itself sound.   By this course he had unconsciously arrayed against him not merely the careless and the profligate, but all who valued the rule of law, and who strenuously objected to a Government which measured the obligations of Englishmen by the length of its own desires.   It was not, however, in England that the doctrine that government should rest on the minority of the well-affected was to be observed in its most glaring colours.   Those who wish to examine its character thoroughly must turn to its extreme development in Ireland.

CHAPTER XLIV

THE CROMWELLIAN SETTLEMENT OF IRELAND

STERN as were the measures needed to secure the reign of what Oliver counted as godliness in England, they were mild-

1651.
English and
Irish.
ness itself in comparison with the drastic measures required to secure its predominance in Ireland. In that unhappy country it was of little consequence whether one party or another gained the mastery at Westminster. In any case Irishmen, whether of Celtic or of Anglo-Norman descent, would be doomed to suffer. Nor is it easy to see how it could be otherwise. More than a century of strife had taught Englishmen to dread lest Ireland should be used as a stepping-stone for the armies of their Continental rivals. It was only in consonance with average human nature that they still preferred forcibly to disable the Irish people, rather than seek to win them over to the side of England, even if, after the past experience by the Irish of English cruelty, it

A plantation
policy.
were any longer in their power to do so. Three generations of English statesmen had striven to secure Ireland by replacing the native population by English settlers, and the policy of Mary and Elizabeth, of Bacon and Strafford, still counted for wisdom on the banks of the Thames. To hold Ireland securely by the extension of the plantation system was the policy which had been handed down to the Long Parliament by preceding Governments. If that Parliament attempted to carry out the same design more completely, it was because Cromwell's sword had made that possible which had been impossible before. Whether Irishmen would be the

better or the worse for this violence not one of these Governments, past or present, either knew or cared. In the eyes of Englishmen, the resistance of the ' Irish enemy ' was no patriotic struggle for independence, no well-justified refusal to bow the neck beneath the yoke of an alien who, apart from his cruelty and his greed, brought with him a religious and political system distasteful to Celtic nature and Celtic traditions, but rather the bestial repugnance of the savage to accept the rudimentary conditions of civilised order.

It is not within the province of the historian to conjecture how things might have fallen out if only the mental habits and the passions of the actors on the stage had been changed. It is sufficient for him to mark the consistency of a policy which sprang from definite causes unremoved during the lapse of years—a policy which led almost inevitably to what is usually known as the Cromwellian settlement, though it was in reality sketched out by the Long Parliament before Cromwell was in a position to make his weight felt. It was Parliament which, roused in 1641 by the tale of horror wafted across the Irish sea, starting from the principle that resistance to Parliament was sheer rebellion against a legitimate Government, proceeded in 1642 to decree the confiscation of the estates of the rebels, and to set aside from the forfeited land 2,500,000 acres for the Adventurers who advanced money for the reconquest of Ireland.[1] To this Act the Royal assent was given just before the outbreak of the Civil War, and, though the money obtained by this means was diverted into other channels, the Adventurers retained their claim to the security on which payment had been made.

Consistency of English policy.

1642. Grant to the Adventurers.

Years passed by before a chance was offered to the Adventurers of converting this claim into possession ; and it was only in 1651, when Ireton set forth to lay siege to Limerick for the second time, that the prospect of reducing Ireland was such as to justify the Lord Deputy and his fellow-commissioners in taking into consideration a scheme

1651. A proposed settlement.

[1] *Scobell,* i. 26.

for satisfying the Adventurers, and for inducing fresh purchasers
to lend money upon the security of lands yet un-
pledged. Military necessities, however, put an end
to the discussion for the time,[1] and it was not till
after Ireton's death that it was possible to resume it
with advantage. To clear the way it was necessary
to secure the emigration of the armed forces of the enemy, thus
rendering the Irish incapable of resistance for at least a generation. According to the best calculation, no less than 34,000
Irish soldiers consented to quit their native soil to serve in
Continental armies, and 6,000 women, children, and priests
brought the number of the emigrants up to 40,000.[2]

Its consideration postponed,

1652. but resumed after Ireton's death.

In January 1652, whilst this emigration was still in the
future, the Commissioners of Parliament—Ludlow, Corbett,
Jones and Weaver—no longer associated with a Lord
Deputy, sketched out a plan of operations. A line
of defence was to be drawn from the Boyne to the
Barrow, and secured by fortifications, within which lands might
be assigned to English and Protestants only, the entire Irish
population being cleared away.[3] It was, however, proposed to
distribute the Adventurers, in accordance with the Act of 1642,
over the four provinces, and to satisfy the soldiers by assigning
to them, in lieu of their arrears, lands in the neighbourhood of
the garrison towns in which they were quartered. An allusion
was made to the classification of Irish lately in rebellion under
several categories or qualifications, in the way in which it had
been proposed to deal with English Royalists in various
negotiations carried on in the course of the Civil War, but it

Jan. 8. Advice of the Commissioners.

---

[1] The Commissioners to Vane, Aug. 2, 1651, *Irish R.O.*, $\frac{A}{89}$ 49,
p. 39.

[2] Petty's *Political Anatomy of Ireland* (ed. 1719), p. 19.

[3] The line was to be drawn 'for securing of the inhabitants within the
said line, the same being once clear of the Irish.' Particulars humbly
offered, Jan. 8, *Irish R.O.*, $\frac{A}{89}$ 49, p. 286. A copy in the Calendar of the
Portland MSS., *Hist. MSS. Com. Rep.* xiii. App. I., pp. 622-25.
substitutes 'enemy' for 'Irish.' If this be accepted the expulsion of
Irish who submitted may not, perhaps, have been contemplated.

does not appear that any certain conclusion was arrived at. In

1652.
April.
Weaver's
mission.

April, Weaver—one of the commissioners—was despatched to England to discuss the scheme with Parliament. On his arrival he found the Adventurers decidedly opposed to any plan which would scatter their homesteads among the Irish, and inclined to ask that the labourers

Aug. 12.
Act of
Settlement.

required to till their lands might be imported from England. The discussion which followed [1] resulted in the Act of Settlement passed on August 12.

By this Act Irishmen, with few exceptions, were placed under one or other of eight qualifications, all who came under

The first
five quali-
fications.

the first five being excepted from pardon for life and estate—in other words, sentenced to be hanged with confiscation of property. The first included not merely persons who had 'contrived, advised, counselled, promoted or acted the rebellion, murders or massacres,' but also those who during the first year of the rebellion had assisted it ' by bearing arms, or contributing men, arms, horse, plate, money, victual, or other furniture or habiliments of war,' unless, indeed, these things had been taken from them by force. The second comprised priests, Jesuits, and other persons in Roman orders who had abetted the massacres or the war; the third, one hundred and six persons of note mentioned by name; the fourth, principals and accessories in the act of killing any Englishman, though an exception was made in favour of those who, being themselves enlisted in the Irish army, had killed soldiers enlisted on the other side; the fifth, persons in arms who did not lay them down within twenty-eight days after the publication of the Act. So far as it is possible to suggest an estimate, we can hardly reckon at less than 100,000 the number of persons sentenced to death on the first and fourth qualifications.[2] No such deed of cruelty was ever contemplated in cold blood by any State with pretence to civilisation.

---

[1] Considerations to be offered by Mr. Weaver, *Portland MSS.*, p. 644. For further particulars on the subject of the transplantation than are given in this chapter see *Hist. Rev.* (Oct. 1899) xiv. 700–734.

[2] 'Petty, . . . in his *Political Anatomy of Ireland*, puts the

There remained to be dealt with those Irishmen who, being of full age or nearly of full age in 1641, had taken no part even in assisting the actors in the first year of the rebellion, or those who were too young to have been responsible agents at that time. A small number of these, who had held high office, civil or military, were sentenced under the sixth qualification to banishment, and to the forfeiture of their existing estates, though lands to the value of a third part were to be granted to their wives and children ' in such places in Ireland as the Parliament, in order to the more effectual settlement of the peace of this nation, shall think fit to appoint for that purpose.' The seventh qualification covered those who, not being included in the former qualifications, had borne arms against Parliament—that is to say, those who had taken part for the first time in the war after November 10, 1642, as regularly enlisted soldiers. These, if they made submission within twenty-eight days after the publication of the Act, were to receive an equivalent of a third of their estates in some part of Ireland appointed by Parliament. The eighth qualification was directed against every person of the Popish religion who, having resided in Ireland at any time between October 1, 1641, and March 1, 1650, had not manifested constant good affection to the Commonwealth, who were to receive the equivalent of two-thirds of their estates in like manner. Others—that is to say, Protestants who had failed to show good affection—from them constant good affection was

The sixth qualification.

Seventh and eighth qualifications.

population in 1652 as 850,000, from which some 160,000 may perhaps be deducted as Protestants of British descent. There remain, therefore, 690,000 Catholic Irish, of whom about 180,000 must have been males old enough to be responsible for their conduct in 1641. Of these 34,000 escaped by emigration the penalties imposed on them, leaving some 146,000 under consideration. If, instead of adopting Gookin's exaggerations, we allow that two out of three of such Irishmen had taken some part in the first resistance, we have about 93,000 liable to suffer death under the first qualification, to which number must be added an incalculable number of Tories who, having shed blood, had come under the fourth qualification, bringing the total up to at least 100,000.' *Hist. Rev.* (Oct. 1899) xiv. 703.

not required—were to forfeit one-fifth of their estates, retaining the remaining four-fifths, without the obligation of exchanging them for land elsewhere. However loose may be the wording of these two clauses, it is evident from the nature of the penalty that persons having an interest in land were alone affected,[1] the object of the Legislature being to clear the soil for the new settlers.

Those having an interest in land alone affected.

The language of the next clause has been the object of much misplaced commendation. "Whereas," it had been declared in the preamble to the Act, "the Parliament of England, after the expense of much blood and treasure for the suppression of the horrid rebellion in Ireland, have by the good hand of God upon their undertaking brought that affair to such an issue as that a total reducement and settlement of that nation may, with God's blessing, be speedily effected; to the end, therefore, that the people of that nation may know that it is not the intention of the Parliament to extirpate that whole nation, but that pardon both as to life and estate may be extended to all husbandmen, ploughmen, labourers and others of the inferior sort, in manner as is hereafter declared—they submitting themselves to the Parliament of the Commonwealth of England, and living peaceably and obediently under their Government—and that others also, of higher rank and quality, may know the Parliament's intention concerning them, according to the respective demerits and considerations under which they fall; be it enacted and declared . . . that all and every person and persons of the Irish nation, comprehended in any of the following qualifications, shall be liable unto the penalties and forfeitures therein mentioned and contained, or be made capable of the mercy and pardon therein extended respectively, according as is hereafter expressed and declared."

Pardon for the poor and landless.

To carry out these promises to the landless man it was, as a matter of fact, enacted and declared 'that all and every

---

[1] "An estate . . . signifieth that title or interest which a man hath in land or tenements," *Cowel's Interpreter*, s.v.

person and persons, having no real estate in Ireland nor personal estate to the value of 10*l*., that shall lay down arms, and submit to the power and authority of the Parliament by the time limited in the former qualifications, and shall take and subscribe the engagement to be true and faithful to the Commonwealth of England, as the same is now established, . . . such persons—not being excepted from pardon, nor adjudged for banishment by any of the former qualifications—shall be pardoned for life and estate for any act or thing by them done in the prosecution of the war.'

The charitable intentions of Parliament in shielding the poor from the consequence of their acts have been often praised. It is, therefore, worth while to ask what was the intention of the Legislature. In the first place, it may be noticed that no remission of personal trans-

What were the intentions of Parliament?

plantation was granted, if only for the simple reason that there is no mention of personal transplantation in any part of the Act. Proprietors of land were to exchange the possessions left to them for estates in some distant part of the country, but were under no obligation to reside on their new property. In the second place, a landless man, whose stock of money and goods did not reach 10*l*. in value, was just as liable to be hanged, if he had assisted the fighting men during the first year of the rebellion, or at any later stage had joined the Tories in killing a single Englishman, as if he had counted his acres by the thousand. Only acts done in prosecution of the war having been mentioned, those alone profited by the clause who, being either too young in 1641 to be mixed up in the troubles of the first year, or having kept themselves singularly aloof from the early troubles, had since taken arms in the regular forces under the Irish leaders. As the great majority of these men elected to emigrate, only a very few can have benefited by this clause, and even those who did gained no more advantage by it than permission to keep the whole of their petty savings ; whereas if they had possessed landed property even below the value of 10*l*., they would have forfeited two-thirds of their estates. It is but a small residuum of the beneficence lavishly attributed by English writers to the framers of this clause.[1]

Immediate interest, however, centred on the question how far the authorities in Ireland would be prepared to carry out the sweeping death sentence pronounced by Parliament. On April 17, some months before the passing of the Act of Settlement, there had been a meeting of officers and civilians at Kilkenny. Irritated by recent military failures, the conference piously concluded that God was for some reason offended with their conduct. " Which," reported the commissioners, " with the sense we have of the blood-guiltiness of this people in a time of peace doth—through dread of the Lord only, we trust—occasion much remorse for particular weaknesses past, in most minds here concerning some treaties which are liable to be attended with sparing when He is pursuing.[2] . . . And whilst we were in debate thereof, and of our dealing with those who yet continue in rebellion, an abstract of some particular murders was produced by the Scout-master-General, who hath the original examinations of them more at large. . . . So deeply were all affected with the barbarous wickedness of the actions in these cruel murders and massacres, being so publicly in most places committed, that we are much afraid our behaviour towards this people may never sufficiently avenge the same; and fearing that others who are at greater distance may be moved to the lenity [to which] we have found no small temptation in ourselves;—and we not knowing but that the Parliament might shortly be in pursuance of a speedy settlement of this nation, and therefore some tender concessions might be concluded through your being unacquainted with those abominations, we have caused this enclosed abstract to be transcribed and made fit for your view."[3]

April 17.
A meeting at Kilkenny.

[1] *Scobell,* ii. 197.

[2] *I.e.* negotiations then in progress for the surrender and transportation of Irish soldiers which might lead to sparing the Irish when God was pursuing them with the purpose of destroying them.

[3] The Commissioners to Parliament, May 5, *Irish R.O.* $\frac{A}{90}$ 50, p. 69 ; Abstract of depositions, *ib.* p. 71.

It may well be that the harshness of the Act of Settlement was in the main due to these representations. That the Effect of its representations. massacre of 1641 cried aloud for punishment, if not for vengeance, was the settled belief of every Englishman who had any connection, official or unofficial, with Ireland. Yet, when the call for repressive action was once reduced into a judicial channel, it soon lost its exaggeration. 1652–54. A High Court of Justice. A High Court of Justice was erected for the trial of murderers. During the two years in which it remained in existence murderers and accessories to murder were sentenced by it—not those who had aided the rebels in their earliest warlike operations. English judges, once seated on the Bench, were steadied in the exercise of their functions, and every latitude was given to prisoners to plead their cause and to produce witnesses in their favour. Though hearsay evidence was, according to the custom of the times, freely admitted, there is no reason to suppose that intentional injustice was inflicted. There was no browbeating of the accused, and there were at least as many acquittals as might be expected in proportion to the numbers tried.[1]

When, at the beginning of September, Fleetwood arrived as Commander-in-Chief with a seat amongst the commissioners, Fleetwood arrives as a commissioner. it might be supposed that something would be done to put the Act of Settlement in force. Yet, except that on October 11 an order was given for its pro- Oct. 11. Order to proclaim the Act. clamation in every precinct in Ireland,[2] no attempt was made to translate the verbal cruelties of Parliament into action. Notice, indeed, was taken that the Act had proved defective in one important respect. A

[1] Judge Lowther's notes of some of these trials are in the library of Trinity College, Dublin, under the press-mark F, 4, 16. Miss Hickson has published a few in *Ireland in the Seventeenth Century*, ii. 171–239. The issue of the Commission for the erection of the court is mentioned in a letter from the Commissioners to Reynolds, Dec. 17, *Irish R.O.*, $\frac{A}{90}$ 50, p. 372. On Jan. 15, 1653, fifty-four persons had been condemned, most of them being considerable men, *ib.* p. 397.

[2] Order by the Commissioners, Oct. 11, *Prendergast*, 96.

body of commissioners despatched north to arrange for the settlement of Ulster appear to have perceived that it would be impossible to deduct the fifth part of the lands owned by the Scots of Down and Antrim so long as the old proprietors were fixed in their old homes. They therefore proposed ' the trans-

1653.
April 9.
Personal
trans-
plantation
proposed.

plantation of popular men . . . of whose dutiful and peaceable demeanours ' they ' had no assurance.' The idea was welcomed by the commissioners, who on July 13 issued orders for the transplantation of

July 13.
Order for
transplant-
ing Scots.

Scottish landowners to the south of Ireland. It was a mere act of executive authority, based upon no legal foundation whatever.[1]

Before this order had been issued the idea of personal transplantation had taken root in England, doubtless in conse-

Spread of the
idea of trans-
plantation.

quence of the unwillingness of the Adventurers to take up lands hampered with the presence of the old proprietors. The government of England was now in stronger hands than those of the Long Parliament, Cromwell having entered in April upon his temporary dictatorship. He was not the man to be content with touching the mere fringe of a great problem, and before laying down his authority upon the meeting of the Nominated Parliament he sketched out with a vigorous hand the policy to be pursued in Ireland. According to the Act passed in 1642 the Adventurers were to receive land scattered over the four provinces, but Cromwell, collecting, as may be believed, the unanimous opinions of the Adventurers themselves, decided that no settlement was possible unless the English colonists were in some way relieved from the dangerous presence of their dispossessed predecessors.

Large
numbers of
Englishmen
to be pro-
vided for.

The difficulty of providing secure homes for those Englishmen who were now invited, either as Adventurers or as soldiers, to take up their abode in Ireland was the greater because those of the latter class

[1] The Commissioners to the Ulster Commissioners [Apr. 13]; The Ulster Commissioners to the Commissioners, Apr. 24; Order by the Commissioners, July 13, *Irish R.O.*, $\frac{A}{90}$ 50, pp. 478, 489; $\frac{A}{84}$ 44, p. 84.

were now found to be far more numerous than had been
expected in the preceding year, when it had been imagined
that adequate provision might be made for their needs by
setting apart for them a certain number of acres in the
immediate neighbourhood of the posts which they would
Cost of the
conquest of
Ireland. continue to guard.[1] The cost of the subjugation of
Ireland had been, and was still, enormous, no less
than 3,509,396*l.* being spent on it between July 6,
1649, and November 1, 1656. Of this sum as much as
1,942,548*l.* had been wrung from starving and devastated
Ireland, leaving 1,566,848*l.* as a burden on the English
Treasury.[2] No wonder there was an outcry in England for a
reduction of expense, practicable by no other means than the
disbandment of soldiers whose just demands could only be
satisfied by the offer of land in lieu of the money due for their
arrears.   As for the Irish, the very self-interest of the
conquerors called for a change of the cruel system actually in
practice, which nothing but military necessity could even
Enormous
taxation. palliate.   "The tax," wrote one who had good
opportunity of learning the truth concerning the
Misery of
the Irish. misery of the Irish, "sweeps away their whole
substance, necessity makes them turn thieves and
Tories ; and then they are prosecuted with fire and sword for
being so.   If they discover not Tories, the English hang them;
if they do, the Irish kill them ; against whom they have nothing
to defend themselves, nor any other that can :—nay, if any
person melted with the bowels of a man, or moved by the rules
of common equity, labour to bring home to them that little
mercy which the State allows, there are some ready to asperse
them as favourers of Tories, coverers of bloodguiltiness ; and,
briefly, in a probable computation, five parts of six of the whole
nation are destroyed ; and after so sharp an execution, is it not
time to sound a retreat ? "[3]

[1] See *supra*, p. 81.

[2] Note by Mr. Firth in *Hist. Rev.* (Jan. 1899) xiv. 105.

[3] Statistical accuracy is not to be expected from Gookin, the writer
of this anonymous work. See *infra*, p. 101. Petty, whose authority in

Ireland, indeed, after the close of the war was in a condition to call for peaceful labour. The greater part of the country was lying waste and desolate. "Frequently," we are told on the authority of the commissioners themselves, "some are found feeding on carrion and weeds, some starved in the highways, and many times poor children who lost their parents, or have been deserted by them, are found exposed to, and some of them fed upon by, ravening wolves and other beasts and birds of prey."[1] The devastation caused by wolves was so great as to call forth public action. In April 1652 the emigrants were prohibited from carrying their wolf-dogs to the Continent. In November a certain Richard Toole was authorised to kill wolves in the counties of Kildare, Wicklow, and Dublin; and in June 1653 orders were issued to the Commissioners of Revenue in every precinct[2] to offer rewards for the destruction of the noxious beasts.[3]

Desolation of the country.

Wolves to be destroyed.

Yet it was to little purpose to destroy wolves unless the blind forces of Nature could be replaced by the protective amenities of civilised life. Whether it would have been feasible to re-establish in their homes what remained of the Irish people, with the expectation that—even if no English colonists were set down amongst them—they would be content to submit for the future to English government, may reasonably be doubted. The rivers of blood that had been shed, and still more the contumely which Englishmen had poured upon Irish thought and Irish habits, stood in the way of such a consummation. Cromwell, at all events, was but in accordance with the unanimous opinion of

The land to be inhabited.

such matters is far higher, calculates that one-third of the Irish 'perished by the sword, plague, famine, hardship, and banishment.' Petty's *Political Anatomy of Ireland* (ed. 1719), p. 19.

[1] *Prendergast*, 307, note 1.

[2] Ireland was at this time divided for military and official purposes into fifteen precincts.

[3] *Prendergast*, 309–311. Orders of the Commissioners, Apr. 27, 1652, June 29, 1653, *Irish R.O.*, $\frac{A}{82}$ 42, p. 202 ; $\frac{A}{84}$ 44, p. 255.

his countrymen in believing that if Ireland was to be brought
within the pale of civilisation, it must be by English
Cromwell
faces the
problem.
hands and brains.   How eager he was to proceed
rapidly with the work is shown by the fact that whilst
he left over every problem relating to England to the
A Crom-
wellian
settlement.
decision of the Nominated Parliament, he took the
case of Ireland in hand during the last month of his
own temporary dictatorship.   It is true that the settlement
thus launched upon the world had little in it that was new,
except the resolute energy of a man determined to enforce his
behests.   On June 1, in co-operation with his impro-
June 1.
A Com-
mittee to
examine the
Adventurers'
claims, and
to hold a
lottery.
vised Council, Cromwell appointed a Committee to
examine the claims of the Adventurers, and to
preside over a lottery which should decide, first, in
which of the three provinces of Munster, Leinster,
or Ulster, their share should fall, and, secondly, to assign those
shares in one or other of ten counties specified in those
provinces.   Negatively, at least, this provision indicated that
Cromwell had made up his mind that Connaught was to be
the part of Ireland assigned in the Act of Settlement for
division amongst the proprietors whose estates had been
forfeited elsewhere; whilst the restriction of the allotment to
certain counties was a concession to the desire of the colonists
that their shares of land might be as near as possible to one
another.[1]

By the army in Ireland the case of the soldiers was held to
be even more pressing than that of the Adventurers, as a disbandment of considerable numbers was now imminent.   On
June 9, a meeting of officers held at Dublin asked
June 9.
A meeting
of officers
in Dublin.
that the soldiers whose services were no longer
needed should at once be put in possession of land
estimated as equivalent to their arrears.   If, when a survey
was completed, it was found that any man had received too
little, the deficiency was to be made good; if he had received
too much, he was to be allowed to purchase the surplus at the

rates laid down in the Act of 1642, namely, an acre in Ulster for 4s., in Munster for 8s., and in Leinster for 12s.   On this

June 22.
A com-
mission
with in-
structions.

advice Cromwell acted.   A new commission was issued to Fleetwood, Ludlow, Corbett, and Jones,[1] as governors of Ireland, accompanied by instructions to appoint surveyors to take a survey of the forfeited lands in the ten counties set apart for plantation—Waterford, Limerick, Tipperary, Queen's and King's counties, Meath, Westmeath, Armagh, Down, and Antrim—dividing them by baronies into two equal parts—the one to go to the Adventurers, the other to the soldiers.   In the meanwhile, 'that the Adventurers, soldiers, and officers should be satisfied, and Ireland planted with as much expedition as may be,' a gross, that is to say a rough, survey was to be taken, in order that the persons interested might receive provisional allotments.   When this survey was completed, complaints of persons alleging that their land had been unduly described as forfeited were to be examined.   The county of Louth, apparently intended to supplement deficiency, was also to be surveyed ; and, finally, the commissioners were empowered to select five other counties— other than those of Dublin, Kildare, Carlow, or Cork—on which to settle disbanded soldiers temporarily till permanent allotments could be assigned to them.[2]

The needs of the settlers having been thus attended to, additional instructions were issued on July 2 to clear their

July 2.
Instruc-
tions for
trans-
plantation.

path from the hampering presence of the old proprietors.   The idea of personal transplantation which had occurred to the Ulster Commissioners[3] now received a development which they had little contemplated.   It was announced that Connaught and Clare were to be the districts to which all who were allowed favour and mercy by the Act of Settlement were to be personally transplanted, and that this transplantation was to be carried out by

[1] Weaver's name had been removed before the dissolution of the Long Parliament.

[2] Commission and Instructions, *Scobell*, ii. 255.

[3] See *supra*, p. 88.

May 1, 1654, on pain of death, thus reading into the Act an injunction and a date which were not found within its four corners. Persons so transplanted were to receive from commissioners appointed for the purpose lands in such proportion to the value of their original property as was set forth in the Act of Settlement, and they 'or others' might take leases, on terms not exceeding twenty-one years, or three lives, under the Commonwealth. These words, 'or others,' are the only indication in these instructions that any one not a landowner or leaseholder was thought of as joining the transplanters; and as the condition as to the length of lease precludes the idea that the presence of mere peasants was contemplated, it may fairly be set down as referring to younger sons of transplanters or to leaseholders voluntarily accompanying them. The whole gist of these instructions shows them to apply to landed men, who were required to make way for the new settlers. The Act of

Sept. 26.
The Act of
Satisfac-
tion.

the Nominated Parliament for the satisfaction of the Adventurers and soldiers, passed on September 26, regulating the details of the scheme of colonisation, gave the force of law to the commission and instructions issued by Cromwell on the subject of the Irish settlement. It was also enacted [1] that, in the event of the ten counties proving insufficient, the Adventurers were to be satisfied in four out of the five baronies of Louth, the soldiers out of other counties to be selected by the commissioners. The further needs of those immediately disbanded were to be met, not, as Cromwell had formerly suggested, by a provisional grant, but by permanent assignments in the remaining barony of Louth and in certain districts in the counties of Cork and Fermanagh. These military settlers were also to occupy a circuit of one mile round the town of Sligo, as well as a belt of land, not more than four miles in breadth, round Connaught and Clare, thus cutting the transplanters off from the hope of receiving relief by sea. [2]

That this Act was passed at Cromwell's instigation hardly

[1] Further instructions, *Scobell*, ii. 257.
[2] *Ib.* ii. 240.

admits of a doubt; and its evidence is conclusive that he had

Cromwell insufficiently acquainted with the Irish problem. not sufficient acquaintance with the Irish problem to treat it as a whole, even from the English point of view. The commissioners, present on the spot, knew well the importance of the question raised by the fact that the High Court of Justice had only condemned a few —perhaps two or three hundred of notorious malefactors— out of the thousands sentenced to death by the Act of Settlement. The problem of the fate to be meted out to tenants at will or labourers who had made themselves liable to death according to that Act, either by giving support to the insurgents in the first year of the war, or by killing an Englishman without being themselves enlisted in the regular forces at a later stage, was a pressing one in Ireland, especially as there was a large party among the officers who called for an entire, or nearly entire, clearance of the land, that it might be handed over to English and other Protestants free from molestation by the older inhabitants.   With this party Fleetwood sympathised, and when, on

Oct. 14. Declaration by the commissioners. October 14, the commissioners issued a Declaration [1] that the Acts would be put in execution, they solved the problem in their own way by transferring to the ranks of the transplanters not merely those who had aided and abetted the rebellion in its first year, but even those who had been concerned as assistants in the first year of the insurrection, though it had not been thought expedient to send them for trial before the High Court of Justice.   A second category was formed of those who had borne arms since the end of the first year, and a third of those whom the transplantation scheme was mainly, if not entirely, intended to affect—persons having an interest in land as proprietors or leaseholding tenants [2]— together with their families, and others who might willingly accompany them.

[1] Reprinted, from a unique copy in the possession of the Marquis of Ormonde, in *Hist. Rev.* (Oct. 1899) xiv. 710.

[2] It was determined on the Instruction of July 2, confirmed by the Act of Satisfaction, that only leaseholders were to be regarded as tenants, *Hist. Rev.* (Oct. 1899) xiv. 716.

If these orders had been carried out literally, Connaught and Clare would have been too small for the multitude which

Irresolution of the commissioners.
would have been driven across the border.[1] The very wording of the Declaration, however, carries conviction that its authors were very imperfectly aware of the effect of their language. On the one hand, they speak of Connaught and Clare as being set apart for the habitation of the Irish nation. On the other hand, they content themselves with directing that certain lands which cannot have been very extensive shall be leased out to such of the newcomers as are not proprietors.[2] When they descend to detail, they are mainly concerned with persons belonging to the landowning class. It is these who are, before January 30, 1654, to announce their claims to the authorities of their precinct and to receive certificates describing the physical peculiarities of those who are to accompany them. It is these who were to hasten to Loughrea by January 30 to secure a provisional assignment of lands in proportion to the stock of corn or cattle they owned, and who were to be busy during the spring months in preparing habitations for those who were to follow them by May 1, a date which, as it corresponded to the 11th in the reformed calendar, would be far enough on the way towards summer to make travel less difficult than it would

---

[1] Of the examinations to prove delinquency, only those relating to the precinct of Athlone have reached us (*Irish R.O.*, $\frac{A}{32}$ 30). Selecting the first and last twenty cases, we find that of forty persons eleven were dead or had gone beyond sea, and that four only had taken the English side. There remain twenty-five, of whom eighteen would have been liable to be hanged by the Act of Settlement, and seven only would have escaped with partial forfeiture of property. By the Declaration of Oct. 14, 1653, the whole of the twenty-five would have been liable to transplantation. No doubt only proprietors and leaseholders appeared at Athlone, and we are left to conjecture as to the men who, being tenants at will or labourers, joined in murders, or had assisted murderers, in the first year, or had borne arms subsequently. But their numbers must have been enormous.

[2] These may be those willingly accompanying the proprietors, leaving not much room for the landless men-in-arms, murderers, &c.

have been at an earlier season. In other respects the sentence could scarcely have been harsher. The cruelty of this Declaration has been sufficiently descanted on. What is hardly less astonishing is that the crime should have been contemplated, in a fit of thoughtlessness, by men who did not give themselves the trouble to ascertain whether they were banishing a nation, or only a selected few.

To the victims the meaning of the Declaration was clear enough. If it was not the entire Irish nation, it was at least a very large majority of it, that was to be crowded into a rocky and inhospitable district, in which it would be impossible to find adequate sustenance. The belief in a general transplantation spread widely. On one estate owned by an Englishman in Munster, the tenants refused to plough or sow till the agent vowed that they at least should be secured against the fate they dreaded.[1] Others bowed before stern necessity, and in crowds gave in their names to accompany the proprietor of the forfeited estate on which they had lived.[2] Yet, when the appointed time arrived, few presented themselves before the commissioners sitting at Loughrea to deal out lands beyond the Shannon provisionally in proportion to the stock of corn and cattle owned. Even in Dublin doubts were expressed whether numbers so large could be compelled to shift their homes. " By the last orders touching transplantation," we are told in February, " it is not intended that any should be sent into Connaught but proprietors and soldiers. The rest stay." [3] Hesitation at headquarters was naturally followed by floods of petitions asking for dispensation, and by an almost universal neglect to comply with the orders of the Government.

A general transplantation feared.

1654. Jan. Large numbers of certificates.

Few actually remove.

Feb. 6. Doubts as to the possibility of carrying out the order.

[1] Dobbins to Percival, Jan. 24, *Egmont MSS.*

[2] In Limerick precinct 339 proprietors received certificates to transplant, on which were noted the names of 3,048 followers—wives, children, tenants, and servants.

[3] Percival to Capt. Gething, Feb. 6, *Egmont MSS.*

On May 1, the day by which all transplantable persons were to have crossed the Shannon, it appeared that certificates

May 1.
Few present
themselves
in Con-
naught.

had been lodged at Loughrea by 1,589 heads of families on behalf of 43,308 persons.[1] It does not follow that those named in the certificates departed at once, or that all of them moved forward at any subsequent time. Petitions claiming exemption poured in, and

Temporary
dispensa-
tions
granted.

the Government, to gain time to examine them, granted temporary dispensations in many cases, but allowed to very few a complete suspension of the order for transplantation. It was still more difficult to deal with the mass, which met the declarations of the will of the Government with sheer inertia. On July 31 the commissioners commuted to transportation to Barbados the death sentence pronounced on one Peter Bath for refusing to transplant. On the other hand, they attempted to make the way easy for the transplanters by insisting that servants left to gather in the crops already planted should not be deprived of a lodging by the new claimants, who were already forcing their way into possession.[2] The result was, however, little or nothing—the transplantation remaining at a standstill during the greater part of 1654. The condition of the country into which the transplanters were required to remove was far from attractive. In Clare, out of 1,300 ploughlands, only forty were inhabited,[3] the remainder being rocky and uncultivated. Connaught had been devastated by both parties, and, where the Irish inhabitants remained in possession, they resented the order to remove to other parts of the province to make way even for persons of their own race.[4]

---

[1] Between May 1 and the end of July only 36 certificates, covering 902 persons, were handed in. Hardinge, Circumstances attending the War, *Trans. of the Roy. Irish Academy* (Antiquities), xxiv. 186.

[2] The Commissioners to the Commissioners of Revenue, May 26, *Irish R.O.*, $\frac{A}{85}$ 45, p. 702.

[3] Grievances of the inhabitants of Clare, *ib.* $\frac{A}{84}$ 44, p. 205.

[4] Hardinge on Surveys in Ireland, p. 34, in *Transactions of the Roy. Irish Academy* (Antiquities), vol. xxiv.

Meanwhile the lot of those who craved a mitigation of their sentences depended to some extent on political develop-

Ireland and the Protectorate. ments in England. Before the end of 1653 Oliver had assumed the Protectorate, and in consequence of rumours calling in question the fidelity of the army, and even of the Government in Ireland, one of his first acts

Henry Cromwell's mission. was to despatch his son Henry to examine the posi- tion.[1] Such an enquiry was the more needed as there were rumours that the Baptists—strong not only in numbers among the officers, but also in the adhesion of Fleetwood—intended to join the Feakes and the Powells in re- pudiating the Protectorate. On both these heads Henry Crom- well was able to bring back satisfactory assurances,[2] and in August Oliver felt himself able to carry out a scheme which he had for some time contemplated, in appointing Fleetwood Lord

Aug. Fleetwood Lord Deputy. Deputy with a Council limiting him in the same way as Oliver was himself limited by the Council in Eng- land.[3] The question of the policy to be pursued in Ireland was far more dubious than the selection of the person of the Governor; though all that is known about the discussions

The ques- tion of trans- plantation discussed at West- minster. in the Council at Westminster is that Lambert on one occasion casually referred to transplantation or not-transplantation as an issue on which no deci- sion had yet been taken.[4] The probability is that Oliver's good sense perceived that the general transplantation decreed by the Declaration of October 14, 1653, was absolutely impracticable, but that, as his manner was, he hesitated long before coming to a decision. At last, on August 17, a clause

Power of dispensation granted to Fleetwood in Fleetwood's instructions gave him and his Council power to dispense with the orders of the ate Parliament or Council of State relating to trans-

[1] See vol. iii. p. 10.

[2] Cromwell to Thurloe, March 8; Lloyd to Thurloe, March 13, *Thurloe*, ii. 149, 162.

[3] Order for the Dissolution of the Board of Commissioners, Aug. 22, *Irish R.O.*, $\frac{A}{27}$ 25, p. 28.

[4] *Clarke Papers*, iii. 207.

plantation, so far as they judged fit for the public service.[1]   At the same time there was a talk of sending Henry Cromwell to Ireland to command the forces in Ludlow's place,[2] and there could be no doubt that his voice would be raised in the Irish Council on the side of moderation.

Such a solution of the difficulty, if loyally carried out in Dublin, would probably have saved the situation, at least ·for the time.   Dispensations for the mass of the peasantry, and for the more inoffensive of the proprietors of land, would have left Connaught and Clare as a residence for the more pronounced enemies of England.   Henry Cromwell, however, remained at Westminster, and neither Fleetwood nor his Council was in a mood to act on the powers conferred upon them.   Fleetwood was himself embittered against the Irish race, and had too little strength of character to shake off the influence of his military surroundings.   " The truth is," he had written to Thurloe in June, "these people are an abominable, false, cunning, and perfidious people, and the best of them to be pitied, but not to be trusted." [3]   He was in the same frame of mind in November.   " We are endeavouring," he and his Council informed the Protector, " to carry on the work of transplanting the Irish proprietors and such as have been in arms." [4]   It was by a mere slip of the pen that the abettors of rebellion did not reappear in this letter.   In a Declaration issued on Novem-

Fleetwood unwilling to take advantage of it.

[1] Instructions to the Lord Deputy and Council, Aug. 17, *Irish R.O.*, $\frac{A}{27}$ 25, p. 38.   A month earlier a well-informed person wrote from London: " I apprehend great mischief likely to accompany this transplantation, not only to Carrig in particular, but also to all the rest of our estate in general. . . . When our new Council goes over—which, it is said, will be suddenly—I believe they will give some stop to the transplantation, it being one of their instructions to moderate it as they shall think fit." Percival to Gething, July 19, *Egmont MSS.*

[2] Percival to Gething, Aug. 1, *ib.*

[3] Fleetwood to Thurloe, June 2, *Thurloe*, ii. 343.

[4] The Deputy and Council to the Protector, Nov. 14, *Irish R.O.*, $\frac{A}{30}$ 28, p. 13.

ber 30,[1] ordering that the transplantation shall be completed

Nov. 30.
Trans-
plantation
to be com-
pleted by
March.

by March 1, 1655, this class of persons is included with the other two. Yet it was necessarily with proprietors, whose estates were required for the new settlers, that the Irish Government was principally con-

Dec. 28.
Commis-
sioners at
Athlone.

cerned, and when, on December 28, a new body of commissioners was directed to sit at Athlone[2] to examine into the character of the delinquency of those who claimed lands beyond the Shannon, it was only with persons having interest in land that they were called on to deal. Indirectly, this commission might be read as an intimation that the transplantation of other than landed men was either dropped or postponed, but no public announcement was made to that effect. So far as the proprietors were concerned the

The trans-
plantation
of pro-
prietors
carried out
in earnest.

Declaration of November 30 was treated as decisive. There was to be no more hanging back in hope of better terms. " The transplantation," writes the Dublin correspondent of a London newspaper, " is now far advanced, the men being gone for to prepare their new habitations in Connaught. Their wives and children and dependents have been, and are, packing away after them apace, and all are to be gone by the first of March next." [3] The emigration, however, was far from complete, even amongst the landowners. Large numbers still held back, and there was some expectation of securing better terms from the Parliament then in session at Westminster.[4] On the other hand, there was a strong opinion amongst the military party that the Government ought to effect a far more general clearance, and this view of the case was expressed in a petition comparing the Irish to the Midianites, whose very neighbourhood was corrupting to the people of God—which was not, indeed, presented

---

[1] This Declaration has not been preserved, but its contents are recited in a later one—*Order by the Lord Deputy and Council*, Feb. 27, B.M. press mark, 806, i. 14, No. 12.

[2] Commission, Dec. 28, *Irish R.O.*, $\frac{A}{26}$ 24, p. 33.

[3] *Merc. Pol.*, E, 823, 5.

[4] This is stated by Lawrence in *The Interest of England*, E, 829, 17.

to Fleetwood till March, but which must have been circulated for signature some time before.[1]

Whilst the policy of the Government was still doubtful a champion of the moderate party appeared in Vincent Gookin.[2]

Gookin pleads for moderation. Gookin, who had sat in the Nominated Parliament as one of the six members for Ireland, was the probable author of the clause giving power to the Dublin Government to dispense with transplantation,[3] which had hitherto produced little effect at Dublin. Towards the end of June he returned to Ireland, and during his visit there *Gookin and Petty.* he seems to have discussed the transplantation with Dr. Petty, a man of varied ability, who, as physician-general of the army in Ireland, had effected a series of far-reaching reforms. Petty, though he is not to be classed among the enemies of English rule, was no admirer of the drastic measures adopted in Ireland. He was, however, by no means inclined to endanger his own prospects by opposition to the Government, and though he seems to have provided Gookin with a few pages of argument directed against general transplantation, he preserved a discreet silence on his authorship, and doubtless enjoined a similar reticence on his friend.[4] Gookin, coming back to England to take his seat for Cork *1655.* and Bandon in the first Parliament of the Protec- *Jan. 3.* *The Great Case of Transplantation.* torate, incorporated Petty's argument with some fiery exhortations of his own, and issued the whole anonymously, on January 3, 1655, under the title of *The Great Case of Transplantation.*

---

[1] The petition is printed in the *Hist. Rev.* (Oct. 1899) xiv. 723.

[2] He was a *persona grata* with the Protector, *ib.* p. 720, note 35.

[3] See *supra*, p. 98.

[4] On Petty's part in Gookin's tract see Lord E. Fitzmaurice's *Life of Petty*, 32, note 3, and *Hist. Rev.* (Oct. 1899) xiv. 721. In after years, at least, Petty was a Unionist of the most pronounced type. He advised that all the marriageable young women of Irish birth, 20,000 in number, as he reckoned, should be transported to England, to become the wives of Englishmen, and that the same number of English girls should be brought to Ireland, to be the wives of Irishmen, and to indoctrinate their children with English ideas. *Political Anatomy of Ireland* (ed. 1691), p. 30.

Accepting the removal of the landed proprietors as needful for the new English settlement, Gookin dwelt upon the good qualities of less exalted Irishmen. English labour, he argued, would never be available to any appreciable extent in Ireland, and, if the settlers were to avoid ruin, they must content themselves with the service of the natives.

1655.
Gookin's
view of Irish
character,
and of the
need of the
employment
of Irish.

"The first and chiefest necessaries," he wrote, "are those natural riches of food, apparel and habitations. If the first be regarded, there are few of the Irish commonalty but are skilled in husbandry, and more exact than any English in the husbandry proper to that country. If the second, there are few of the women but are skilful in dressing hemp and flax, and making of linen and woollen cloth. If the third, it is believed to every hundred men there are five or six masons or carpenters, at least, of that nation, and these more handy and ready in building ordinary houses and much more prudent in supplying the defect of instruments and materials, than English artificers." [1] Yet, if the bulk of the Irish population was to be retained as tenants and servants of the English settlers, how was the difficulty raised by the military party to be met? With what feeling of confidence could the settlers establish themselves in their new homes, amidst an Irish population far outnumbering their own families, and alienated from them by every sentiment by which human action is governed? Gookin met these questions in that spirit of unfounded optimism which marred his usefulness as a political adviser. The Irish, he argued, deprived of their priests and of their landlords, would readily accept the religion and habits of their conquerors. [2]

His expecta-
tion of the
conversion
of the Irish.

At Dublin these sanguine hopes found but little echo. "There is," wrote Fleetwood, "a very strange, scandalous book, *Arguments against Transplantation*, [3]

Feb. 7.
Fleetwood's
opinion of
Gookin.

[1] *The Great Case of Transplantation*, p. 17, E, 234, 6.

[2] *Ib*. pp. 18–20.

[3] Fleetwood cannot have studied it very deeply, or he would have given the title more correctly.

that is now come forth, which doth very falsely and un-
worthily asperse those that did and now do serve the State
here. The person who is said to write this will, I doubt, as
much deceive your estimation in England as he hath been
disingenuous to us here, who have been ready on all occasions
to show respect to him; but those who know him better than I
do have, before this time, bespoken what manner of spirit he
was of, which I, in too much charity, did hope had been otherwise. It will be a great discouragement to the State's servants
if such may be allowed their liberty to traduce them." [1]   The
indignation, which Fleetwood shared with his military advisers,

March.
Petition for
a universal
transplanta-
tion.

March 9.
Lawrence's
pamphlet.

found a voice not only in the petition demanding a
universal transplantation, which was presented to him
about the middle of March,[2] but also in a pamphlet
published in London on the 9th of the same month,
under the title of *The Interest of England in the
Irish Transplantation*. This pamphlet, written by
Colonel Richard Lawrence, a brother of the President of the
Council, and himself a member of several Committees upon
which the work of transplantation devolved in Ireland, is notable
as giving away the case of those whom Gookin attacked, by
maintaining that that writer was in the wrong in charging the
Dublin Government with having even contemplated a general
transplantation. The orders given, he alleged, had referred to
no more than the removal of proprietors and men who had been
in arms. The proprietors, he asserted, were not 'near the
twentieth part of the people of Ireland,' whilst the greater number of those who had borne arms had been sent abroad; 'so
that, though it be hard to determine the number of these two
sorts of persons, yet any man that knows the state of Ireland
must acknowledge they are probably so inconsiderable that they
will not be missed or discerned as to their numbers from whence
they remove.' [3]   The attempt to include the numbers who had
borne arms but had laid them aside before the final surrender,

---

[1] Fleetwood to Thurloe, Feb. 7, *Thurloe*, iii. 139.
[2] See *supra*, p. 100.
[3] *The Interest of England*, p. 17, E, 829; F, 17.

as well as the far greater numbers who had aided or abetted the rebellion in its beginnings, was thus tacitly dropped by the mouthpiece of the Irish Government ; and Gookin could but reply in *The Author and Case of Transplanting . . . Vindicated*, that whatever might be the intentions of the Irish Government, its public declarations embraced a more sweeping system of transplantation, and that there was nothing to prevent them from stepping on some future occasion beyond the limits which, according to Lawrence, they had imposed on themselves for the present.[1]

1655.
May 12.
Gookin's
reply.

The policy of the Government with respect to transplantation was necessarily affected by the progress made with the new settlement. So far, indeed, as landed men were concerned, the increasing necessity of disbandment placed their sentence beyond recall. In the summer of 1652 the strength of the army was 34,128, exclusive of commissioned officers.[2] Towards the end of 1654 the Deputy and Council gave their opinion that the garrison of Ireland could not, consistently with safety, be reduced below 15,600.[3] Some small numbers, indeed, had been disbanded in 1653 ; but it was not a moment too soon to complete the work, as Parliament was at this time crying out for a diminution of military expenses in all the three countries, and the revenue of Ireland was no more than 197,000*l.*, against an expenditure of 630,814*l.*, thus leaving a deficit of 433,814*l.* Of the expenditure incurred, no less than 523,842*l.* was needed on account of the army.[4]

Necessity
of disband-
ment.

1652–54.
Strength of
the army.

Financial
difficulties.

Under these circumstances the Irish Government had been diligently preparing for the assignment of land to disbanded

---

[1] *The Author and Case of Transplanting*, published on May 12. E, 638, 7.

[2] Statement by the Commissioners, Aug. 11, 1652, *Irish R.O.*, $\frac{A}{90}$ 50, p. 215.

[3] The Deputy and Council to the Protector, Nov. 14, 1654, *ib.* $\frac{A}{30}$ 28, p. 14.

[4] Hardinge on Surveys in Ireland, p. 7. *Trans. of the Roy. Irish Academy* (Polite Literature), xxiv.

soldiers.   In August 1653 the Surveyor-General, Benjamin

Aug.   Worsley, was directed to make a gross survey—or,
A gross   as it would now be styled, a rough survey of the for-
survey
ordered.   feited estates.   Profitable lands were to be set forth,
with their acreage and boundaries ; unprofitable lands to be
mentioned but not measured.   Such, at least, had been the
scheme adopted in the instructions embodied in the Act of
Satisfaction.[1]   So far as can be conjectured by the result, even
less precise instructions were given in Dublin, as it seems, from
the few returns preserved, that Worsley and his subordinates
contented themselves with setting down the estimated acreage
of the land, as well as the rent due from it at the time and also
in 1641, together with its estimated value at the outbreak of
the rebellion.[2]

The survey had not proceeded far when the commissioners
who at that time governed Ireland were startled by a suggestion

Doubt as to   that the forfeited land would be insufficient.   Ac-
the suffi-   cording to existing Acts the grant of an acre would
ciency of the
forfeited   cancel a debt of 12s. in Leinster, of 8s. in Munster,
land.   and of 4s. in Ulster.   It was calculated that the
acreage of forfeited lands was 2,697,000, and that, after setting
aside 565,000 acres for the Adventurers, there would remain
2,131,500, of which, if the lands reserved for the Government
in the four counties of Dublin, Kildare, Carlow, and Cork
were deducted, only 1,727,500 would be available to meet a
debt to the soldiers of 1,550,000l., to which was to be added
200,000l. due to other public creditors ; so that the whole debt
to be satisfied amounted to 1,750,000l.   Unfortunately, at the
rates set down in the Act the disposable acres were worth no
more than 802,500l., leaving an unsecured debt of 947,500l.

Nov. 21, 22.   In this difficulty the commissioners took the sense of
A council of   a council of officers which met in November and re-
officers agree
to raise the   commended that the rates should be raised—in other
rates.   words, that the acres dealt out should be estimated at

[1] *Scobell*, ii. 252.

[2] Hardinge's Survey in Ireland, 9–13, 39–41.   *Trans. of the Roy.
Irish Academy* (Polite Literature), xxiv.

a higher sum than the Act prescribed—on the understanding that the new rates should be separately appraised in each county, according to the nature of the soil.[1]

By the end of 1653 the gross survey had proceeded so far that Worsley was able to send in an estimate of the acreage of the several baronies, though without specifying what lands were forfeited or unforfeited, profitable or unprofitable.[2] Rough as this calculation was, the Dublin Government announced in May that 4,711 soldiers would be provided with land before the end of June.[3] These lands, however, could only be provisionally assigned till a more exact admeasurement had been taken, and the officers, having grown impatient of the loose methods of the gross survey, obtained from the Government a commission to take what is known as the Civil survey, in which Crown lands, Church lands and lands forfeited by private owners were to be distinguished from one another. On June 2 commissions for surveying the ten counties were issued, seventeen other counties being subsequently added. The surveyors were instructed to take the baronies assigned to soldiers first.[4] Still, however, it was felt that there was room for improvement in the methods pursued, and a Committee appointed on September 8 to consider the whole question resulted on December 11 in the acceptance of an offer made by Dr. Petty to survey the forfeited lands in the three provinces in a far more accurate manner than had hitherto been attempted. The *Down Survey* as it was called, simply because its results were set down on a map, and not merely described in words and figures, was to be completed in thirteen months dating from February 1, 1655—that is to say,

Marginal notes:

Dec. 1653. The division of lands ordered.

1654. May 4. The settlement of soldiers begun.

June 2. The civil survey begun.

Sept. 8. A Committee to examine the whole question.

Dec. 11. An agreement with Petty for the *Down Survey.*

---

[1] The Commissioners to the Council of State, Dec. 16, 1653, *Irish R.O.*, $\frac{A}{90}$ 50, p. 587.

[2] *Ib.* $\frac{A}{85}$ 45, p. 80.

[3] Instructions to Rowe and Kindon, May 4, *ib.* $\frac{A}{85}$ 45, p. 341.

[4] Petty's *Down Survey*, 382, 383. Hardinge on Surveys in Ireland, 14, in *Trans. of the Roy. Irish Academy* (Polite Literature), xxiv.

by March 1, 1656. As might have been expected, the substi-

Petty's con-
troversy
with
Worsley. tution of Petty for Worsley led to violent recrimina-
tions between them. Petty described Worsley as
ignorant and grasping, whilst Worsley described
Petty as a charlatan without practical knowledge of the surveyor's art. The truth seems to have been that Worsley was
an ordinary surveyor, incapable of rising to the height of his
gigantic task, whilst Petty was possessed of unusual organising
skill, with a keen eye for the requirements of a new situation.[1]

Pending the completion of the new survey the officers
agitated for immediate possession of the lands assigned to

The officers
demand
immediate
possession. them, at least in some provisional fashion. Nor did
they find Fleetwood and his Council obdurate. On
May 10, 1655, they received an engagement that

1655.
May 10.
More
baronies for
the soldiers. several additional baronies would be set apart to satisfy
their claims.[2] On the 22nd the Government allowed
the officers to withdraw their offer of a higher rate
by counties,[3] and to revert to the rates established in

May 22.
Immediate
possession of
lands to the
value of two-
thirds of the
arrears. the Acts of Parliament by provinces. At the same
time they directed that they should be placed in
immediate possession of lands to the value of two-
thirds of their arrears, a limitation obviously prudent
in view of the uncertainty as to the real acreage of any lands
that were now available for division. The officers were, however, to state the order in which the regiments were to be disbanded, so that the survey might proceed with the baronies

July 9.
Dissatisfac-
tion of the
army agents. assigned to those regiments in the same order.[4]
With this arrangement, however, the agents appointed
by the army to treat with the Government were

July 20.
Concessions
by the
Government. altogether dissatisfied, and on July 20 the Deputy
and Council, though still refusing to give immediate
possession of unsurveyed lands to individual soldiers,

[1] Petty's *Down Survey*, 4–30.

[2] Order by the Deputy and Council, May 10, *Irish R.O.*, $\frac{A}{5}$ 5, p. 154.

[3] See *supra*, pp. 105, 106.

[4] Order by the Deputy and Council, May 22, Petty's *Down Survey*,
64.

agreed to allow the rents of the soldiers' moiety of lands in the whole of the ten counties to be received by the army agents, with assurance that the land itself would be divided in due course as soon as the Down Survey was complete. The rents of other baronies assigned as collateral security, to be divided amongst the soldiers if it appeared that the ten counties were insufficient, were to be collected on behalf of the Government, but set aside, to be divided amongst the soldiers in the event of the lands in these districts being required for their use.[1]

The approaching completion of the settlement necessarily led to increasing stringency in the removal of the old proprietors.

1655.
March 7.
Seizure of
the corn of
those neg-
lecting to
transplant.

Soon after the first of March the corn of those who had neglected to remove was seized, and sold for the benefit of their compatriots who had already started for Connaught.[2] On March 19 courts-martial were established for the trial and execution of transplantable persons still to be found in any of the three provinces ;[3] but at the same time the courts were instructed to substitute transportation to the colonies for the death penalty whenever they considered it desirable, and in any case to send no prisoners to execution without special approval by the Government. On

April 2.
Hether-
ington's
execution.

April 2, however, the Government, resolving to make at least one example, gave its consent to the execution of a certain Edward Hetherington. The sentence passed on him was solely for not transplanting, but it was alleged against him that he had taken part as a Tory in the slaying of Englishmen.[4] On the following day he was hanged.[5]

1654.
Ravages
of the
Tories.

The Tories, in truth, were even greater obstacles to the success of the plantation than the recalcitrant proprietors. Their bands, lurking in the fast-

---

[1] Petty's *Down Survey*, 66–80.

[2] Declaration by the Deputy and Council, March 7, B.M. press-mark, 806, i. 14, No. 14.

[3] Declaration, March 19, *Irish R.O.*, $\frac{A}{26}$ 24, p. 75.

[4] Resolution of the Deputy and Council, Apr. 2, *ib.* $\frac{A}{5}$ 5, p. 114.

[5] *Carte Papers*, vii. fol. 6.

nesses of the bogs and mountains, consisted of the hardiest of the natives who refused to submit to the strangers' yoke. Swooping down upon English habitations, and with still greater delight on the habitations of Irishmen who had submitted, they plundered and slew to their hearts' delight. Fear, or reluctance to betray countrymen, rendered the Irish peasant slow to give information which might lead to the capture of the marauders. To check the complicity of the natives orders were given in Cork precinct that the Irish remaining in their old quarters should be collected in villages, in which at least thirty families were to be drawn together, and that these villages should not be within half a mile of wood, bog, or mountain. Care, too, was to be taken for the appointment of a head-man, with the duty of bringing in the cattle every night and setting a watch over them.[1] A few weeks later a party of Tories murdered an Irishman who served the English as a constable at Timolin. As the Tories were countenanced by the inhabitants of the neighbourhood, and no information had been given, all Irish Papists in Timolin were ordered to transplantation as a punishment, their cabins being burnt and rates levied on the barony for the relief of the widow.[2] Later on, perhaps in revenge for this punishment, another band of Tories swooped down on eight English surveyors at Timolin, carried them into the woods, and there murdered them.[3] In vain prices were set on the heads of the leaders of the Tories.[4] If some were brought in and hanged, others quickly slipped into their places. At last, in January 1655 the Government denounced the ingratitude of the Irish rebels, who, notwithstanding the mercy and favour of Parliament to all who would live peaceably under English

May 12. Irish to be collected in villages.

July. Murder of an Irish constable at Timolin,

1655. March? and of eight surveyors.

---

[1] Instructions touching the Irish, May 12, 1654, *Irish R.O.*, $\frac{A}{85}$ 45, p. 361.

[2] Order by the Deputy and Council, July 21, *ib.* p. 505.

[3] Order, Dec. 25, 1655, *Prendergast*, 206, note 3. Prendergast says that no murder was committed, but does not give his authority.

[4] Instances are given in *Prendergast*, 343–4.

rule, nevertheless continued in their evil courses, disturbing all

1655.
Jan. 27.
Courts-
martial
established. who desired to live peaceably by 'murders, spoils, rapines, and thefts.' The officers in each precinct were therefore ordered to act as a court-martial to judge summarily in such cases. No quarter was any longer to be given.[1]

So the renewed struggle was carried on in all its horrors. As in the days when Bruce was holding out against the officers

The
struggle
continued. of Edward I., the men who were thieves and murderers to the one side were heroes and patriots to the other. Not to submit to the contemptuous alien was the resolution which armed the heart of the Irish Tory. If he walked in darkness, it was because open resistance had ceased to be possible. He at least would not justify Gookin's dream of a submissive Ireland waxing fat under English landlords, caressing the hand that chastised him, and making sport for the master who loathed and despised him.

Again and again in the course of this inglorious struggle did the Government at Dublin attempt to reduce the number of its enemies. Thinking in terms of English law, it was never

Vagrants
to be
trans-
ported. weary of decreeing that vagrants and other persons who refused to work were to be disposed of in the English colonies beyond the sea—to New England, Virginia, the West Indies, and especially to Barbados. The first instance appears to be one in which Messrs. Sellick and

1653.
Oct. 25. Leader, of Bristol, offered in the autumn of 1653 to ship 250 Irishwomen between the ages of 15 and 50 to New England. At the instance of Lord Broghill this proposal was set aside in favour of another to send out persons, both men and women, from the county of Cork. The persons so sent were to be such as 'live like beggars and vagabonds, and follow no lawful vocation.' Permission was accordingly granted to search for such persons ' of the Irish nation that are rogues and vagabonds, idlers and wanderers, and such as have

---

[1] Order of Deputy and Council, Jan. 27. 1655, *Irish R.O.*, $\frac{A}{26}$ 24, p. 27.

no means to get their livelihood by labour or otherwise, or such
as, being able to labour, shall refuse to do so.'　In January

1654.
Further
orders
for trans-
portation.

1654 the governors of certain towns were directed to
hand over to three merchants of Waterford, for
transportation, all rogues and vagrants, whether men
or women, taking care that no one was sent off who
was living in a family and whose good behaviour was certified
by the master of that family.　In April one Norris was to
transport rogues and vagabonds from Limerick precinct to the
Caribbee Islands, and the same class of persons from Galway
precinct to Virginia.　In June a similar order was given to the
same person to transport to Barbados.[1]　These orders, which
were followed by others to the same effect, were obviously

1655.
Abuses
detected.

liable to abuse, and in 1655 we hear of directions to
search a ship lying in Dublin harbour, on suspicion
that persons had been forcibly carried on board
though they were neither rogues nor vagrants.[2]

That the persons condemned to transportation were doomed
to a lifelong slavery is a delusion propagated by writers un-

The trans-
ported
servants
not slaves.

acquainted with the social condition of the colonies.
The system of service prevailing in Barbados was
applicable, at least in the more northern colonies, to
free emigrants as well as to persons sent abroad under compulsion, and both there and in the West Indies the service came
to an end at the expiration of a fixed term of years, the money
paid to the shipper by the master who acquired these limited
rights being supposed to be paid for the expenses of the
voyage, which the servant, on his part, was bound to repay by
his labour.[3]　No doubt the passage across the Atlantic was

[1] Orders by the Commissioners, Oct. 25, 1653; Jan. 23, April 21,
April 24, June 7, 1654, *Irish R.O.*, $\frac{A}{84}$ 44, p. 663; $\frac{A}{85}$ 45, pp. 66, 298, 301,
436.

[2] Order by the Deputy and Council, July 6, 1655, *ib.* $\frac{A}{5}$ 5, p. 188.

[3] In June 1654 the commissioners write to Col. Phayre that they have
been unable to transport some of O'Dwyer's soldiers intended for service
on the Continent but that men are wanted in Barbados and other West
Indian islands, ' where they will have as good condition as any English or

accompanied with considerable hardship, and those who were
assigned to a rough and cruel master had to endure suffering
for a time; whilst even under more favourable circumstances
the servant in Barbados had to work under a tropical sun.
Nor would it be possible to deny that women cut adrift from
family life were subject to peculiar perils. Yet, when their
term of service was expired, the paucity of numbers of white
women enabled them to command their own price, and there
is every reason to believe that the greater number of them
ultimately settled down as the free wives of free men.[1]

other servants there, and after 4 years are to be free men to act for their
advantage.' They add that 14s. a head will be paid to the officers who
accompany them, 'which otherwise is to be allowed to every such Irishman as voluntarily goes abroad upon this contract.' The same is to be
paid by the Undertaker to each ' of the said Irish now kept together upon
the charge of the country as shall be put aboard, who are to have the like
provision and accommodation; and for such women as shall go abroad,
they are to be provided for as to apparel.' If the number did not reach
400, it was to be made up by apprehending vagrants and idle persons
judged to be such by justices of the peace. The Commissioners to Phayre,
June 15, 1654, *Irish R.O.*, $\frac{A}{90}$ 50, p. 708. On the evidence that the
service to which Irishmen and others were sent was temporary servitude,
not slavery, see vol. iii. p. 309, note 1. In Virginia, a special Act was
passed in 1655 that all Irish servants that, from ' the first of September,
1653, have been brought into this colony without indenture... shall serve
as followeth, viz., "all above 16 years old to serve six years, and all under
to serve till they be 24 years old."' Hening's *Laws of Virginia*, i. 411.
In his *Historical Sketch of the Persecution suffered by the Catholics of
Ireland*, Cardinal Moran takes the usual view, that the transported
Irishmen were slaves, supporting it almost entirely on the evidence of
priests and others in Europe, who had no personal knowledge of the
colonies. An apparent exception is a statement that ' when the Rev.
John Grace visited these islands in 1666, he found that there were no
fewer than 12,000 Irish scattered amongst them, and that they were
treated as slaves.' Fortunately, Cardinal Moran has published the letter
on which this statement is founded, and in that letter there is nothing
about slavery. The men had been sent by Cromwell ' in agrorum culturâ
ministratum, cum quibus misere et crudeliter agitur tum in temporalibus
tum maxime in spiritualibus.' *Spicilegium Ossoriense*, p. 485.

[1] Prendergast gives the most gloomy account of the fate of the women
transported, telling us that ' the West India sugar planters . . . desired

Next to the elimination of Tories, no subject was deemed
more important to the success of the plantation than the
securing of centres of trade in English hands. On
May 10, 1655, orders were given that 'Papists and
other superfluous Irish' should be expelled from
Dublin.[1] A year earlier, in 1654, the Roman Catholic inhabitants of Kilkenny, Wexford, and Clonmel

Towns to be in English hands.

Cases of Dublin, Kilkenny, Wexford, and Clonmel,

the men and boys for their bondsmen, and the women and Irish girls, in a
country where they had only Maroon women and negresses to solace
them.' Writing again of a later project of sending 1,000 boys and 1,000
girls to Jamaica—a project which, as will be seen (see *infra*, p. 218), was
never carried into effect—he says that the 'boys were to go as bondsmen, and the girls to be bound by other ties to these English soldiers in
Jamaica' (*Prendergast*, 89, 93). To these reckless statements we may
oppose the fact that Ligon gives us an account of the expenses of an
estate in Barbados, reckoning those of ten white women servants, 'four to
attend in the house,' and 'the other six that weed and do the common
work abroad yearly' (*Hist. of Barbados*, 115). Mr. Bruce's very full
account above referred to puts the matter in a clear light so far as Virginia
is concerned. 'A certain degree of liberty in the sexual relations of the
female servants with the male, and even with their masters, might have
been expected, but there are numerous indications that the general sentiment of the colony condemned it, and sought by appropriate legislation
to restrain and prevent it.' The marriage of a woman servant during her
time of service without her master's consent was punishable, because it
deprived the master of her services. Speaking of a somewhat later time,
when women of bad character were transported in large numbers,
Mr. Bruce writes: "The women who were exported from England to
the colony had unusual opportunities of advancing their welfare in life.
If they enjoyed an honourable reputation, they found no difficulty in
marrying into a higher station than they had been accustomed to. Bul-
lock," in 1649, "mentions the fact that no maid whom he had brought
over failed to find a husband in the course of the first three months after
she had entered into his service. The fortunes of these imported women
were frequently superior to their deserts, for a large proportion of them
were considered to be worthless" (Bruce's *Economic Hist. of Virginia*,
ii. 51). The eagerness with which women were sought in marriage in
Barbados is shown by a statement made in 1654, by an English visitor,
that 'a whore, if handsome, makes a wife for some rich planter' (Whistler's Journal, *Sloane MSS.* 3926, fol. 9).

Order by the Deputy and Council, May 7, *Irish R.O.*, $\frac{A}{5}$ 5, p. 147.

were expelled, with the exception of a few artisans and fishermen, though they were almost all of English descent.[1] In their case, however, the Government was content to allow the expelled families to reside outside the walls in the neighbourhood of their old homes, without insisting on transplantation. In Galway, houses deserted by their owners in 1652 were seized by the Government; and in July 1655, on the ground that the articles of capitulation had provided for the expulsion of the inhabitants if their presence was found to endanger the security of the place, all Irishmen, with the exception of the sick and infirm, were ordered to leave, the value of their property being provided for them elsewhere.[2]

of Galway,

Limerick, at the mouth of the Shannon, was of special importance, and in May 1654 it was ordered that no more than forty artificers and fishermen might remain, and they only if they had not borne arms and were not proprietors of land.[3]

and of Limerick.

To weaken Papists and to strengthen Protestants was the chief object of the Government in Dublin and Westminster. For erring Protestants the path was made easy by two ordinances issued by the Protector before the meeting of Parliament—the one covering with an indemnity those of Munster who had supported Ormond and Inchiquin in 1648, on the ground that they had brought their province over to the Commonwealth in 1649; the other letting off Protestants in other parts of Ireland with a fine, in lieu of the confiscation of one-fifth of their property adjudged to them by the Act of Settlement.[4] Taking the two together, and noticing

1654. May–Sept. Concessions to Protestants.

---

[1] Prim's Men of the Family of Langton, *Kilkenny Archæological Journal*, New Series, iii. 85; Orders by the Commissioners, March 6, 13, 15, 1654, *Irish R.O.*, $\frac{A}{84}$ 44, p. 62; $\frac{A}{85}$ 45, pp. 157, 179.

[2] Order by the Commissioners, March 15; Order by the Deputy and Council, Oct. 18, 1655, *ib.* $\frac{A}{82}$ 42, p. 705; $\frac{A}{5}$ 5, p. 254.

[3] Order by the Commissioners, May 15, 1654, *ib.*, $\frac{A}{85}$ 45, p. 363.

[4] *Ordinance for Protestants of Munster*, Aug. 1, 1654. E, 1064, 27; *Ordinance for Protestants in Ireland* Sept. 2, *Scobell*, ii. 359.

that they were nearly coincident in point of time with the grant

Coincidence
with the
grant of a
dispensing
power.

of the power of dispensation from transplantation to Fleetwood on August 17,[1] it would seem that the Protector was at that time inclined to adopt a policy of conciliation on both sides; though it was only to be expected that conciliation should go very much further in the case of Protestants than in that of Catholics. Nor is this all. That Gookin was the warm advocate before the Council of the

June 23.
Land
granted to
Gookin in
Ireland.

Munster indemnity is beyond dispute.[2] It is equally beyond dispute that in June 1654 the Protector showed his favourable opinion of Gookin by conferring on him a grant of land in Ireland; and that Fleetwood

Fleetwood's
opposition
to Gookin's
views.

manifested his hostility by refusing for a twelvemonth to carry the grant into effect.[3] On November 30, 1654, in spite of the dispensing power conferred on him, Fleetwood had issued that sweeping order for transplantation[4]

1655.
May 23.
Complains
of having no
letter.

which rendered the crisis acute. On May 23, 1655, he complained of being discountenanced in England, and pleaded for a letter from the Protector to encourage him in the prosecution of the work of transplantation.[5]

The fact was that Fleetwood's conduct as Deputy had given cause for much searching of heart at Whitehall. In addition

Differences
between
Fleetwood
and the Pro-
tector.

to the difference of opinion between Fleetwood and the Protector in the matter of the transplantation, the Deputy's notorious patronage of the Baptists, to which sect he himself belonged, and who were numerous and influential in the Irish army, could not but give umbrage to a Government which had had experience of the revolutionary tendencies of many of their co-religionists in England.[6]

---

[1] See *supra*, p. 98.   [2] *Egmont MSS.*

[3] *Hist. Review* (Oct. 1899), xiv. 734.   [4] See *supra*, p. 100.

[5] Fleetwood to Thurloe, May 23, *Thurloe*, iii. 468.

[6] " In Ireland they " (*i.e.* the Anabaptists) " were grown so high that the soldiers were many of them re-baptised as the way to preferment ; and those that opposed crushed with much uncharitable fierceness. To suppress these he sent hither his son, Henry Cromwell, who so discountenanced the Anabaptists, as yet to deal civilly by them, repressing

The first remedy which occurred to the Council was to send Henry Cromwell in the room of Ludlow, whose continuance in office was incompatible with the Protectoral system.   Accord-

1654.
Aug. 24.
H. Cromwell
to command
the army
under
Fleetwood,

Dec. 25.
and to be a
Councillor.
ingly, on August 24, 1654, at the request of the English Council, Henry Cromwell received a commission to command the Irish army under Fleetwood, with the title of major-general;[1] and on December 25 he was named a member of the Irish Council.[2]   The delay in sending the new commander to Ireland was probably due to a desire on the part of the Protector to conciliate his son-in-law.[3]   Subordinate as Henry Cromwell would be in both capacities, his relation to the Protector could hardly fail to give him a preponderating influence in the Council.

The opposition between the Protector and the Deputy increasing in the spring of 1655, the young commander was at

1655.
July 9.
H. Cromwell
in Ireland.
last despatched to his duties, landing in Dublin on July 9.   He was preceded by a letter which, in its involved arrangement, testifies to Oliver's embarrassment.   Embedded in the midst of pious remarks is his disclaimer of an intention, which had been attributed to him, of sending Henry as Deputy in Fleetwood's place.   Then, after a further instalment of religious observations, the real object of the letter is slipped in :—" If you have a mind to come over with your dear wife, &c., take the best opportunity for the good

their insolencies, but not abusing them or dealing hardly with them.'
Rel. Baxterianæ, i. 74.

[1] Order of Council, Aug. 22, *Interr.* I, 75, p. 523, O.   Cromwell's *Memoirs of the Protector*, 693.

[2] He had been recommended for this post by the English Council. Order of Council, Aug. 23 ; Commission, Dec. 25, *Fourteenth Report of the Deputy Keeper of Records in Ireland*, p. 28.

[3] Mr. Firth, in the *Dict. of Nat. Biogr.*, Art. ' Henry Cromwell,' attributes the delay to the Protector's unwillingness to advance so near a member of his own family.   If so, why did he name him to the command on Aug. 24?   The membership of the Council could hardly be separated from that post.

of the public and your own convenience." [1]   It is easy to read between the lines. Though the Protector had no wish to deprive his son-in-law of his high dignity as Lord Deputy, he would be glad if he would voluntarily abandon the personal ful-

June 19.
Gookin to
receive his
land.
filment of its duties. This letter was emphasised by another, written only three days earlier, ordering Fleetwood to place Gookin in possession of the land which had been granted to him twelve months before.[2]

Fleetwood's temper was none the more amiable for this expression of the Protector's sentiments. On July 14, five

Fleet-
wood
defiant.
days after Henry Cromwell's arrival, he issued two declarations which, taken together, showed his determination to carry out his transplantation policy in

July 14.
His
definition of
men in arms.
the most extreme way. One of these took the form of a reply to certain queries sent to him by the Protestants of Limerick, in which he defined those who had borne arms as including persons who had attended any rendezvous, or had kept watch and ward, even if they had been ' forced or pressed ' into the service.[3] The other was an order issued by him as Commander-in-Chief, reminding officers and soldiers that they had not only neglected to search

Soldiers to
search for
transplant-
able persons.
for persons condemned to transplantation under the three qualifications, but had entertained such persons as tenants or servants. If they did not amend their ways they would be sent before a court-martial, to be dealt with in accordance with the articles of war.[4]

The resistance of the officers and soldiers to the attempt

---

[1] The Protector to Fleetwood, June 22, *Carlyle*, Letter cxcix. It should be said that the correspondence in the *Lansdowne MSS.* furnishes proof that Fleetwood was desirous of coming over on personal grounds, though he may have wished to pay no more than a temporary visit. See also Fleetwood's own letter in *Thurloe*, iii. 602.

[2] The Protector to the Deputy and Council, June 19, *Irish R.O.*, $\frac{A}{28}$ 26, p. 64.

[3] Answers to Queries, July 14, *ib.* $\frac{A}{5}$ 5, p. 199.

[4] Declaration by the Deputy, July 14, B.M. press-mark, 806, i. 14, No. 24.

to deprive them, in their quality of present or future proprietors, of the service of Irish labourers or tenants

The resistance of the soldiers to Fleetwood's policy.

lay at the root of Fleetwood's difficulties. During
the last few months he had encountered the same
opposition nearer Dublin, where an attempt to clear
off the native Irish from what were popularly known as the

The five counties.

Five Counties—that is to say, Wexford, Wicklow,
and Kildare, together with parts of Dublin and
Carlow—had broken down before the resistance of the new
proprietors.[1] For some weeks Fleetwood hung on at Dublin.
By the beginning of August his retirement was a matter of
common talk. The crowd which had hitherto followed him in

Fleetwood and Henry Cromwell.

his attendance on the service of the Baptist congregation now followed Henry Cromwell to the lately
deserted 'public service' instituted by the Instrument of Government. The Provost of Trinity College hailed

Sept. 6. Fleetwood leaves Dublin.

the son of the Protector as the future ruler of the
country.[2] It was impossible to hold out longer,
and on September 6 the Lord Deputy took shipping
for England.

The departure of Fleetwood was a turning-point of the
Cromwellian policy in Ireland. It indicated a policy of
distrust of those officers who arrogated to themselves

Significance of the change.

the title of 'the godly,' and announced at least an
intention to introduce a more secular *régime*. It
signified, too, the abandonment of the plan of sweeping the
large majority of the Irish population out of three provinces,
and supplying their places by English labourers. Under the
influence of Henry Cromwell no more is heard of the large
class of those who had taken part in or had given assistance to
the rebellion in its earliest stage, the Government being
content with the transplantation of landowners and men who
had borne arms, the latter class being, as Colonel Lawrence

[1] Orders by the Deputy and Council, May 21, June 7, B.M. press-
mark, 806, i. 14, No. 21 ; *Irish R.O.*, $\frac{A}{5}$ 5, p. 173.

[2] Letters from Dublin, Aug. 1, 13, 19, Sept. 5 ; *Merc. Pol.*, E, 851,
8 ; E, 852, 18 ; E, 853, 22 ; *Perf. Diurnal*, E, 852, 15.

had argued,[1] comparatively a small one. For the earlier and more extensive plan, regarded from a merely English point of view, there had been something to be said. To put an end to the constant resistance of Irishmen to the imposition of English government and English custom by replacing the natives of three-fourths of Ireland by Englishmen seemed a desirable end to men to whom Irishmen appeared to stand outside the pale of civilisation, and who doggedly believed that Irishmen were alone to blame for the catastrophe which had shocked the whole of England in 1641. Fortunately for the progress of the race nature does not allow any people to regard the fate of another purely from its own point of view. The English project had recoiled partly because the grip of the native population on the soil could not be shaken loose, but still more because the English population was not prepared to rush in where no vacuum had been created. The new project, of retaining the mass of Irishmen, whilst depriving them of their natural leaders, and so tempting them to be as Englishmen, remained yet to be tried, though with little chance of success.

[1] See *supra*, pp. 103, 104.

CHAPTER XLV

HISPANIOLA AND JAMAICA

ALTHOUGH the speech in which the Protector had set forth the delinquencies of his first Parliament as a justification of its

1654.
The purpose
of the
fleets. approaching dissolution contained no reference to the two fleets which had by that time left the shores of England, its silence can safely be ascribed to prudential motives. Second in Oliver's mind only to his desire to protect 'the people of God' was his resolution to extend beyond the seas the power of England, a resolution which with

July 20.
A blow at
Antichrist
projected, him assumed, to some extent, the character of a Divine mission. "We consider this attempt," he had said in recommending the West Indian expedition to his Council, "because we think God has not brought us hither where we are, but to consider the work that we may do in the world as well as at home." [1] To weaken the grasp of Spain on the New World was to strike an effectual blow at the dominion of Antichrist, and Oliver could not fail to be bitterly mortified when he found the Parliament, on whose co-operation he had looked with hope, leaving this holy enterprise without financial support.

Yet, with all his religious enthusiasm, Oliver never lost sight of the practical objects to be attained by the destruction of Antichrist; nor did he fail to perceive that, if the enterprise was to be justified in the eyes of the world, it must be justified on other than religious grounds. The commercial interests of

---

[1] See vol. iii. p. 159, and also *Clarke Papers*, iii. 207.

England led him to challenge the claim of Spain, not, indeed,
as has often been erroneously alleged, to refuse to
Englishmen the right of trading with Spanish colonies,
but to seize English ships and to maltreat English
crews merely because they were found in some part or another
of the Caribbean Sea, even though they might be destined for
some island in actual possession of an English colony.[1] Setting
aside, therefore, the religious grounds of strife, the impending
conflict based itself on a conflict between two opposing
principles. For England the right of possession rested on
effective occupation.[2] For Spain, so far as America was concerned, it rested on the arbitrament of Alexander VI. Taking
his view of the position for granted, Oliver assured Venables of
the righteousness of his mission. "Either," he argued, "there

and also the defence of trade.

---

[1] Oliver's views on this subject are clearly set forth in the commission
issued by him to the five commissioners charged with the control of the
West Indian expedition. "We having taken into our serious consideration the state and condition of the English plantations and colonies in the
western parts of the world called America, and the opportunity and
means which God hath betrusted us and this Commonwealth with both
for securing the interest we already have in those countries which now lie
open and exposed to the will and power of the King of Spain—who
claims the same by colour of a donation of the Pope—at any time when
he shall have leisure to look that way ; and also for getting ground and
gaining upon the dominions and territories of the said King there ;
whereunto we also hold ourselves obliged in justice to the people of these
nations for the cruelty, wrongs and injuries done and exercised upon them
by the Spaniards in those parts. Having a respect likewise in this our
undertaking to the miserable thraldom and bondage, both spiritual and
civil, which the natives and others in the dominions of the said King in
America are subjected to and lie under by means of the Popish and cruel
Inquisition and otherwise, from which, if it shall please God to make us
instrumental in any measure to deliver them, and upon this occasion to
make way for the bringing in the light of the Gospel and power of true
religion and godliness into those parts, we shall esteem it the best and
most glorious part of any success or acquisition it shall please God to
bless us with." Commission of the Commissioners, Dec. 9, *Narrative of
Venables*, 109.

[2] The Protector had here adopted Raleigh's view. *Hist. of England*,
1603-1642, iii. 39-41.

was peace with the Spaniards in the West Indies or there was not. If peace, they had violated it, and to seek reparation was just. If we had no peace, then there was nothing acted against articles with Spain." [1] The expedition once resolved on, Oliver had no thought of limiting it to the seizure of any single port or island. He was bent on bringing under English dominion the track of the gold convoys across the Isthmus of Panama. [2] This scheme was a reversion to the Elizabethan gold-hunt, as opposed to the agricultural and commercial settlements of more recent years. There was nothing strange in the adoption of such a policy. What was strange was that Oliver should have thought it possible to cut off the supplies through which alone Spain was able to save herself from bankruptcy, and yet to remain at peace with her in Europe. It is to be presumed that the long-suffering with which Philip II. had postponed hostile action, in spite of Drake's roving exploits in American waters, led him to forget that the hesitating and inactive character of that Philip was unlikely to be reproduced in his grandson ; and also that his personal experience of his relations with France had convinced him of the possibility of carrying on warfare by sea without coming to a formal breach which would carry with it the opening of hostilities in a wider sphere. However this may have been, Oliver seems to have thought that he could justify an attack on the treasure-house of the world by the happy results which his action was likely to produce on the balance of power amongst the churches of Europe. In New England the great enterprise was discussed with approval, Cotton's satisfaction taking the form of a prediction that it would lead to the drying up of the river Euphrates foretold in the Apocalypse. To Captain Leverett, fresh from service in New England, Oliver had used much the same language, adding that 'he intended not to desist till he came to the gates of Rome.' [3]

Scope of the expedition.

[1] Venables' *Narrative*, 3.

[2] Instructions to Venables.   Burchett's *Complete History of . . . Transactions at Sea*, 385.

[3] See an article by Mr. Strong in the *American Historical Review*

If there is anything which at first sight appears unaccountable in the history of this expedition, it is Oliver's belief that its
Oliver ex-
pects its task
to be an
easy one.
task of conquest was an easy one, though such heroes as Hawkins and Drake had never been able to accomplish more than the sacking of a few towns and the temporary occupation of a few ports. Partly, perhaps, he was influenced by a not unnatural, though misplaced, confidence in the superiority of regular troops and a national fleet over the crews brought together by private adventurers, but
He is misled
by Gage and
Modyford.
still more by the representations of two men who had had personal experience of the West Indies, and whose information passed current at Whitehall as undisputed truths. One of these—Thomas Gage—had been sent out to Spanish America by the Dominican order, of which he had become a member, but had returned to England in 1641, where he had announced his conversion to Protestantism, after which he took the side of Parliament and adopted the career of a minister. In 1648 he published, under the name of *The English-American*, an account of the West Indies ; and in the summer of 1654, or even earlier, he laid before the Protector a memorial in which he recapitulated the conclusions of that work, assuring him that the Spanish colonies were thinly peopled, and that the few white inhabitants were unwarlike, and scantily provided with arms and ammunition. He alleged that the conquest of Hispaniola or Cuba would be a matter of no difficulty, and even that Central America was not in a condition to resist long.[1] Colonel Modyford, who was a member of the Council of Barbados, recommended, on the other hand, an

(Jan. 1899), iv. 2. The Diary of Samuel Sewall is there quoted as evidence that Leverett was to have been Governor of Hispaniola. It is most improbable that a mere captain would have been destined to such a position, and it must not be forgotten that the conversation in which the statement was made did not occur till 1696.

[1] Gage's observations, *Thurloe*, iii. 59. For a fuller account of Gage, see his life in the *Dict. of Nat. Biogr.*, and Mr. Strong's above-mentioned article, where it is demonstrated that neither Gage's nor Modyford's papers can have been handed in so late as December, under which date they are placed in the printed *Thurloe*.

attack on Guiana ; but he too regarded the enterprise—comprising the occupation of the coast as far westward as Cartagena —as ' very easily compassed.' [1]

Though Oliver was led astray in a matter of which he had no personal experience, he was well aware of the existence of one source of danger against which it behoved him to provide. When Drake or Raleigh sailed for the Indies, the commander-in-chief exercised undisputed authority over every single person on board. The differentiation between the naval and military services made it no longer possible to follow their example in this respect. Even as early as in 1589 the division of the command between Drake and Norris had been attended with disastrous results to the expedition they conducted against Lisbon. Yet it was impossible to revert to the earlier system. To appoint either Penn or Venables to the supreme command over the land and sea forces would but spell instant ruin, and, with this problem to face, the Protector fell back on a solution which, if not ideally the best, was probably the best of which circumstances admitted. The general conduct of the expedition was to be entrusted to five commissioners, of whom Penn and Venables were to be two, the General and Admiral each retaining executive authority in his own service. Such an arrangement had little in common with the often-condemned blunder of appointing a body of civilian commissioners to control a single general. It was intended to supply a means of keeping a double command in tolerable harmony ; whilst the inclusion of Penn and Venables themselves in the number of the commissioners afforded each of them a means of pleading his own cause within doors, instead of being driven to accept or reject orders, definitely given by a merely civilian authority which claimed superiority over the professional heads of the expedition.

Danger from the division of authority.

Five commissioners appointed, of whom Penn and Venables were two.

Yet, though no better provision suggests itself as available, the contrivance was at the best a clumsy one, and required the

---

[1] A paper of Col. Modyford, *Thurloe*, iii. 62.

utmost care in the selection of the three external commissioners. Unfortunately, one only even approached the necessary condi-

Winslow, Searle, and Butler commissioners.

tions. Edward Winslow, who had been one of the adventurous band which sailed for New England in the ' Mayflower,' had three times served as Governor of Plymouth Colony, and had returned to England in 1646. Though he had sided with Parliament at the time of its expulsion in 1653, his knowledge of colonial affairs, together with the repute of his abilities and character, had gained for him the confidence of the Protector.[1] The choice of Daniel Searle, the Governor of Barbados, would, but for one circumstance, have been as satisfactory as that of Winslow. He was a capable man, but necessarily hampered by his relations to the colony whilst the expedition remained at the island, and after it left he would be unable to leave his post to accompany it into action. His absence would be of the greater consequence because Winslow's other colleague, Captain Gregory Butler, selected apparently on account of his local knowledge, was, by the testimony of all who came into contact with him, weak in those qualities of temper and discretion which are indispensable in a councillor.[2]

Some time before the sailing of the fleet it had become evident that the danger of a misunderstanding between Penn

Relations between Penn and Venables.

and Venables was by no means imaginary ; and the instructions issued on December 9 to all concerned must have served to increase that danger, Penn's services being therein limited to the conveyance of the land forces to their destination, to the employment of the fleet in

[1] See Mr. Firth's account of his career in the Preface to Venables' *Narrative*, x.

[2] Mr. Firth has collected the statements of those who served with him. " Truth is," wrote Major-General Fortescue after the force had landed in Jamaica, " I know not of what use he is, unless to make up a number. . . . If I may without offence speak it, he is the unfittest man for a commissioner I ever knew employed ; I suppose His Highness and Council had little knowledge of him." And again, " He may very well be spared, his whole business having been to engender strife and create factions among the officers," Venables' *Narrative*, xii.

the destruction or capture of French or Spanish vessels, and to the promotion of the design against the Spaniards in the West Indies. That design was to be carried out, as the Protector informed his Admiral, ' in the manner expressed in our instructions to General Venables, which he is to communicate to you.' [1] As a matter of fact, the instructions given to Venables were in far greater detail than Penn's. The object of the expedition, he was told, was ' to gain an interest in that part of the West Indies in possession of the Spaniards.' He was not, however, bound to any definite plan. It had been proposed, he was told, to seize on Hispaniola or Puerto Rico, or even upon both ; after which Havana might be won, a place invaluable as the port of call for the homeward-bound treasure-fleet on its way from Panama to Europe before it entered the Bahama Channel.[2] An alternative scheme was a landing at some point between the mouths of the Orinoco and Porto Bello, with the intention of ultimately securing Cartagena. Yet a third proposal was to begin with San Domingo or Puerto Rico, and afterwards to attempt Cartagena instead of Havana. It was, however, left to those on the spot to decide which, if any, of these schemes should be carried out.[3]

Plan of the design.

It is not strange that Penn, captious as he was,[4] and already prejudiced against Venables, took umbrage at the fulness of instructions which, having been withheld from himself, were to be communicated to him by his military colleague. Even before the issue of these instructions the Protector, anxious to conciliate him, had confirmed a grant of Irish land made to him in September, and accompanied his concession with pressing

Penn's dissatisfaction.

*Dec. 4.
A grant of Irish land to him.*

---

[1] Penn's instructions, *Mem. of Penn*, ii. 23. Penn's commission, which these instructions accompany, is there dated Oct. 9. Mr. Firth shows (Venables' *Narrative*, ix., note 1) that this must almost certainly be an error for Dec. 9.

[2] Corbett, *Drake and the Tudor Navy*, i. 90.

[3] Instructions to Venables, Burchett's *Complete History*, 385.

[4] This was Winslow's opinion of him. Winslow to Thurloe, March 16, *Thurloe*, iii. 249.

letters to the authorities in Dublin to see that the matter was not neglected. After this Oliver felt himself justified in [1]

Oliver recommends two kinsmen to Penn. recommending two young kinsmen of his own for appointments in the fleet, and even in sharply reprimanding the Admiral for giving to one of his own relatives a place which he had promised to the Protector's nephew.[2]

On December 20, when the fleet was almost ready to sail, Oliver made one final appeal to Penn's better feelings. " I

Dec. 20. An appeal to Penn. understand," he wrote, " so much of your care and industry in this business that I cannot but acknowledge it, and let you know how much you make me beholden to you ; and I pray you persist therein. I do humbly hope the Lord will have an eye upon this business, and will bless it. And therefore, if it be His business, it will certainly provoke every good heart to eye Him in it, and to be able to overcome every thing in a man's own heart that may anywise lie as an impediment in the way that may hinder the bringing of it to its perfection ; and in this I have full assurance of you, notwithstanding I have had some knowledge of a little dissatisfaction remaining with you, which I hope by this time will be removed, and I desire you it may be so. You have your own command, full and entire to yourself, nothing interfering with it, nor in the least lessening you. The command at land is also distinct, and there the General at land must exercise his authority ; and thus I trust you will both consent to carry on the public work without hesitation ; and God forbid that any thing, either in you or him, should in the least hinder that. I hope it shall not ; and know assuredly, upon the experience you have had of me, that I shall be as tender of your honour, as sensible to uphold your quality, as you shall be to desire me. The Lord make your journey prosperous and bless you ! " [3]

---

[1] *Mem. of Penn*, ii. 19.

[2] The Protector to Penn, Dec. 1, Jan. 15, Portland MSS., *Hist. MSS. Com. Rep.*, xiii. App. ii. 88, 89.

[3] The Protector to Penn, Dec. 20, *Hist. MSS. Com. Rep.*, xiii. App. ii. 88.

For the time being this pleading was not without effect. Before the sailing of the fleet Winslow was able to write to Thurloe that that sore was easily cured ; and after his arrival in the West Indies he could report that the demeanour of the General and Admiral mutually towards ' each [1] other at sea was sweet and hopeful.' [2] The wound, however, still rankled, and when the time of action arrived it was likely to break out again, with disastrous consequences.

Far more damaging than Penn's jealousy was the Protector's own blunder in ignoring the strength brought to an army by regimental discipline and comradeship. Instead of taking complete regiments the Government resolved that the army for the West Indies should be composed of drafts from the regiments serving in different parts of the country, and, what was worse still, that these drafts should be selected by the colonels of the regiments in which they had served. The natural consequence was that the men chosen for foreign service were for the most part those of whom their colonels were most anxious to be rid, and when the numbers thus supplied were found insufficient, an attempt was made to fill the vacant places with the riff-raff of the London streets. In vain Venables pleaded that the men he was to command might be raised from the seasoned regiments with whose martial qualities he had been familiar in Ireland ; or, if this might not be, that volunteers might be drawn from the troops in England.

Character of the land forces.

Such proceedings, inexplicable to Venables, can only be explained by the brevity of the time available for the collection of the forces. The Protector had been warned by Gage that the rainy season began in May, and when November, and even December arrived, his anxiety to see the last of the fleet must have been intense. As for the employment of volunteers, tropical service was none too popular in the army, and it is probable that, if Venables' advice had been

Necessity of haste.

---

[1] Misprinted ' every.'

[2] Winslow to Thurloe, March 16, *Thurloe*, iii. 249.

taken in this direction, he would have found himself without any following worthy of consideration.[1]

The same conviction of the value of time which made it impossible to send to Ireland for soldiers stood in the way of

A muster refused.

compliance with the request of the General that he should be allowed to hold a general muster of his soldiers at Portsmouth before their embarkation. " Before I came thither," he bitterly complained, " some were shipped and sent away, and all were reproached for not shipping faster than wind and tide and boats would serve us." [2] Whatever may have been the causes of this haste, the consequences bade fair to be disastrous. The army from which so much was expected was without cohesion and without confidence in its commander. Everything that it most behoved soldiers to know would have to be learnt, not merely in the presence of the enemy, but under climatic conditions against which neither they nor those who sent them knew how to provide. It had not been by gathering a mob and styling it an army that Oliver had beaten down his enemies at Marston Moor and Naseby.

Nor was it only from the deficiencies of the force thus hurriedly brought together that danger was to be expected.

The force to be strengthened in the Indies.

According to the accepted plan, Venables was to have taken with him 3,000 men—though the number was found, in fact, to be no more than 2,500—and this body was to form the nucleus of an army to be made up by recruits in Barbados and the other English islands. What likelihood, however, was there that these raw levies would find in a force composed as was the one now hurried on shipboard a nucleus round which to rally ? The case was the more hope-

The soldiers led to expect an easy task.

less as both officers and men were under the impression that their object was less to defeat an enemy than to found a colony. Even Venables was left

---

[1] F. Barrington to Sir J. Barrington, July 14, *Hist. MSS. Com. Rep.*, vii. 571.

[2] Venables' *Narrative*, 6 ; *A Brief and Perfect Journal, Harl. Misc.*, iii. 513.

under this delusion. The city of San Domingo, according to his instructions, 'not being considerably fortified,' might 'probably be possessed without much difficulty'; and he gave evidence of his belief that little danger was to be feared by carrying with him his wife, whom he had recently married as a mature widow, pleading subsequently that 'his Highness did only intend a plantation, where women would be necessary.'[1]

On December 20 the first portion of the fleet put to sea, and the remainder followed on the 25th. Two storeships which were to have carried necessaries for the soldiers failed to arrive in time ; whilst the provisions already placed on board for their use, being found defective, Venables threw the blame on Desborough, who had been appointed to arrange for the supplies, and whom he charged—probably without foundation—with acting in collusion with the victuallers.[2]

The outward voyage to Barbados was uneventful, and on January 29 the fleet cast anchor in Carlisle Bay. The arrival of a hostile force could hardly have been more unwelcome to the planters, who had been in the habit of importing goods in Dutch bottoms in defiance of the provisions of the Navigation Act. Almost immediately after their arrival the commissioners made seizure, by the Protector's orders, of a number of Dutch vessels lying in the bay, and that, too, in virtue not only of the Navigation Act, but also of another Act which prohibited all foreign trade with the colony in consequence of its adhesion, at the time when the Statute was passed, to the Stuart cause.[3] Such a proceeding could only be justified by the clause in the Navigation Act forbidding the importation into an English colony of goods not the produce of the countries in which the ships bringing them were owned, a clause which had been violated by the Dutch ship-masters if, as is highly probable, they had carried negro slaves across the Atlantic.[4] Angry at

1655.
Jan. 29.
The fleet at
Barbados.

Seizure of
Dutch
vessels.

---

[1] Memoranda of Eliz. Venables, *Chetham Soc. Misc.* iv. 9–28.
[2] Venables' *Narrative*, 5–7, 102.   [3] See vol. i. 317.
[4] Winslow to Thurloe, March 16, *Thurloe*, iii. 249 ; Venables' *Narrative*, 8.

this interruption of their trade the colonists raised difficulties
Enlistment
of men. when an attempt was made to enlist volunteers to
make up the numbers required to complete the army.
The planters, not unreasonably, cried out against the induce-
ment offered to their servants to desert their work, and it was
only after the commissioners had entered into an engagement
that freemen only should be entertained that the enlistment
made any progress.[1]　The engagement, however, was in many
cases evaded, and in one way or another, so far as numbers were
concerned, the force under Venables began to present a for-
March 21.
A muster
taken. midable appearance.　At a muster taken on March 21
it was found to reach 6,873,[2] including a troop of
horse raised in Barbados to supply the place of one
which had been detained by contrary winds in an Irish port.
March 31.
The fleet
sails. When the fleet put to sea on March 31, it picked up
some 1,200 volunteers at Montserrat, Nevis, and St.
Kitts; to whom must be added a naval regiment of
about the same strength, serving under Vice-Admiral Goodson
Numbers
of the army
on board. as its colonel, thus bringing the entire force above
9,000 men,[3] now divided—including the seamen—
into eight regiments.

The quality of the new levies, with the notable exception
of the sea regiment, was not commensurate with their numbers.
Bad quality
of the new
levies. " Our planters," wrote Venables after the catastrophe
had occurred, " we found most fearful, being only
bold to do mischief, not to be commanded as soldiers,
nor to be kept in any civil order, being the most profane,
debauched persons that we ever saw, scorners of religion ; and,

[1] The freemen are described as ' such as [had] served in the country
for freedom, or paid their passage when transported from England.'
J. Barrington to Sir F. Barrington, *Hist. MSS. Com. Rep.*, vii. 572. I
have added ' had ' on my own responsibility, as the sentence makes
nonsense without it.

[2] Venables' *Narrative*, 122.　Mr. Firth makes the number 100
more, having omitted to take into account his own correction on the same
page.

[3] The question of numbers is fully discussed by Mr. Firth in his
Preface to Venables' *Narrative*, xxx.

indeed, men kept so loose as not to be kept under discipline, and so cowardly as not to be made to fight." If Venables' words may be thought to be exaggerated, as those of a man on his defence, they were at least no harsher than those of more impartial witnesses. "To say the truth," wrote three of the commissioners to the Governor of Barbados, "your men and the men of St. Christopher's lead all the disorder and confusion." The testimony of Captain How to the worthlessness of the Barbadians is to the same effect. "The men we had from thence," he declares, "for the most proved good for little. I dare say that 1,000 of our soldiers that came out of England or Ireland is better than 5,000 of them."[1] Their discipline, too, was shaken by the difficulty of procuring arms for more than a part of the army. Gunsmith's tools had been left behind, and the wood of the island was not such as to enable the pike-heads brought from England to be fitted with shafts of the usual length. The result was that it was only for a short time at the end of the stay at Barbados that the whole force in the island could be drilled.[2] The evil was complicated by the ineffectiveness of many of the officers, who had been brought together without sufficient discrimination before the troops left England. Food, too, was running short, and on the voyage the landsmen were put on half-rations, a circumstance which again roused the spirit of contention between Penn and Venables, the latter declaring that the best bread was reserved for the sailors, the worst being served out to the soldiers.[3]

On one important subject, however, Penn and Venables were agreed. Knowing the motives which actuated the large Question of majority of the soldiers, they proposed that the pillage. plunder should be brought into a common stock, to be divided amongst all who were concerned in its capture. To this, however, the other commissioners took exception. It had San been resolved that the city of San Domingo should Domingo to be the object of the first attack, and on April 13, be attacked. when the expedition was nearing the coast of

---

[1] Venables' *Narrative*, 30, 40.   [2] *Ib.* 12.   [3] *Ib.* 13.

Hispaniola, Venables was compelled to issue an order offering to the soldiers six weeks' pay in lieu of pillage. The reason for such an unpopular decision was plainly given. " Whereas," the General declared, " the city of Domingo, where we design our first attempt, is intended by His Highness for a colony of

Apr. 13.
Plunder to
be com-
muted. the English, which, if destroyed by pillage, ruineth the whole design, making us incapable to reap the fruit of our success, if the Lord shall please to bless us with the same : I do therefore order and require officers and soldiers under my command not to pillage or plunder any money, plate or jewels whatsoever, or to waste or destroy any houses, tame cattle, or any other goods or things which are necessary for us to plant within the country, or to improve with the best advantage of his Highness the present design." [1] The men to whom these words were addressed were as unfit to be colonisers as to be soldiers, and preferred the wild gamble of pillage to the distribution of an evenly divided sum of money.[2] The order of the General led to an outcry, which portended little less than a mutiny when the time should arrive for putting it in force.

On April 13, the day on which the order was issued, the fleet was off San Domingo, near enough to the coast to descry

The fleet
off San
Domingo. the inhabitants hurrying to take refuge in the city. The commissioners had sensibly agreed that the troops should be landed near the mouth of the river Jaina, at the spot chosen by Drake on his famous expedition. This was far enough from the city to avoid the danger of surprise before the whole force had been put ashore, and near enough to it to enable the men to approach the object of their

Prepara-
tions for
landing. enterprise without a long and wearisome march. It was found, however, that a heavy surf rendered landing impracticable at this point, and the greater part of the army was therefore sent to the westward, to find a

---

[1] Venables' *Narrative*, 14. Order by Venables, Apr. 13, Portland MSS., *Hist. MSS. Com. Rep.*, 13, ii. 91.

[2] Whistler's Journal, in the Appendix to Venables' *Narrative*, 150.

safer landing-place at the mouth of the Nizao,[1] whilst a regiment and a half, under Colonels Holdip and Buller, was to be sent ashore to the east of the city, where they would be cut off by the river Ozama from any chance of joining in the assault, though they might render service by blocking the place on that side.

On the 14th the bulk of the army was landed at the mouth of the Nizao without opposition, where there was a march of some twenty miles to the Jaina, and of about ten more from the Jaina to the city walls.[2] Orders had been given to supply the men with provisions for three days ; but the orders were but superficially carried out, as the sailors themselves were on short allowance and the naval authorities took care to put the soldiers on shorter allowance still. Even more distressing was the want of water. Not, indeed, that it was altogether lacking. Dry beds of streams had a few pools remaining in them, from which it was possible to drink, and occasionally a fuller stream slipped sluggishly past towards the sea. It had, however, never occurred to those in authority in England to furnish vessels in which water could be carried.[3] Venables, whose military experience had been gained in a land in which food was scarce and water plentiful, awoke too late to the gravity of the danger. "Whoever," he wrote, "comes into these parts must bring leather bottles, which are more needful here than knapsacks in Ireland." Yet, toilsome as was the march in the drought and heat, its hardships were not without alleviation. For seven

Apr. 14.
The army landed.

Apr. 14-16.
A toilsome march.

---

[1] The narratives on which my account is based are either printed by Mr. Firth in Venables' *Narrative*, or are referred to by him in the Preface. Venables held that the change of place was entirely due to Penn's carelessness or misconduct ; but the account given above is far more probable, as Penn had nothing to gain by endangering the success of the expedition.

[2] As the crow flies it is about fifteen miles to the Jaina and about seven more to San Domingo, but the winding of the track must have lengthened the distance. Contemporary narratives naturally make it still longer.

[3] See the list of stores in *Thurloe*, iii. 203.

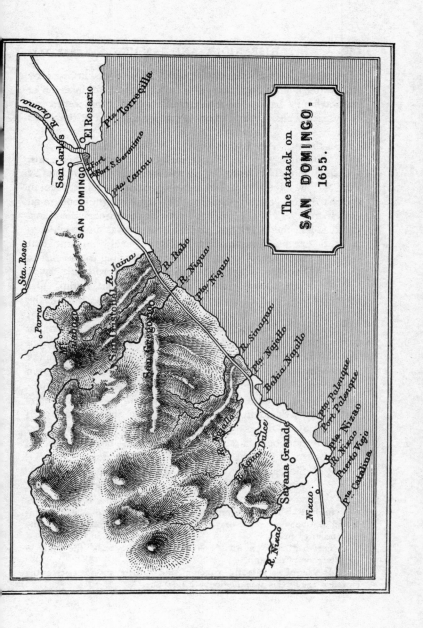

The attack on
SAN DOMINGO.
1655.

R. Orozoro

El Rosario

Pta. Torrecilla

San Carlos R.

San Carlos

Fort

Fort S. Geronimo

SAN DOMINGO

Pta. Canou

SAN DOMINGO

Sta. Rosa

R. Jaina

R. Isabo

R. Niguay

o Parra

Pta. Niguay

R. SanTiago

San Tiago Mayo

R. Sinagua

Pta. Nigello

R. Bella

Babia Nigallo

Rivas Dulce

Savana Grande

Ptas Palenque
Port Palenque

Nixao

R. pta. Nixao
R. Nixao

Puerto Vejo

Pta. Catalines

R. Nixao

miles the soldiers tramped along a lane overshadowed by orange trees, tempting them with fruit hanging within reach of the wayfarer's hand. In many cases over-indulgence brought on dysentery and fever, and not a few dropped out of the ranks to die.

On the way the regiments stumbled on a deserted monastery. The image of the Virgin with the Saviour in her arms, rendered more attractive by the gold and jewels which stiffened her robe, was torn from its place in the chapel and pelted with oranges by these rough intruders on the sanctuary.[1] When, on the third day's march,[2] the Jaina was reached, the water was so high that it was impossible to cross it except by swimming.[3] Here Venables learnt that Buller, having failed to effect a landing to the east of San Domingo, had come on shore with his 1,500 men near the mouth of the Jaina, but, finding that the Spaniards had evacuated a small fort commanding the landing-place, had, in spite of instructions to the contrary, marched off in the direction of the city, taking with him the only guide. Buller would have done better if he had prepared the way for his commander by examining the river which the main army had to cross, as in default of such aid the afternoon and evening were spent by the wearied regiments in search of a ford. When darkness fell with tropical swiftness, the wanderers had not only failed in achieving their object, but had straggled from the river banks. Consequently, their three days' provisions having been already exhausted, they had to pass the night without food or water. When morning dawned the search for the ford was resumed, and the army was at last able to cross the river at some distance

A deserted monastery.

Apr. 16.
Buller's escapade.

Apr. 17.
A fresh advance.

---

[1] In the Rawlinson MS. printed in Venables' *Narrative*, p. 130, this is said to have taken place near the Jaina. The same scene may easily have occurred twice.

[2] They had started at 4 P.M. on the 14th, and reached the Jaina in the afternoon of the 16th.

[3] As want of water is still spoken of, and as there was a bar across the entrance, the estuary was, no doubt, a tidal one.

from its mouth ; after which a plantation was reached, which provided water and a certain amount of food. In the afternoon the men resumed their march, tempted by a captured Irishman, who offered to bring them to the Ozama at a point above the city where they would find a sufficiency of water and be in a position to attack the place on its least guarded side.

The march from the Jaina was even more trying than that of the preceding days. Not a single stream now crossed the A terrible path, and what wells there were had either been march. rendered useless by the Spaniards or were under the protection of fortifications. The road, for some way at least, no longer led under the shade of orange trees, but was broad and hard, reflecting the rays of the glaring sun. Again and again, in disobedience to their officers, the men refused to march till they had rested. The return of Buller's men with a tale of suffering did not tend to raise their spirits, and when, at the parting of two roads, their Irish guide persuaded them to take the right-hand turning, which led, not to the Ozama, but in front of the fort of San Geronimo, which was situated on the sea-coast and commanded the way to the city, the want of water was hardly likely to be overcome. It might, however, be expected that 9,000 armed men could defend themselves from attack. The country was but thinly populated, most of the few inhabitants being cow-killers, who were armed with long lances for slaughtering the wild cattle which roamed amongst the woods and were valuable for their hides and tallow alone. As Venables, who was himself suffering from dysentery, was reconnoitring the fort, a party of these men An attack dashed unexpectedly from an ambuscade on the repulsed. advanced guard—or, as it was then called, the forlorn—and broke through it ; after which they found little resistance till the seamen's regiment stood firm, and by their superior discipline converted what bid fair to be a rout into an assured victory. It was the only regiment in the whole army in which the bond of tried comradeship was strengthened by the habit of obedience to officers long known and trusted.[1] The material difficulties of the enterprise were not, however, lessened by the repulse of the enemy, and though the Spaniards evacuated a smaller fort beyond San Geronimo, they first rendered its well unserviceable.   In the evening Venables

The city approached. found himself in front of the wall of San Domingo unprovided with appliances for an attack, and with his men dropping fast from hunger and thirst.   In spite of the

A retreat ordered. remonstrances of some of the old soldiers he had no resource but to order a retreat to the plantation where the troops had found refreshment in the morning.

The check was not altogether owing to the unmilitary qualities of the private soldiers.   It was at least partially due

Cause of the failure. to the mistake of trusting to the word of a perfidious Irishman and marching hastily to the Ozama, instead of waiting near the mouth of the Jaina till arrangements had been made with the fleet for the supply of necessaries to the soldiers.   If Venables' memory is to be trusted, the mistake had arisen in consequence of his allowing himself to be over-ruled by Butler, who, as a single commissioner, had no authority to give orders to a colleague.

[1] Confidence in the account which assigns the merit to the seamen is strengthened by its being found in the journal of an officer of Fortescue's regiment. Whistler writes : "There did fly forth of the woods a party of the enemy which did lie in ambush upon our forlorn, and General Venables being one of the foremost, and seeing the enemy fall on so desperately with his lances, he very nobly ran behind a tree ; and our sea regiment having this day the forlorn hope, did fall on most gallantly and put the enemy to fly for their lives, and coming where General Venables was got behind a tree, he came forth to them, but was very much ashamed, but made many excuses, being so much pressed with terror that he could hardly speak." Venables' *Narrative*, 154. Whistler, however, was not present, and is clearly in the wrong in representing the seamen as being in the 'forlorn.' Moreover, his malicious account—which no doubt reflected the ill-will of the fleet towards the soldiers—is explained by the writer of the letters printed in App. D. of Venables' *Narrative*, who tells us that after the skirmish ' the General came out of the wood . . . where he had lain hid beyond the enemy's ambush.' Evidently he had gone too far in advance, and had been cut off from his army by the men attacking from the ambuscade.

The mischief was now remedied. Communications were opened with the fleet, and arrangement made that pro-

The fleet to furnish provisions. visions and other stores should be landed near the mouth of the Jaina, or sent in boats to meet the troops on the completion of their next advance. Venables himself took advantage of the delay to go on board

Venables on ship-board. to be nursed by his wife, a proceeding which drew down on him the rude jests of the men, many of whom were suffering from the same disease as him-self, and who had no shelter or assistance as they lay on the bare ground. Their condition was rendered worse by the

The rains set in. rainy season, which had now set in, and which threatened a rapid increase of the sickness whose ravages had been already felt. On the 24th, the much-needed

Apr. 24. The army starts again. supplies having been delivered, though ships were detached to take up their stations off the city and San Geronimo, their fire proved ineffectual, as, either from bad gunnery or because the men-of-war stood too far out to sea, no damage was done on either side. On the same day the army, dragging a mortar, and carrying provisions for six days, once more started, it might seem under more favourable omens. Yet it had accomplished but two miles when daylight failed. The rain had ceased for a time, and the night was passed without water, as no streams now crossed the line of march, and the supply from the fleet was not to be counted on till the neighbourhood of the city was reached.

On the morning of the 25th the exhausted troops once more addressed themselves to their enterprise. Slow and toil-

Apr. 25. The march resumed. some was the march, and it was only in the after-noon that San Geronimo was in sight. Once more Venables took no precautions to search the woods on either side of his march, and just as the head of the army was passing the fort, and all eyes were fixed on its guns, a party

An un-expected rout. of cow-killers whom no estimate reckons above 200 dashed from behind the trees and charged the front ranks under the command of Colonel Murphy, an Irishman, eager, we may well believe, to avenge the wrongs of his suffering nation. The short pikes manufactured in Barbados were no match for the long lances of the Spaniards, and again the advanced guard turned and fled, carrying away one regiment after another in its rush of headlong panic. In vain Major-General Heane attempted to stem the tide. Isolated among the enemy, with but two comrades at his side, he fell mortally wounded, whilst one of his companions, wrapping the flag of England round his body, perished with him. Venables, weakened by disease, and only able to stand with the help of two men, did his best vainly to check the flight. Once more the steadiness of the naval regiment saved the army. Opening out to allow the fugitives to stream through its ranks, it then formed up, and drove the assailants into the woods.

After such a disaster all thought of renewing the attempt upon the city was of necessity abandoned. The army regarded Venables as an inefficient commander, and with even greater justice Venables regarded his troops as a disorganised rabble. Adjutant-General Jackson, a man of low character, prone to vicious indulgences, who had been the first to fly, was cashiered and sent to the hospital ship to swab the decks for the wounded. Other officers were also broken. Their disgrace could not restore discipline amongst the unruly mob which had followed them in flight. Bad as was the character of many of the men brought from England, that of the West Indian levies was even worse. It was to no purpose that Penn offered the assistance of the fleet, and actually rendered every service in his power. The spirits of the men had fallen too low for further exertion. In their flight they had thrown away their arms, and even the provisions they carried. On their return to the Jaina, as a party of 1,500 had thrown themselves on their faces to drink of the stream, the appearance of two of their own negro attendants scared them into the belief that the enemy was upon them. Numbers took to flight, and others leapt into the water, three being drowned before they could be rescued. On the 28th three of the commissioners—Penn, Winslow, and Butler—acknowledged that every single officer was of opinion 'that these

Apr. 28.
Officers punished.

Apr. 28.
The commissioners acknowledge the task hopeless.

people will never be brought to march up to that place again.'
In consequence of this conviction it was resolved to try whether
an attempt upon Jamaica might be more successful. It was,
however, difficult to keep order amongst the men till the fleet
was able to receive them. By their fevered imaginations the
noise made by the land-crabs as they moved down towards the
shore was taken as the rattling of the bandoliers of a hostile
army, whilst parties sent out to forage allowed themselves to
be slaughtered with impunity by the smallest groups of the
enemy. The rain poured down in torrents ; hunger, too, was
added to their miseries, and every horse was slaughtered for
food before the island was abandoned.[1]

At last, on May 4, the remains of the expedition embarked
for Jamaica, the sagacious Winslow unfortunately
dying on the voyage. On the 11th the noble
anchorage now known as Kingston Harbour was
reached. Three small forts on its western side were
at once battered by Penn's guns, and as soon as the
troops began to land the garrisons abandoned their posts.
Venables, still under the power of disease, watched the landing
from on board, muffled in his cloak, with his hat slouched over
his face, not deigning to cast a glance on the men to whose misconduct he attributed his failure.[2] The next day
the English occupied Santiago de la Vega—the
Spanish Town of the present day—some six miles
distant from the sea. The Spanish population of the island
did not exceed 1,500 persons, of which 500 at the utmost were
fighting men, who abandoned all thought of active
resistance. The terms offered by Venables to these
Spaniards were hard enough—emigration within
ten days on pain of death, together with the forfeiture of all
their property. These terms, however, were no more than the
counterpart of those exacted from the English settlers in

Marginal notes:

May 4.
Hispaniola abandoned.

May 11.
The fleet at Jamaica.

May 12.
Santiago de la Vega occupied.

May 13.
Terms offered,

---

[1] The Commissioners to Searle, April 28, Venables' *Narrative*, 30.
[2] According to Whistler, he looked ' as if he had been a student of physic more than like a general of an army.'

Providence[1] when the Spaniards made themselves masters of that

May 17.
and ac-
cepted. island in 1640. It was only on the 17th that they were accepted, and the Spanish Governor—so at least

A Spanish
trick. it was believed—surrendered himself as a hostage. Before long, however, it appeared that the Spaniards had merely entered into the negotiation to gain time to withdraw with their families and property to the hills, and that the pretended Governor was but an old man of no repute.

In the meantime the military settlers were learning that colonisation has its dangers as well as war. Penn sent on shore

Distress
for food. every pound of biscuit he could spare, as, though herds of cattle were pastured on the Savannah, this would not meet the demand for bread. On the 19th, indeed, the two long-expected storeships arrived, but the supplies brought by them were limited, and it was resolved to appeal for assistance to New England, and meanwhile to send home the larger ships, in order to diminish the number of mouths, leaving the frigates to remain on guard, or to cruise on the look out for prizes. Penn, disgusted at the failure in Hispaniola, and on bad terms with Venables, was easily persuaded that it was his duty to return in order to report in person on the situation, and on June 25, after appointing Goodson as his

June 25.
Penn sails
for England,
and is fol-
lowed by
Venables. successor, he sailed for England with the homeward-bound division of his fleet. With far better excuse Venables, whose life was despaired of, resolved to follow his example, making over the military command to Fortescue, a capable and devoted officer, who had acted as major-general since the death of Heane.

Long before this catalogue of troubles reached the Protector the comparative failure of his great enterprise had been brought home to him. The first news of the rout before San Domingo

July 24.
News from
the West
Indies. reached him on July 24. The resolution to despatch the expedition had been forced through the Council by his own personal resolution, and its failure, therefore, stung him more sharply than any other catastrophe of equal importance would have done. For a whole day he shut himself

[1] Now New Providence.

up in his room, brooding over the disaster for which he, more than anyone else, was responsible.[1] On August 4 a letter from Venables announced the occupation of Jamaica, an island which, to save appearances, was given out either as part of Hispaniola, or at least as standing in the same relation to Hispaniola as the Isle of Wight to England.[2] No attempt to show that, island for island, Jamaica was more fit than Hispaniola to be the seat of an English colony could assuage the bitterness of Cromwell's meditations. He had aimed—in opposition to the common-sense of Lambert—not merely at planting one more colony in the Indies, but at making himself master of at least so much of the West India Islands and the American continent as would dominate the trade-route of the Spanish treasure-ships, and towards that end Jamaica, held—if held it could be—by a disorganised and cowardly mob, could contribute little or nothing.

Aug. 4.
A letter from Venables.

The Protector's annoyance.

In such a mood Oliver was hardly likely to be very complaisant to the two commanders who had left the post of danger to others. On September 1 Penn arrived at Portsmouth, bringing with him a doubtful rumour that Venables was dead. On the 10th, however, Venables reached Plymouth, very weak, but in a hopeful way of recovery, and, continuing his voyage, notified his arrival at Portsmouth in a letter to Thurloe.[3] On the 20th both commanders were summoned before the Council to answer the charge of having deserted their posts. For Penn there was little to be said, as his presence was manifestly required at the head of the fleet remaining in the Indies, and which, weak as it was, might yet

Sept. 1.
Arrival of Penn,

Sept. 10.
and of Venables.

Sept. 20.
Penn and Venables before the Council.

---

[1] *Merc. Pol.*, E, 850, 10; *The Weekly Intelligencer*, E, 851, 3; Cardenas to Philip IV., $\frac{\text{July 25}}{\text{Aug. 4}}$, *Simancas MSS.* 2529.

[2] Letter of Aug. 4, *Clarke Papers*, iii. 47; *A Perfect Account*, E, 851, 5.

[3] Penn to the Protector, Aug. 31, *Mem. of Penn*, ii. 131; Mabbott to Clarke, Sept. 8; *Clarke Papers*, iii. 51; Venables to Thurloe, Sept. 12, *Thurloe*, iv. 27.

have to play its part in the defence of the new settlement in the not improbable case of a Spanish attack. Venables, on the other hand, was guilty at the most of saving his own life at a time when hundreds of his officers and men were perishing. It was out of the question that he could have lived long enough to render efficient service in Jamaica.

What Penn had to say for himself there are no means of knowing. Venables, truly enough, represented his own return Venables questioned by the Protector. as authorised by the officers serving under him. "Have you ever read," replied the Protector, "of any general that had left his army, and not commanded back?" Venables pleaded his health as affecting his historical memory, but after some hesitation produced the instance of the Earl of Essex of Elizabeth's day. "A sad Both commanders sent to the Tower. example!" was Oliver's curt reply.[1] In the end both he and Penn were committed to the Tower. There was no intention of dealing harshly with either of them, but Oliver had made up his mind not to set them at liberty till they had formally acknowledged their offences and Oct. 25. Liberation of Penn, had surrendered their commissions. Penn complied with these conditions on October 25. Venables, Oct. 31. and of Venables. who was far less to blame, held out longer, and did not pass the prison gates till the 31st.[2]

Turning to the larger question of responsibility for the failure at Hispaniola, there is little to be said against Penn. Conduct of Penn, He may have been to some extent jealous of his colleague, and he seems to have taken care that in the distribution of provisions the sailors should have a preference over the soldiers. After the final retreat, too, he, not unnaturally, expressed his contempt for the poltroons on shore, and that, too, not merely in words, but also by slackness in supplying the provisions of which they were in urgent need.

---

[1] Venables' *Narrative*, 71–88.

[2] Council Order Book, *Interr.* I, 76, pp. 296, 345, 353; Mabbott to Clarke, Sept. 22, *Clarke Papers*, iii. 52; Thurloe to H. Cromwell, Sept. 25, *Thurloe*, iv. 55; Penn's Petition, Oct. 25, *S. P. Dom.* ci. 76.

In the actual conduct of the forces confided to him he was without reproach, ready, so long as hope was left, to aid and support the military forces to the utmost of his power. It is more difficult to characterise the behaviour of Venables, because the extreme physical weakness to which he was reduced leaves little opportunity of judging what energy he might have shown if his state of health had been other than it was. Yet, so far as it is possible to form an opinion, there appears to be no reason to object to the view which would relegate him to a place in that numerous body of officers who make excellent subordinates, but display their inefficiency in supreme command.

and of Venables.

It is the less necessary to pursue this subject further as the principal cause of failure must evidently be sought elsewhere than in the misconduct of the commanders. It was not, indeed, to be expected of the Protector, overwhelmed as he was with political and administrative anxieties, that he should have applied himself—as he would have applied himself twelve years earlier, when he was a simple colonel of a cavalry regiment—to the details of service ; that he should, for instance, have inquired into the provision of longer shafts for the pikes, or of leather bottles for the carrying of water. But—in all probability from sheer ignorance of tropical conditions—he had sent forth an army to establish England's supremacy in the Indies which, in the military sense, was no army at all. He had been told of the weakness of the Spaniards, and had a sincere conviction that he had Providence to friend. Of the war against the burning sun and of the waterless roots of the hills he had no conception. It was said, probably with truth, that out of the 9,000 who landed in Hispaniola there were but 1,000 old soldiers ;[1] the rest were the rejected of English regiments or, still worse, the offscourings of the West Indian colonies, not one of whom had seen service in any shape or form. Oliver, as ever, trusted in God. For once in his life he had forgotten to keep his powder dry.

The fault mainly the Protector's.

[1] Venables' *Narrative*, p. 44.

CHAPTER XLVI

THE BREACH WITH SPAIN

GREAT as was the indignation of the Spanish Government at the proceedings of Penn and Venables in the Indies, that

1654.
Oct. 8.
Blake sails
for the
Mediter-
ranean. aroused by Blake's action on the coast of Spain could have been no less. The attack on Jamaica was but an act of war committed without previous announcement; whilst Blake's hostility was but thinly veiled under the mask of friendship. All that can be said on the part of the Protector is that when he sent forth his two fleets he was still under the extraordinary delusion that he would be allowed to fight Spain in America whilst remaining at peace with her in Europe. At all events, at the time of Blake's final putting to sea on October 8, 1654,[1] more than two months before Penn's departure, England and Spain had a common enemy in France, so far as maritime captures were concerned, and for some time to come it would be to the interest of Spain to give comfort and support to Blake, whose first object was the ruin of

Aug. 5.
The Protec-
tor writes to
Philip IV. French commerce in the Mediterranean. On this basis Oliver had on August 5 despatched a letter in advance to the King of Spain, requesting him to receive Blake as the admiral of a State in amity with himself.[2] How useful to Spain was the appearance of the English fleet in the Mediterranean at that conjuncture may be gathered from

[1] Blake sailed originally for Plymouth on Sept. 29, but was driven back by a storm. Weale's Journal, *Sloane MSS.* 1431, foll. 7–10.

[2] The Protector to Philip IV., Aug. 5, 1654, *Guizot*, ii. 486.

the fact that the Duke of Guise was preparing to sail from Toulon at the head of an expedition designed for the
conquest of Naples, and that Blake was ordered to
frustrate that undertaking by attacking and ruin-
ing his fleet.[1] Having this object in view, Blake
naturally met with the most friendly reception in the
Spanish ports.[2] If his design was not carried out,
it was simply because on his arrival at Naples he

The Duke
of Guise's
designs on
Naples.
Blake's in-
structions.

Dec. 12.
His arrival
at Naples.

[1] Blake's instructions are not known to exist, with the exception of
one of July 22, 1654, relating solely to his mission to Algiers, of which
a copy, misdated 1656, and so calendared by Mrs. Everett Green, occurs
in *Entry Book*, Charles II., No. iv. p. 17. I suspect that it was originally intended to send him merely to Algiers, which would account for the
language reported by Sagredo. See *infra*, p. 214. Blake's employment
against the Duke of Guise, which was probably an afterthought, is men-
tioned in a letter of Mazarin to Bordeaux of $\frac{\text{Dec. 23}}{\text{Jan. 2}}$, *Thurloe*, iii. 41.
Cardenas, too, in his despatch of $\frac{\text{Dec. 25}}{\text{Jan. 4}}$, speaks of Blake's instructions to
fight the Duke as well known. *Simancas MSS.* 2529. Compare an
extract from a letter from the secretary of the Grand Duke of Tuscany
published by Mr. Whitwell in the *Hist. Rev.* (July 1899, xiv. 536).

[2] According to Burnet (*Hist. of His Own Time*, i. 80), Blake had an
altercation with the Spanish Governor of Malaga about an English sailor
who had insulted the Sacrament; telling him that ' an Englishman was
only to be punished by an Englishman.' The account given by Weale
shows that the fleet arrived in Malaga Road about six in the evening of
the 22nd, and left at noon on the following day. It may, therefore, be
taken for granted that no shore-going was allowed during so short a stay ;
and Weale himself certainly remained on board, as is shown by his
description of the general appearance only of the town. *Sloane MSS.*
1431, fol. 14. Weale's account of his landing at Alicante shows the
footing on which the English were with the Spaniards : " This day went
Mr. Whitchote, Mr. Eades and myself, and several of our officers ashore,
this being a very great holiday amongst them. We saw their procession-
ing, and were very courteously entertained by an English Father ; his
name is Thomas, a Jesuit amongst them. We did eat with them
pomegranates and prepared quinces in abundance, and he gave us some at
our coming away or departure." Weale, however, made his own comments : " It would have melted a heart of stone to have seen how the
poor people went after and followed their deceivers, ravening wolves,
anti-Christians ; how they were obedient to all their follies ; how they
sang and played in public places, and carried about their Virgin Mary

found that the Duke had abandoned his attempt, and had returned discomfited to Toulon.[1]

Before undertaking further enterprises Blake was compelled to provision his ships, and he therefore sailed with the greater

Dec. 21.
Blake at
Leghorn.

part of his fleet to Leghorn, which he reached on December 21.[2] He was there hospitably received, though forbidden for some days to hold communication with the shore [3]—a prohibition due to his having brought in two French prizes which had taken on board their lading at infected ports. The Grand Duke must have been the more satisfied with Blake's friendly bearing as he was aware that the

A Genoese
intrigue.

Genoese had been urging the Protector to transfer the trade of his countrymen from that port to Genoa. It was true that some dissatisfaction had been caused in London by the sale at Leghorn of some prize goods captured by Prince Rupert from an English trader, and by the measures of retaliation taken by the Tuscan authorities in the time of the Dutch war, when the 'Phœnix' was recaptured by English sailors within the Mole of Leghorn. Oliver, however, though outwardly courteous to Ugo Fiesco, the Genoese ambassador who had been sent to make the proposal, refused, after consulting the merchants, to countenance it in any way, though the Genoese had done their utmost to stir up ill-will in London by spreading the false news that English vessels were no longer

through their town. The Churchmen and their friars did look like bull beef on us." *Sloane MSS.* 1431, fol. 14b. The last expression must mean that they looked as if they would like to eat them.

[1] A Letter of Intelligence, Dec. $\frac{6}{16}$; Longland to Thurloe, Dec. $\frac{8}{18}$, Boreel to the States General, Jan. $\frac{12}{22}$, *Thurloe*, iii. 10, 12, 102.

[2] Weale's Journal, *Sloane MSS.* 1431, fol. 17b.

[3] Blake to the Commissioners of the Admiralty, Jan. 15, *Add. MSS.* 9304, fol. 99. On the legend of Blake's exaction of money from the Grand Duke, and its probable origin in a diplomatic invention of the Genoese, see *Hist. Rev.* (Jan. 1899), xiv. 109. Even in the absence of the testimony there cited the truth would appear in the expression of the Tuscan secretary that the English fleet was in the port of Leghorn 'con i soliti termini di buona corrispondenza con S. A.' Extract from Gondi's letter to Banducci, Jan. $\frac{13}{23}$, *ib.* xiv. 536.

safe in the port of the Grand Duke.[1]   The truth was that the

Friendly feeling between the Protector and the Grand Duke. relations between the two Governments were on so friendly a footing that, a few days before Blake sailed from Plymouth, the Master of the Ceremonies called on Salvetti, the Grand Duke's minister in London, requesting in the name of the Lady Protectress that his master would send her his own portrait, together with those of the Grand Duchess and his young son, that she might add them to her collection.[2]   Not only was this complied with, but a present of a cask of the choicest wine of Tuscany accompanied the portraits, a present which was received with gratification, though, in consequence of the delicacy of its flavour, the wine was ruined by the sea voyage, and proved undrink-

A request to build a church at Leghorn refused. able.[3]   One request, indeed, made not by Blake, but by Longland, the agent of the Levant Company at Leghorn, met with a refusal.   Asking—doubtless by

---

[1] The despatches of Ugo Fiesco, published by Signor Prayer in *Atti della Società Ligure* (xvi. 209–281) should be compared with Salvetti's information, from which extracts are given in the *Hist. Rev.* (Jan. 1899, xiv. 110).   That the story of Blake's exactions was of Genoese origin appears from the way in which it is mentioned in the newspapers: "From Genoa we hear that General Blake is about Leghorn, where, it is said, he doth expect some satisfaction from the Great Duke of Tuscany for the losses which the English have received before that port some few years since." *A Perfect Account*, E, 826, 15.   In another newspaper we have as news from Genoa: "General Blake is still at Leghorn, from whence, it is said, he will not depart till he has received 150,000 crowns that the Great Duke of Tuscany is to pay for the damages done heretofore to the English ships within his port.   Yet this is not believed." *Merc. Pol.*, E, 826, 16.   The last-mentioned newspaper, being a Government organ, was doubtless better informed than its contemporary, and added the note of warning at the end.   "Da che," wrote Salvetti, "si vede assai chiaramente i buoni uffizii che vengono fatti dai Genovesi per rovinare il porto di Livorno . . . ma io spero che non sia per riuscirgli ; non ostante che questo lor ministro facci qui quanto puol mai per ottenere il suo intento fino ad offerire di prestare quà grossa somma di denari." Salvetti to Gondi, Feb. $\frac{2}{12}$, 1655, *Add. MSS.* 27,962 O, fol. 382.

[2] Salvetti to Gondi, Oct. $\frac{6}{16}$, 1654, *ib.* fol. 324b.

[3] The history of these presents may be traced through Salvetti's despatches of 1655.

the Protector's orders—for permission to erect a Protestant church at that port, he was told that the Grand Duke would take the matter into consideration whenever a similar demand was conceded in other parts of Italy.[1]

Having thus knitted firmly the good relations which, but for a passing cloud, had long existed between England and Tuscany, Blake found himself at leisure to fulfil another point of his instructions[2] which bound him to do his utmost to compass the liberation of Englishmen held in captivity by the Barbary pirates. The condition of these unfortunate prisoners, kept in slavery in Algiers, Tunis, Tripoli, and Sallee, had long called out sympathy in England, and in 1646 Edmund Casson had been sent out to the Mediterranean to negotiate for their liberty. At Algiers he was so far successful that he procured a treaty with the Dey assuring freedom of trade to English merchants, and an engagement that no Englishmen should in future be condemned to slavery. The treaty, indeed, would not affect the lot of the 650 English slaves captured before the date of its signature, but Casson was permitted to ransom some 240 of them with the consent of their masters, and it was only lack of means which prevented his bargaining for the remainder. From that time, though it is impossible to affirm that no English slaves were surreptitiously landed, the Algerines are at least known to have set free some which had been brought in by their ships. It is not improbable that similar treaties were concluded at Tunis and Tripoli, but we have no certain information on the subject.[3]

Blake's next object.

English captives of the Barbary pirates.

1646. Casson's treaty with Algiers.

[1] Longland to Thurloe, $\frac{\text{Jan. 26}}{\text{Feb. 5}}$, *Thurloe*, iv. 464. This letter is wrongly placed amongst those of 165⅝.

[2] See *supra*, p. 147, note 1. No doubt the instructions there referred to, which only relate to Algiers, were afterwards enlarged so as to include the other Barbary ports.

[3] A copy of Casson's treaty, with additions subsequently made by Blake, is in *S. P. Barbary States—Algiers*, ii. fol. 252. Compare *A Relation of the Whole Proceedings concerning the Redemption of the Captives of Algiers and Tunis*, 1647, B.M. press-mark, 1432, i. 4. In a letter of Nov. 16, 1646, Casson writes of 'the business to be acted at

Unfortunately, if any understanding had been arrived at with Tunis, it was brought to an end by the villainy of an English sailor. In 1651 a certain Mitchell, having engaged to carry thirty-two Turks on board his ship to Smyrna, had scarcely left Tunis when, falling in with some galleys of the Knights of Malta, he sold his helpless passengers to their most deadly enemies, who sent them to tug at the oar in their galleys. Intelligence of Mitchell's conduct had no sooner reached Tunis than the whole city was stirred with well-merited indignation. The English Consul, Boothouse, was thrown into prison, whilst his countrymen went about in fear of their lives.[1] Luckily for him, Penn's fleet, which was at that time cruising in the Mediterranean,[2] made its appearance in Tunisian waters, and obtained leave to remove him, on condition that he would do his utmost to procure the redemption of the kidnapped Turks. Boothouse scraped together about 2,500*l.* and made his way to Malta, where he was baffled by the refusal of the Knights to liberate their slaves for less than 10,000*l.* Inflamed with anger at this failure to restore to freedom the men who were suffering through the violation of an Englishman's word, the Dey, not unnaturally, took his revenge by suffering his cruisers to bring in Englishmen as captives wherever they could light upon them.[3]

Marginal notes: 1651. Villainy of Stephen Mitchell. | Indignation in Tunis. | June 17. The English consul imprisoned, | June 25. but allowed to go to Malta.

Tunis,' and of sending the Parliament's letters to the consul and merchants there. It is therefore to be presumed that he carried on negotiations there, but this is all that can be said.

[1] Boothouse's complaint of his treatment at Tunis was heard in the Council on July 27, 1654. Council Order Book, *Interr.* I, 75, p. 454.

[2] See vol. i. 315.

[3] Boothouse's Narrative, *S. P. Tunis.* Penn in his Journal mentions taking him on board on June 29, *Mem. of Penn*, i. 346. [Boothouse printed in 1653 a tract called *A brief Remonstrance of Several National Injuries perpetrated on the public Ministers and Subjects of this Commonwealth by the Dey of Tunis.* It gives an account of his negotiations at Malta for the redemption of the Tunisian captives, and states the circumstances of their capture more favourably to Mitchell.]

Accordingly Tunis was the object to which Blake's attention was first directed. Neither he nor the Protector appears to have taken into account the irritation which the wrong done by Mitchell had aroused. It was enough for them that Englishmen were held in slavery. Tunis itself, however, was unassailable by sea so long as the Fort of Goletta remained untaken, it being placed astride on the narrow channel forming the only entrance into the basin at the extremity of which the city stands. When, therefore, on February 8, Blake, with eighteen of his ships, arrived in Tunis Road, his object was merely to open negotiations with the Dey for the release of some sailors who had been captured in an English vessel named the 'Princess.' Finding him obdurate, Blake passed on to Porto Farina, where so much of the ancient harbour of Utica as had not yet been silted up sheltered nine of the Dey's men-of-war. These ships, as could be perceived from the sea, lay close inshore under the protection of a strong fort, whilst additional batteries were being thrown up and guns carried on board. A considerable body of troops had also been brought to the place, in expectation that the English admiral would land troops in support of his naval operations. Blake, however, had no such intention, and an immediate attempt on the ships seems to have been considered out of the question, perhaps in consequence of the direction of the wind. On the 22nd a council of war decided that before making the attack the bulk of the fleet should be temporarily withdrawn to provision itself at a Spanish port, the beef which had been brought from England proving defective, and the stock of bread and liquor having fallen very low. On the following morning, therefore, Blake sailed for Cagliari, in the island of Sardinia, leaving eight frigates behind to blockade the Gulf of Tunis.[1]

Marginal notes: 1655. Feb. 6. Blake aims at Tunis. — Feb. 8. He anchors in Tunis Road. — Feb. 13. Blake off Porto Farina. — Feb. 22. A resolution to provision the fleet before attacking.

---

[1] Blake to Thurloe, March 14, *Thurloe*, iii. 232 ; Blake to the Admiralty Commissioners, March 14, *Add. MSS.* 9304, fol. 103 ; Weale's Journal, *Sloane MSS.* 1431, fol. 20b–22b.

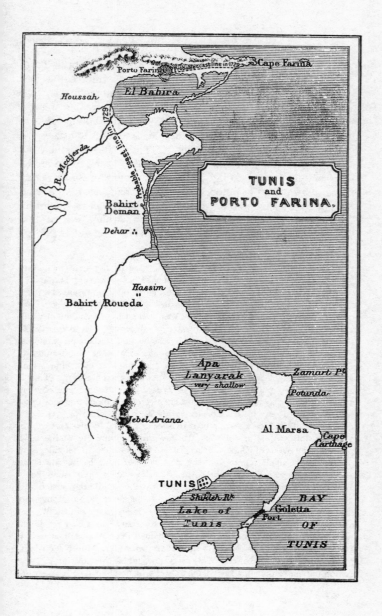

TUNIS
and
PORTO FARINA.

It was not till March 18 that Blake was once more in Tunis Road, where he made yet another attempt to induce the Dey to yield. Finding him still impracticable, the Admiral made sail for Trapani, near the western extremity of Sicily, to take in water, hoping also to disguise by his departure his intention to attack the ships in Porto Farina.[1] There he remained till March 31. On April 2 a council of war, held as the fleet was beating up against a south-westerly gale,[2] resolved to enter Porto Farina as soon as the wind was favourable. On the 3rd Blake cast anchor in the Roads outside that harbour, which was at that time a fairly wide-mouthed bay.[3] At daybreak on

Mar. 18.
Blake again off Tunis.

Mar. 23.
He sails for Trapani.

Mar. 31.
He makes for Porto Farina,

April 3.
and anchors in the Roads.

---

[1] Blake to Thurloe, April 18, *Thurloe*, iii. 390.

[2] One would think that, unless the violence of the gale was exaggerated, the captains must have come on board before leaving Trapani.

[3] Porto Farina, as laid down in the charts of the present day, is a shallow lagoon with an entrance so narrow that Blake could never have escaped from the trap when the action was over without a change of wind, unless the enemy had been utterly disabled. Moreover, it is inconceivable that the Turks, having so many weeks in which to make their preparations, would not have raised batteries at the entrance after the fashion of Goletta. There was, however, as late as 1729 an older coast-line, which was very different from the one given in our present charts. This is shown by a map published in Shaw's *Travels*, which were published in 1738, but which, as it was founded on his own observations taken in 1729, must be held to refer to that date (*Sloane MSS.* 3986, foll. 54, 55). His description of the locality, contained in a letter written by him on Oct. 10, 1729 (*ib.* fol. 56), is as follows: "A few miles within Cape Zibeeb," a point to the west of Cape Farina, "is Port Farina. The village, at present, is of small repute, but the port is a beautiful basin, safe in all accidents of weather, and where the Tunisians keep their small navy. Before the port is a large pond formed by the Medjerda, which discharges itself here into the sea. . . . As the shore is all along very shallow, and as the mud brought down by the Medjerda is always in great abundance, there seems to be nothing extraordinary why this river might not have shifted itself in time from one channel to another, till at last it retired to where it now is, and where those winds," *i.e.* the N.E. winds, "can give it no disturbance. Yet, even now, under this position, there is reason to believe that in a few years only it will be obliged to look out for

the 4th, favoured by a light westerly breeze,[1] he made his way

April 4. The attack on Porto Farina. inside with fifteen sail to attack the enemy's nine ships, lying inside two moles, on which batteries had been placed in support of those in the large fort. Favoured by the sea breeze, which blew the smoke of the Tunisian guns into the faces of the gunners, he easily overpowered the batteries on the moles, and after a longer time also silenced those in the fort. In the meanwhile, the enemy being thus occupied, boats were despatched to set the Tunisian ships on fire. This object having been successfully accomplished, the English fleet had merely to fire an occasional shot into the burning mass in order to keep in check any attempt of the enemy to extinguish the flames. When all was over Blake's ships were warped out of the harbour, as the wind,

another channel; for the pond or anti-harbour spoken of above, which was formerly an open bay or creek of the sea, till the Medjerda by degrees circumscribed those limits, is now almost filled up by the mud lodged there continually by the river; and the bar or mouth of it, which would likewise some years ago admit of vessels of the greatest burden, and a great number at the same time, is now so shallow and narrow that one vessel only of a hundred tons runs a great risk in entering it, and the cruisers of thirty or forty guns discharge all their lumber, guns and ballast while they lie at anchor without." I suppose there can be little doubt that the basin described by Shaw is the port within the moles, and the pond the existing harbour, though not then in its present form. I also notice that it was in Shaw's time difficult of approach on account of the narrowness of the entry. Shaw, however, speaks of a bar, not of points of land approaching one another, and though his language is ambiguous, I am inclined to interpret his description as implying two banks approaching one another, but both still under water. This, however, is of little importance for my purpose, as Shaw states that 'vessels of the greatest burden, and a great number at the same time,' could enter 'some years ago,' and therefore at the time of Blake's attack. The map on page 153 is founded on Shaw's map, though the moles have been added from a plan dated 1756 in *Add. MSS.* 13,959, No. 80. There is also a drawing of Porto Farina, dated 1777, in the British Museum, marked K. 117 (66).

[1] This is implied by Weale's statements that on the morning of the 3rd they had 'an indifferent fair gale' on the way from Trapani, and that the fleet warped out after the action on the 4th. Blake, too, in the letter cited in the last note, speaks of having 'a gentle gale off the sea.'

continuing in the same quarter, did not permit the fleet to make its way back to the Roads under sail. Its loss was found to be no more than twenty-five killed and forty wounded, most of whom had been struck down by small shot aimed at the men in the boats.[1]   The design, evidently planned with care, had been executed with a precision which left nothing to be desired.   Students of naval history may look upon the

Blake's achievement. achievement as a rehearsal of the destruction, two years later, of the Spanish fleet at Santa Cruz, and may count it as the first successful attempt to over-power shore batteries by the guns of a fleet.[2]   No doubt, at Porto Farina as at Santa Cruz, failure to silence the enemy's guns would have been attended by mischievous, and probably by disastrous, consequences.   It is the incommunicable attribute of genius not to be the slave of theoretical rules, but to judge how far they are applicable to each case as it arises. The superior gunnery of English ships [3] and the superior discipline of their crews gave Blake his chance, and of that chance he was not slow to avail himself.   Within a few days after he had brought off his ships from a complete victory Penn and Venables were approaching the coast of Hispaniola to meet as complete a failure.   If we are tempted to draw a contrast between the two enterprises, it is at least well to remember that Blake's task, hard as it was, was at least the easier of the two.

---

[1] Blake to Thurloe, April 14, *Thurloe*, iii. 390; Letters from the Fleet, April 9, 18, *Perfect Diurnal*, E, 840, 11; Weale's Journal, *Sloane MSS.* 1431, fol. 26.   Weale distinctly speaks of the fleet as warping out. Blake's statement is that 'the same favourable gale continuing, we retreated out again into the Road.'   He can only have intended to refer to the lightness of the wind, not to its direction, as the wind was, by his own account, off the sea at the time of his entrance.   He contrasts it with the stormy weather mentioned afterwards as following.

[2] Fort Puntal was attacked by Wimbledon's guns in 1625, but it only surrendered to a land force.

[3] Blake was able to estimate the weakness of the gunnery opposed to him, as he had seen a good deal of it when he was last off Porto Farina, many shot having been then fired at his ships without any appreciable result.

He had undivided command over his own force, and he was not hampered by military considerations. He was placed at the head of a purely naval force, and in his hands a purely naval success, which left nothing more to be accomplished from a naval point of view, was the result.

Unfortunately, the object of Blake's presence in these waters was unattainable without the assistance of a strong military force. On his reappearance before Tunis the Dey stiffly refused to make the least concession. The destroyed ships he alleged to be the property of the Sultan, and it was with the Sultan that Blake would have to reckon. If the English Admiral wished to negotiate, let him come ashore.[1] Blake knew better than to trust himself in such a trap, and as he also knew that his guns would not carry far enough to reach any part of Tunis, there was nothing for it but to return to Cagliari, though he had not procured the liberty of a single captive.[2] If Blake was led to express himself in apologetic language in his report to Thurloe, hoping that the Protector would not be offended at what had been done, 'though he expected to hear of many complaints and clamours of interested men,'—he was certainly influenced not merely by a supposed defect in his instructions, to which he had pointed in an earlier letter, but also by the knowledge that trade with Tunis, which had hitherto been carried on in spite of the captures made by Tunisian freebooters,[3] was likely to be brought to an end in consequence of the blow that he had struck.[4]   Nor

He fails to procure freedom for the slaves in Tunis.

---

[1] The Dey to Blake [April 7], *Merc. Pol.*, E, 841, 3.

[2] Blake to Thurloe, March 14, April 18, *Thurloe*, iii. 232,390.

[3] Weale's Journal shows that at the time of Blake's first arrival off Tunis an English ship was lying in the harbour, *Sloane MSS.* 1431, fol. 21. Blake, too, in his despatch of April 18, mentions sending a letter to Constantinople by 'the "Merchant's Delight" of London, which was then, by Providence, in the road of Goletta.' I do not know why some vessels were captured by the Tunisians and others not. Can it have been that only those bound for Tunis were spared?

[4] The best comment on this is to be found in the following information from London after the story of Blake's action was known there: " Il danno che l' Ammiraglio Blake ha fatto ai Turchi di Tunis ha messo

was the trouble predicted by the Dey as likely to arise in Constantinople by any means imaginary. In London, at least, credit was for some time given to a rumour that the English ambassador in that city, Sir Thomas Bendish, had been put to death, together with all Englishmen on whom the Sultan was able to lay his hands, and that the massacre had been followed by a general confiscation of English property. In time, however, it was discovered that the report was without foundation, and that the Sultan had no inclination to take up the quarrels of a vassal so independent as the Dey of Tunis.[1]

Reported massacre at Constantinople.

After once more replenishing his stores at Cagliari Blake made for Algiers.[2] The Dey of that place, whose fortifications lay within reach of the English guns, and who had no offence received from English sailors to avenge, accorded him a most friendly reception. Since Casson's treaty[3] he had remained on fairly good terms with such English merchants as had visited his dominions, and had recently agreed to the ransom of a considerable number of English captives in the hands of his subjects. Blake's arrival quickened his good resolutions, and on May 2 Casson's treaty was renewed, with two additional clauses, of which the first extended protection to inhabitants of Scotland and Ireland, whilst the second declared that the agreement was not intended to cover the cases of Englishmen serving for wages on board foreign vessels.[4] After this numerous captives were given over to Blake

Apr. 10.
Blake leaves Tunis,

Apr. 28.
and anchors off Algiers.

May 2.
Casson's treaty renewed.

questi mercanti di Levante in grande apprehensione d' avere a suffrire gran perdite in quelle parti, come anche rovinare affatto il lor gran commercio che hanno in quelle parti, come al certo seguirebbe mentre detto Ammiraglio Blake continuasse a minacciare quei barbari." Salvetti's *Newsletter*, $\frac{May\ 25}{June\ 4}$, *Add. MSS.* 27,962 O, 432b. On the further history of this question see *Thurloe*, iii. 637, 663, 726.

[1] Salvetti's *Newsletter*, July $\frac{6}{16}$, *ib.* 455b.

[2] Weale's Journal, *Sloane MSS.* 1431, fol. 26b-28.

[3] See *supra*, p. 150.

[4] Treaty, May 2, *S. P. Algiers*. Nieupoort, in his despatch of $\frac{June\ 29}{July\ 9}$, mentions a subsequent treaty with Tripoli. It is, however, certain from

upon payment of their value. A difficulty occurred when forty

Captives
ransomed. Dutch slaves made their escape from their masters and swam out to the fleet, as Blake had no money to buy the freedom of any who were not his fellow-countrymen.

The sailors
subscribe
to free
Dutch
fugitives. It was got over by the offer of his sailors to subscribe a dollar apiece for the freedom of these venturous Dutchmen. The tender was thankfully accepted by the Algerine masters, who may have thought it improbable that they would regain their living property, and the amount, at the motion of the sailors themselves, was deducted from their pay after their return to England.[1]

Hitherto, whenever a chance offered, Blake's ships had picked up French prizes, whilst the assistance which he received

Blake sup-
ported by
Spain. from the Spanish authorities at Trapani and Cagliari had alone rendered his enterprise feasible. All through the winter the attitude maintained by the

1654.
Dec.
The Pro-
tector's
attitude. Protector in his relations with the ambassadors of the two countries had failed to show even an appearance of friendliness towards France, either because he wished to drive as hard a bargain as possible with Mazarin, or because, in spite of his knowledge of the intentions with which he had sent forth Penn and Venables, he was slow to realise the inevitable result of their attack on the Spanish islands in the Indies, and no less slow to accept the alliance of a Power which he believed to be ill-disposed towards the Huguenots, and which, if it succeeded in wresting Flanders from Spain, would occupy ports threatening English commerce. " Oh," he had said to Stouppe in December, " if there were but means

He wishes
Condé were
a Protestant. to bring the Prince " of Condé " over to our religion, it would be the greatest blessing that could befall our Churches. I hold him to be the greatest captain, not merely in our own age, but in many ages past. It is

Weale's Journal that Blake did not go near that place. As Nieupoort writes of the escape of the Dutch slaves as having occurred at Tripoli, it may be taken that he was really thinking of the treaty with Algiers.

[1] Longland to Thurloe, June $\frac{8}{18}$, *Thurloe*, iii. 526 ; Blake to the Admiralty Commissioners, Oct. 2, *S. P. Dom.* ci. 2.

unfortunate that he should have engaged himself to those who seldom keep their promises." [1] Evidently, if he could have had his way, Oliver would have been as ready to take up arms against France as against Spain. Distrust of the French Government, however, did not imply any confidence in Spain.

Cardenas gains no information about Penn's object.

It was hardly possible that it should. Cardenas at that time was doing his utmost to worm out the secret of Penn's destination. He complained to his master that none of the confidants from whom he usually derived his information had been allowed to participate in the secret. All he could say was that there were rumours abroad that Penn was to sail in the direction, as some said, of Rochelle, or, as others said, of Madagascar. Reports of his object being either Cuba or Hispaniola, however, gained consistency as time went on. [2] An attempt to put a direct question to Oliver himself was naturally repelled. The ambassador could obtain no other answer from the Protector than that it was unheard-of for the minister of a foreign State to expect information on the secret designs of the Government to which he was accredited. [3]

However dissatisfied Cardenas may have been, the complaints of Bordeaux were pitched in as high a key. All through the winter and the early spring his negotiation dragged on. It was in vain that he announced that Mazarin was prepared to expel the Stuarts from France on condition of the expulsion from England of the agents of Condé and the city of Bordeaux; and that he would also consent to a mutual engagement between the two Governments to give no assistance to one another's enemies or rebels. Against this last con-

Oliver will not abandon his claim to defend the Huguenots.

dition Oliver took his stand. Never, he said, would he sign away his right to help the Huguenots against their Government if at any time their persecution

---

[1] Barrière to Condé, Dec. $\frac{15}{25}$, Chantilly Transcripts, *Add. MSS.* 35,252, fol. 227.

[2] Cardenas to Philip IV., Dec. $\frac{18}{28}$, *Simancas MSS.* 2529.

[3] Bonde to Charles X., Oct. 19, 1655, *Stockholm Transcripts.* The story was told by Cardenas to Bonde, showing that he had no charge to bring against Oliver for having verbally deceived him.

should be renewed. Bordeaux was powerless to alter his resolution. Week after week he had to report that he had made no progress; and though he attempted to emphasise his own determination by demanding his passports, he repeated the request so frequently, without acting upon it, that he merely displayed his reluctance to break off his negotiation.[1]

1655.
Bordeaux
often asks
for his
passports.

There can be little doubt that Oliver trusted to the blows he was striking at French commerce to bring Mazarin to what he conceived to be reason; and amongst those blows must be counted one which had been struck in North America in the course of 1654. On February 17 in that year, at a time when the Dutch Government was still resisting the English demand for the disqualification of the Prince of Orange from office, the Protector had commissioned Major Sedgwick to invite the New England colonies to raise a force for the conquest of the Dutch settlement of New Amsterdam, now known to the world as the city of New York. Sedgwick had done no more than make preparations for the execution of his orders when the news that peace had been concluded with the Dutch reached America. His commission, however, included what at that time was the usual clause empowering him to make reprisals on the French.[2] The New Englanders were accordingly glad to take the opportunity of serving under him in order to settle in their own favour a dispute about the border-line between their own settlements and the French colony of Acadia, which at that time included not merely the later Nova Scotia, but also the coasts of the present New Brunswick and Maine. With this object in view Sedgwick was so well supported that he was

Oliver hopes
to bring
Mazarin to
reason.

1654.
Feb. 17:
Sedgwick's
commission.

[1] The despatches of Bordeaux for the first four months of 1655 should be compared with those of the Dutch ambassador in De Witt's *Brieven*, iii. 5-61.

[2] Sedgwick to the Protector, July 1, 1654, *Thurloe*, ii. 418. The commission, however, seems only to have given him leave to seize French ships, not to attack French settlements. Leverett to the Protector, July 4, *ib.* ii. 425.

able to possess himself of the three forts held by the French
in Acadia, and was consequently received by the
colonists on his return with the warmest manifesta-
tions of their gratitude.   The Protectorate revealing
itself in such a guise had no warmer supporters than in New
England, where it was accepted as a working of Divine
Providence.[1]   When the news reached England in October,
Bordeaux found to his sorrow that the Protector
showed no signs of an intention to surrender his new
acquisition, and though for some months he lost no
opportunity of pressing his claim for its restoration,
he was forced to acknowledge that he had little prospect of
success.[2]

July.
Seizure of
three forts
in Acadia.

Oct.
The Pro-
tector will
not hear of
restoring
them.

If Bordeaux continued to believe that, so far as his main
object was concerned, time was fighting on his side, it was
because he suspected that the Protector would
ultimately be driven into war with Spain.   Suspicion
must have been changed into certainty when, towards
the end of March, news reached London of Penn's
arrival at Barbados,[3] and when, about the same time, the
Protector warned the merchants trading with Spain not to
embark their capital too deeply in that treacherous country, a
warning which was repeated in the course of the following
month.[4]   Yet it is doubtful whether even at this late
hour Oliver had positively determined to break with
Spain.   It was known that a Spanish ambassador, the
Marquis of Lede,[5] was on his way towards England, nominally
with a message of compliment, but in reality in the hope of
renewing the good understanding which had formerly prevailed

1655.
Bordeaux
thinks that
time is on
his side.

April.
Oliver still
hesitates.

---

[1] Leverett to the Protector, Sept. 5, *Thurloe*, ii. 583.

[2] Bordeaux to Brienne, Oct. $\frac{16}{26}$, $\frac{\text{Jan. 25}}{\text{Feb. 4}}$, *French Transcripts*, *R.O.*

[3] Salvetti's *Newsletter*, $\frac{\text{March 30}}{\text{April 9}}$, *Add. MSS.* 27,962 O, fol. 410b.

[4] Bordeaux to Mazarin, $\frac{\text{March 29}}{\text{April 8}}$, April $\frac{19}{29}$, *French Transcripts*, *R.O.*

[5] Bordeaux gives his name as Leyde, and the mistake has been
followed by Guizot and later writers.   The family name of the Marquis
was Bette.   See Gobelinus, *Preuves de la Maison de Bette*.   Lede is in
East Flanders, near Alost.

between the two countries. It is probable that before finally making up his mind Oliver wished to hear what the Marquis had to say, in the hope that Spain might be prepared at last to

May 11. give way on the two main points in dispute. On
Lede refuses
to give way May 11, when Lede announced distinctly that, what-
on the Indies ever else might be conceded, his master would never
and the
Inquisition. give way either on the Inquisition or the Indies, all
hesitation was at an end. The ambassador in vain engaged that his master's troops would join the English forces in recovering Calais, on condition that Oliver would join the Spaniards in recovering Bordeaux for Condé.[1] The French ambassador was at once informed that the commissioners appointed to treat with him were ordered to draw up a treaty with France. " I have never," he wrote to Mazarin, " had any

The nego- word so positive before." [2] It was obviously to gain
tiation with
France to time to take the measures required by this change of
be seriously front that the answer to Lede's proposition was
pursued.
delayed ; and it was only on June 6, after a com-
June 6.
The Pro- plaint from both the Spanish ambassadors,[3] that they
tector's
answer to were informed that the Protector would come to no
Spain.
terms with them unless they were empowered to give

way on the questions of the Indies and the Inquisition, and also to make certain concessions to English trade in Spain, notified in a paper which had been placed in their hands about a fortnight before.[4] To this Lede had no reply to give except to refer the

---

[1] Papel presentado al Ser^mo Protector, May $\frac{11}{21}$. It is published in *Remarques sur la reddition de Dunkerque* (ascribed to Hugues de Lionne), p. 5.

[2] Bordeaux to Mazarin, May $\frac{17}{27}$; Bordeaux to Brienne, May $\frac{17}{27}$, *French Transcripts, R.O.* The ambassador's first meeting with the commissioners was on the 16th ; but he had expected them on Monday the 14th, so that the resolution must have been promptly taken—perhaps on Saturday the 12th, the day after Lede's audience.

[3] Lede and Cardenas to the Protector, *Thurloe*, iii. 154. The letter is undated, but was evidently written not long before June 6.

[4] The proposals on commerce are to be found in *Certain Passages*, E, 840, 7. Cardenas's despatch of June $\frac{8}{18}$, giving an account of this negotiation, is not to be found at Simancas, but its purport can be gathered from the instructions issued to him on Sept. $\frac{5}{15}$.

Protector to the King of Spain ; and though, when the special ambassador took his leave on the 12th, he was dismissed with every expression of friendliness, he could discover no sign that Oliver had the slightest disposition to modify his demands.[1]

The effects of the failure of Lede's negotiation were most strongly felt in the instructions given to Blake. Scanty as is the evidence which has reached us, it is known that about the middle of April the Protector informed Blake that a supply of provisions for three months would shortly be forwarded to him—no doubt because the friendly offices of Spanish governors would not be available much longer ; and there is reason to suppose that he at the same time added instructions for him to proceed to Cadiz Bay. At all events, these instructions were repeated and confirmed on or about April 30.[2] Yet, even if these

April.
A message to Blake.

April 30 ?
It is confirmed.

---

[1] Cardenas to Philip IV., $\frac{\text{June 21}}{\text{July}}$, *Simancas MSS.* 2570.

[2] The Protector in his letter of June 13 (*Thurloe*, iii. 547) speaks of two messages, one sent by sea in a ketch, and the other, which appears to have been written in confirmation of the first, by way of Leghorn. The former is shown by this letter to have been sent off before April 28. The proximate date of the other is known from a letter of Lawson's of May 1 (*S. P. Dom.* cviii. 9), in which he mentions sending on a despatch for Blake by Captain Nixon. Nixon was in command of the 'Centurion,' a large ship, and so can have had nothing to do with the ketch. He must have taken the messenger to some port on the other side of the Straits, and have sent him on to Leghorn overland. [The facts stated above are not quite correct. The Protector mentions two communications—(1) 'former despatches by way of Leghorn' ; (2) 'those sent by a ketch immediately from hence.' Both were apparently duplicates of the same despatch, containing, as Cromwell writes to Blake, an order 'for your coming to Cadiz Bay with the fleet' (*Thurloe*, iii. 547). The ketch 'Sea Adventure,' Capt. Abraham Pearse, sailed about the beginning of April, and had reached Malaga by April 19 ; but the exact date when Pearse reached Blake's fleet does not appear (*Cal. S. P. Dom.* 1655, pp. 136, 452, 459, 525). As to the overland despatch, the post from London to Leghorn took four or five weeks. Longland, the agent at Leghorn, sent the 'Warwick' pinnace on May $\frac{1}{11}$ to Alcudia Bay with letters to Blake from Thurloe (*Thurloe*, iii. 422). They seem to have reached Blake at Formentara on May 16, and on May 17 he started for Cadiz (Weale's Journal,

instructions contained a definite order to attack the home-ward-bound treasure-fleet, Blake knew too well that the prize he sought to grasp was not to be expected in European waters so early in the year, and, leaving Algiers on May 10, he remained cruising off the Balearic Isles for some days before he made for the Straits. That he contemplated a breach with Spain in the near future as probable is shown by his despatching on the 18th, two frigates to Cartagena to take on board the guns of Rupert's ships wrecked there in 1650, which he claimed as the property of the English Commonwealth. The request was promptly complied with, and when on the 30th the frigates rejoined Blake, who had by that time anchored off Cadiz, the Admiral found himself in possession of fifty additional pieces of ordnance.[1]

May 23. Rupert's guns secured.

On June 4 Blake put to sea. On the 12th, as he was lying off Cape Santa Maria on the Portuguese coast, he acknowledged to the Protector the receipt of secret instructions in confirmation of earlier ones, instructions which appear to have reached him before he left Cadiz, and must, therefore, so far as we can judge by the date, have been drawn up after May 11, the day on which Lede's memorial put it out of doubt that the King of Spain had no intention of giving way on the two points at issue between himself and the

June 4. Blake puts to sea on the receipt of secret instructions.

Sloane MSS. 1431). Captain Nixon did not carry either of these despatches. He with the 'Centurion' and the 'Dragon,' convoying victuallers for Blake's fleet, sailed about the end of April. The despatch sent by him was a later one: probably that containing the 'secret instructions' acknowledged by Blake in his letter of June 12, and distinguished there from 'a former instruction touching the silver fleet' (*Thurloe*, iii. 541). This 'former instruction' was apparently the duplicate despatches sent off at the beginning of April.]

[1] Weale's Journal, *Sloane MSS.* 1431, foll. 29b–31. Weale does not say that the guns had been Rupert's, but he treats them as belonging to the Commonwealth, and I cannot imagine that they can have been demanded on any other ground. The King of Spain had allowed the claim put in by Blake in 1650 for the contents of the wrecks. See vol. i. 305. That the two frigates also brought off some anchors points in the same direction.

Protector.[1] Blake now wrote that the Plate Fleet was expected in four or five weeks, and that he intended to range the sea between the Portuguese and African coasts in the hope of intercepting it.[2] Lede's pronouncement on May 11 had thus led to definite instructions for the capture of the homeward-bound Plate Fleet, whilst his departure on June 12 led to no

June 13.
Blake to stop supplies for the West Indies.

less definite instructions, given to Blake on the following day, to hinder, by the seizure of outward-bound ships, any relief or assistance being given to the Spanish possessions in the Indies. The order was accompanied by a full acknowledgment of Blake's services at Porto Farina, thus setting at rest any doubt as to their acceptance.[3] A paper of instructions added on the 14th directed him to send home part of the fleet, whilst keeping his station

Extension of the limits of war.

with the remainder.[4] Almost imperceptibly the war was spreading beyond the limits originally designed. The claim to defend traders in the Indies was first held to justify an English admiral in intercepting, even in European waters, supplies sent to Spain from the Indies, and then to give a right to intercept supplies sent from Spain for the defence of the Indies. It could not be long before war would be openly avowed.

It was not Blake's fault that he was unable to gratify the

[1] The 'Amity,' which no doubt conveyed Blake's letter of the 12th, parted from the fleet on that day. She was, however, 'designed home' on the 1st. Weale's Journal, *Sloane MSS.* 1431, foll. 31b, 32b. She may not have been ready to sail ; or Blake may have wished to keep her till he could announce that he was actually on the look-out. A message sent later from England on June 14 reached Blake on July 1, or in seventeen days. Blake to the Protector, July 4, *Thurloe,* iii. 611.

[2] Blake to the Protector, June 12, July 4, *ib.* iii. 541, 611.

[3] The Protector to Blake, June 13, *ib.* iii. 547. The letter as printed begins with an acknowledgment of Blake's letter of March 25, as containing an account of the affair at Porto Farina. As this did not take place till Apr. 3, there must be a mistake of some kind. Blake's despatch relating to it was dated Apr. 18.

[4] These instructions, which have not been preserved, are referred to in Blake's reply, *Thurloe,* iii. 611.

Protector.   The Plate Fleet, alarmed by the threatenings of war,

July.
Preparations
at Cadiz.

had held back from crossing the Atlantic.   In the meanwhile there was anxiety at Cadiz and a determination not to leave it to fall unsuccoured into the hands of the English.   On July 6 Blake announced that a fleet was being got together in the harbour, and that Dutch and French ships had been taken up to strengthen it.[1]   On

Aug. 12.
A Spanish
fleet off Cape
St. Vincent.

August 12 he heard that it had actually sailed, and, having slipped past him, was beating up and down off Cape St. Vincent.   Blake at once followed it up,

Aug. 15–18.
It avoids an
engagement.

and for four days did his best to bring on an action. The Spaniards, however, having no reason to commence a war unless in defence of their own treasure-ships, were successful in avoiding an engagement.   " These checks of Providence," reported Blake, " did put us upon second thoughts."

Aug. 18.
A council of
war.

A council of war was called, when the instructions from home were carefully scanned without finding any authority to attack a fleet not bound for the Indies. Blake accordingly resolved to leave the Spaniards alone, all the more because his ships were foul from having been so long at sea, while his liquor was running short, some of his ships not having more on board than would serve for four days.   Yet

Aug. 22.
Blake makes
for Lisbon,

he kept the Spaniards in sight till the 22nd, and then, being assured by one of their captains that they had no order to begin the war, and also that they

Aug. 24.
and arrives
there.

knew nothing of the coming of the Plate Fleet, made the best of his way to Lisbon, where he arrived on the 24th.

On August 30 Blake announced to the Protector his purpose of returning to his station, if only his needs could be supplied.

Aug. 30.
His com-
plaint.

His account of the condition of his fleet was indeed pitiable.   "How these passages of Providence," he wrote, "will be looked upon, or what construction

---

[1] Blake to the Protector, July 6, *Thurloe*, iii. 620.   The line only partially deciphered should be read : ' to set forth a force of ships to secure the Plate Fleet.'   Compare Weale's Journal, *Sloane MSS.* 1431, fol. 37.

our carriage in this business may receive I know not—although it hath been with all integrity of heart—but this we know, that our condition is dark and sad, and without especial mercy like to be very miserable : our ships extreme foul, winter drawing on, our victuals expiring, all stores failing, our men falling sick through the badness of drink, and eating their victuals boiled in salt water for two months' space, the coming of a supply uncertain—we received not one word from the Commissioners of the Admiralty and Navy by the last—and though it come timely, yet if beer come not with it we shall be undone that way. We have no place or friend, our recruits [1] here slow, and our mariners—which I most apprehend—apt to fall into discontents through their long keeping abroad. Our only comfort is that we have a God to lean upon, although we walk in darkness and see no light. I shall not trouble your Highness with any complaints of myself, of the indisposition of my body or troubles of my mind ; my many infirmities will one day, I doubt not, sufficiently plead for me or against me, so that I may be free of so great a burden, consolating myself in the mean time in the Lord and in the firm purpose of my heart with all faithfulness and sincerity to discharge the trust while reposed in me." [2]

The Protector's reply, written on September 13, was a model of the considerate treatment due to a faithful servant of his Government. Without concealing his persuasion that an attack on the Spanish fleet off Cape St. Vincent would have been in accordance with the Admiral's instructions, or that it would be desirable to carry it out even now, he left it to Blake to decide whether it would be best for him to remain at sea or to return to England. It was not, he explained, his fault that provisions had not reached the fleet. They had been sent away, but the ships carrying them had been driven back by a storm.[3] How great was Oliver's disappointment at Blake's avoidance of an

Sept. 13.
The Protector leaves him to stay or return as he may think best.

---

[1] *I.e.* supplies to make up deficiencies.
[2] Blake to the Protector, Aug. [30], *Thurloe*, iii. 719.
[3] The Protector to Blake, Sept. 13, *ib.* i. 724.

action may be gauged from the very date of his letter. On September 13 Penn and Venables were already before the Council, and the whole miserable story of the failure of the attack on San Domingo was publicly known. It would have been something to have been able to set off against that disaster a victory over a Spanish fleet, however profitless that victory might have been. When, therefore, Blake, having come to the conclusion that it would be ruinous to keep the sea longer,

Oct. 6.
Blake's return.

anchored in the Downs on October 6,[1] the talk in London was that he would find his way to the Tower.[2] Those who spread the rumour had little knowledge of Oliver's skill in the judgment of men.

It is not improbable that, in his interpretation of his instructions to Blake, the Protector was influenced by his growing assurance that the general war, which he deprecated, could not be avoided much longer. When the news from Hispaniola

July.
The effect of the news from Hispaniola on Cardenas.

reached England on July 24, Cardenas, though qualifying Oliver's proceedings as infamously hypocritical, clung to the hope that he might be so alarmed at his danger on the one hand from Spanish fleets in the Indies, and on the other from English merchants exasperated by the ruin of their trade, as to draw back from the course on which he had entered. Unwilling to thrust himself forward at such a crisis, the Spanish ambassador sent Barrière to White-

Aug.
Barrière's interview with the Protector.

hall about the middle of August to urge these considerations on the Protector. Barrière could, he thought, speak more freely as the representative of Condé, who had everything to lose from a breach between Spain and England. Whatever may have been the language used on both sides at that interview, the civility of the reception which Oliver accorded to the agent of one for whom he had the profoundest admiration was such as to lead Cardenas to imagine that a restoration of Jamaica was not impossible.[3] At Madrid no such illusions were cherished. The Spanish

---

[1] Weale's Journal, *Sloane MSS.* 1431, fol. 39.

[2] Sagredo to the Doge, Oct. $\frac{12}{22}$, *Venetian Transcripts, R.O.*

[3] Cardenas to Philip IV., July $\frac{16}{26}$, Aug. $\frac{2}{12}$, $\frac{20}{30}$, *Simancas MSS.* 2529.

Government persistently, and not unreasonably, believed that Oliver was determined on war.

War, it may fairly be assumed, could at this stage only have been averted by Philip's acceptance of the conditions which Oliver had laid down in his answer to the Marquis of Lede.[1] Such concessions, entirely opposed to the principles which had animated the Spanish councils for more than a century, could never have been made by Philip, even if there had been no seizure of Jamaica and no threatening appearance of an English fleet off his own coasts. In the instructions to Cardenas drawn up on August 26, and finally despatched to him on August 31,[2] that ambassador was directed to demand an audience for the purpose of taking leave, and to cross the sea to Flanders as soon as possible. If the reason of this sudden departure were asked, he was to ground it on the claims, put forward in the answer made to Lede, to free commerce in the Indies, to an extension of the consideration hitherto shown to the consciences of Englishmen, and to commercial privileges unheard of in any former treaty. If anything was said about Jamaica, the Protector was to be told that what had happened there was in itself a breach of the peace, and that he knew it to be so. Nothing short of his abandonment of the three points, and offering reparation for the events in the Indies, could be accepted as satisfactory ; but even in that case Cardenas was not to defer his leave-taking. If any fresh negotiations were opened, they must be conducted through some other channel.[3]

On September 17, before these orders reached the ambassador, it was known in London that Philip, not contenting himself with a mere demonstration of his resentment, had laid an embargo on all English goods and vessels in his dominions.

Philip will not give way.

Aug. 26 / Sept. 5 Instructions to Cardenas.

Sept. 17. Embargo in Spain known in London.

---

[1] See *supra*, p. 163.   [2] $\frac{\text{Aug. 31}}{\text{Sept. 10}}$, as we learn from Cardenas's reply.

[3] Instructions to Cardenas, $\frac{\text{Aug. 26}}{\text{Sept. 5}}$, *Simancas MSS.* There is a translation of them in *Guizot*, ii. 548, incorrectly dated October. That the earlier date is right is shown by the action taken by Cardenas when he received them on Oct. $\frac{8}{18}$.

Loud was the outcry amongst the London merchants, and when, on October 9, Cardenas demanded an audience for the purpose of taking leave, those cries were redoubled, and found an echo in the clothing districts, where goods were largely manufactured for export to Spain. The Protector, in answer to the complaining merchants, reminded them that he had already warned them of their danger,[1] and he now advised them to set out a fleet of privateers to recoup themselves at the expense of Spain. The proposal fell on deaf ears, and Oliver was forced, if he went to war, to wage it on the now scanty resources of the Government. Yet he was aware that the feeling of the merchants was shared by many influential members of the Council, and it was probably this knowledge that led him to interpose delays in the way of the departure of Cardenas. On October 15 the Council met to take into consideration the Spanish demands, and some influential voices, among which it may safely be conjectured Lambert's was heard the loudest, were raised in favour of a policy of abstinence from aggression and the maintenance of peace. Oliver, however, spoke strongly against the abandonment of his great design, and, as usually happened when he was himself in earnest, he brought over the majority to his side. On the 17th Cardenas received his passport, but so clogged with unusual conditions that he refused to make use of it ; and when at last these obstacles were removed, and he was able to leave London on the 27th, the officials of the Custom House at Dover, surely not without a hint from Whitehall, broke open his chests and searched his baggage in the hope of discovering prohibited goods. It is to be hoped that this outrage was due to the misplaced zeal of some subordinate, and not to the Protector himself.[2]

Marginal notes:
Oct. $\frac{9}{19}$. Cardenas demands an audience to take leave.
Dissatisfaction of the merchants.
Oct. 15. The Council decides on war.
Oct. 17. A passport sent to Cardenas.
Oct. 27. He leaves London.

[1] See p. 162.

[2] Cardenas to Philip IV., Sept. $\frac{17}{27}$, $\frac{Sept. 25}{Oct. 4}$, Oct. $\frac{8}{18}$, Oct $\frac{15}{25}$, $\frac{Oct. 22, 30}{Nov. 1, 9}$. Before leaving Cardenas took care to secure the services of two intelligencers ; whilst Barrière, who was left in England by Condé at the special request of Don Luis de Haro, remained till April 1656. Fiesque

On October 26, the day before Cardenas began his journey, the Protector ordered the issue of a manifesto in justification
Oct. 26.
The Pro-
tector's
manifesto. of his breach with Spain. The wrongs which Englishmen had suffered from the Spanish Government were recounted at large, and it was energetically asserted that Spain, not England, had begun the war in the Indies. As usually happens when contending parties put forward diametrically opposite views on the line of conduct pursued by themselves or their adversaries, it is necessary for those who desire to form an independent judgment to seek out the unexpressed axioms on which these various judgments are founded. In this case the search is attended with no difficulty. Nature of
the Spanish
claim. In Spain it was held as an axiom that the Indies, land and sea, were the property of the King of Spain. In England it was held with equal tenacity that the sea at least was free to all. These differences of opinion once admitted to exist, it is intelligible that Philip should believe it to be within his rights to make captives of Englishmen who traded in his seas without permission, and to put Englishmen to death who, in the teeth of his prohibition, were found as colonists on islands which, from his point of view, were as much his own as the seas which washed their coasts.

To Oliver also the case he was resolved to maintain appeared beyond dispute. " The just and most reasonable The English
claim. grounds," he began, " of our late enterprise upon some islands possessed by the subjects of the King of Spain in the West Indies are very obvious to any that shall reflect upon the posture wherein the said King and his people have always stood, in relation to the English nation in those parts of America, which hath been no other than a continual state of open war and hostility ; at the first most unjustly begun

to Condé, Nov. $\frac{7}{17}$, Condé to Fiesque, Jan. $\frac{5}{15}$, $\frac{\text{March } 22}{\text{April } 1}$, 1656, Chantilly Transcripts, *Add. MSS.* 35, 252, foll. 239, 241. License of transportation, *Interr.* I, 72, pp. 299, 301. The issue of the Declaration was kept back till after Cardenas was gone. Nieupoort to the States General, Nov. $\frac{2}{12}$, *Add. MSS.* 17, 677 W, fol. 176. A translation wrongly dated is in *Thurloe,* iv. 117.

by them, and ever since in like sort continued and prosecuted,
contrary to the common right and law of nations and
the particular treaties between England and Spain."

The war
begun by
Spain.

The English, he continued, had of late years been
so patient that some might regard the recent expedition as an
act of aggression rather than, as it really was, an act of defence
against the Spaniards, "who, as oft as they have
opportunity, without any just cause or provocation
at all, cease not to kill and slaughter, nay sometimes

The mis-
deeds of
Spain re-
counted.

in cold blood to murder the people of this nation, spoiling their
goods and estates, destroying their colonies and plantations,
taking also their ships, if they meet with any upon those seas,
and using them in all things as enemies, or rather as rovers
and pirates; for so they . . . brand all nations, except themselves, which shall presume to sail upon those seas, upon no
other or better right or title than that of the Pope's donation,
and their first discovering some parts of the West Indies;
whereupon they would appropriate to themselves the sole
signory of the new world."

In Oliver's eyes it was no small justification that he was
reverting to the policy of the Elizabethan sea-kings. Yet he
never failed to fall back from general considerations

A reversion
to Eliza-
bethan
policy.

upon particular facts. "As to the state of our
quarrel in the West Indies," he explained, "whereas
we have colonies in America as well in islands as

Attacks on
Englishmen
in the West
Indies.

upon the continent upon as good and a better title
than the Spaniards have any, and have as good a
right to sail in those seas as themselves; yet without any just
cause or provocation—and when the question of commerce was
not at all in the case—they have notwithstanding continually
invaded in a hostile manner our colonies, slain our countrymen, taken our ships and goods, destroyed our plantations,
made our people prisoners and slaves, and have continued so
doing from time to time, till the very time that we undertook
the expedition against them."

Omitting the very numerous acts of violence cited by the
Protector as having been committed before the last peace in

1630, there were quite enough to justify his indictment. Providence and Tortuga had in 1627, at a time of war
with Spain, been occupied by Englishmen as unin-
habited islands. When peace was made in 1630 the
case of these islands was passed over in silence ;
whereupon Charles I. had not hesitated to grant them
both to a colonising company, which despatched settlers to
occupy them. The Spaniards, however, refused to regard the
occupation as legitimate, attacked one of the company's ships
in 1633, and in the following year invaded Tortuga, destroyed
the property of the colonists, and hanged, shot, or carried away
as captives all the Englishmen in the island. In 1635 a similar
attempt was made on Providence, and, though it ended in
failure, it was renewed in 1640, when the colonists agreed to
abandon the island with the loss of all their property. In 1651
another body of English settlers was attacked in Santa Cruz,
and about a hundred of them killed ; whilst the remainder,
who hid themselves in the woods, gave up all hope of resistance,
and made their escape to other islands. Then followed a tale
of ships driven by stress of weather into Spanish ports, only to
be seized with their cargoes. One ship was even captured on
the high seas and carried into Havana, with the goods on board,
where ship and goods were confiscated, 'and most of the men
kept prisoners and forced to work in the bulwarks like slaves.'
Another vessel, having sprung a leak off the coast of Hispaniola
as she was returning from an English plantation, the crew were
forced to put themselves ashore in a boat, where they were
taken by the Spaniards 'and made to work like slaves in their
fortifications.'

As such conduct could only be defended on the plea that
the whole of the Indies was a Spanish preserve into which no
one of foreign nationality could rightfully intrude, Oliver
proceeded to deny that Spain could base any such claim either
upon the arbitrament of Alexander VI., or upon prior discovery of lands she had never possessed or planted. The
conclusion of this part of the manifesto was a stirring appeal to
his countrymen. "We need not enlarge our discourse upon

this subject; for there is not any understanding man who is not satisfied of the vanity of the Spaniards' pretensions to the sole sovereignty of all those parts of the world; but we have opened a little the weak and frivolous pretences whereupon the Spaniards ground all their cruel and unworthy dealings with the English in the West Indies—enslaving, hanging, drowning, and cruelly torturing to death our countrymen, spoiling their ships and goods, and destroying their colonies in the times of the greatest peace, and that without any just cause or provocation at all—that the English nation, reflecting upon the indignity of such proceedings against their own flesh and blood and the possessors of the same true Christian religion with them, might consider with themselves how the honour of this nation would lie rotting as well as their vessels of war, if they should any longer suffer themselves to be used, or rather abused in this manner, and not only excluded from commerce with so great and rich a part of the world against all right and reason, but also be accounted and executed as rovers and pirates for offering to sail or to look into those seas, or having any intercourse—though with our own plantations only—in those parts of the world." [1]

On these words—appealing to our own generation even more than to Oliver's contemporaries—must be founded the justification of the policy on which the Protector had at last

Oct. 17. Cardenas in self-defence.

definitely embarked. Cardenas, in defending his master's conduct in a conversation with the Swedish ambassador before leaving England, had nothing to say on the Spanish ill-treatment of English colonists, except that Providence had been a mere nest of pirates; whilst he naturally inveighed against the Protector for his stealthy attack on Hispaniola and Jamaica, and spoke of the idea that it was possible for the two nations to be at war in America and at peace in Europe as too childish to be discussed. [2] It is on

[1] *Declaration*, Oct. 26, E, 1065, 1. The composition was probably the work of Fiennes, to whom other State Papers of the time are attributed.

[2] Bonde to Charles X., Oct. 19, *Stockholm Transcripts*. The dates

these latter grounds, if at all, that our sympathies must be with the Spaniard. If Oliver had good cause for war, he did not open hostilities in honourable fashion. Though he was not bound to inform Cardenas of the destination of his fleets, he was bound, on the grounds of common honesty, to let him plainly understand, at the earliest possible moment, that an attack on Spain in some quarter of the globe would be the result of a refusal to grant the concessions he demanded.

show that Cardenas's words cannot be taken as a direct reply to the Declaration published nine days after they were spoken; but the Protector's complaints about the conduct of the Spaniards in the West Indies must have been conveyed to him verbally many times during the previous months.

CHAPTER XLVII

THE PROTESTANT INTEREST

As the outbreak of war with one country necessarily affects the relations of the belligerent Power with all others, it was inevitable that Oliver should be drawn closer to France as the distance widened between his own Government and that of Spain. In May, almost immediately after Lede's memorandum had made it certain that Philip had no intention of giving way,[1] Bordeaux found reason to believe that the commissioners appointed to treat with him had been instructed to apply themselves seriously to the settlement of outstanding disputes ; and but for an unfortunate occurrence it is almost certain that a satisfactory conclusion would have been reached in a much shorter time than was in reality the case. The commissioners, who on May 16 had left a satisfactory impression on the French ambassador,[2] informed him before taking leave that information had been received of a persecution of Protestants in the dominions of the Duke of Savoy, the cruelties exercised having been not only suggested by the French ambassador at Turin, but carried out by English regiments in the service of the King of France. If this proved to be true the Protector would be unable to enter into an alliance with the oppressor of his co-religionists, and he therefore required an explanation before he could proceed further in the matter.[3] Bordeaux naturally

Marginal notes:

1655.
Effect of the breach with Spain on the relations between England and France.

May 16.
Bordeaux informed of the persecution of Protestants in Piedmont.

---

[1] See *supra*, p. 163.   [2] See *supra*, p. 163.

[3] " Ils me dirent que son Altesse et le Conseil avait appris avec beaucoup de ressentiment la persecution des Protestans de Savoye, que

retorted that as Catholics were persecuted in England his master was not bound to give account of the persecution of Protestants in his own dominions, far less in those of another
French mediation demanded. prince. Finally, the commissioners told Bordeaux that all that His Highness desired of him was to convey to his master a hope that he would interpose in any way he pleased in favour of the injured Protestants.[1]

Though the story told by the commissioners was in some respects exaggerated, and the persecution was in nowise due to
The Vaudois of the Alps. the instigation of Servien, the French ambassador at Turin, it was not far from the truth. Westward of Turin, the two Alpine valleys of the Pellice and the Chisone were inhabited by peasants whose ancestors had early in the thirteenth century imbibed the ascetic doctrines taught by the Waldenses or followers of Peter Waldez. Though from time to time subjected to persecution, the inhabitants of the valleys succeeded in maintaining their existence as a religious community under the name of Waldensians or Vaudois, but, coming in the seventeenth century under the influence of Geneva, they dropped their older tenets in favour of the more recent doctrines of Calvin. Holding such opinions,

suivant les advis de ce pays l'Ambassadeur de sa Majesté l'avoit suggeré et ses troupes, entr'autres quelques Regimens Anglois, executé avec un esprit de vengeance, que nos ennemis se servoient de ce prétexte pour refroidir les bonnes intentions de son Altesse, luy representant que la bienseance ne luy permettoit pas de s'unir avec sa Majesté dans le temps qu'elle faisoit persecuter lesdictz Religionnaires, et qu'ilz avoient ordre de me demander quelque satisfaction sur ce sujet." Bordeaux to Brienne, May $\frac{17}{27}$, *French Transcripts, R.O.* The commissioners diplomatically asserted that the enemies of France were making use of the affair of the Vaudois to keep up the estrangement between the two countries; but, considering what happened afterwards, it is justifiable, as I have done in the text, to lay the warning at Oliver's own door. Bordeaux says that the news was brought by Stouppe, and requested the commissioners to ask him ' ce qu'il avoit fait chez l'Ambassadeur d'Espagne samedy dernier et pour quel service il en avait reçeu deux mille francs ce mesme jour.' Saturday last was May 12, and the news must therefore have reached England not later than that day.

[1] *Ib.*

they had their full share of persecution; but the Dukes of Savoy, in whose Piedmontese territories their valleys were situated, had found it difficult to subdue them, and in 1561

1561.
Edict of toleration.

Philibert Emmanuel granted them toleration within certain well-defined geographical limits. These limits did not include La Torre, Luserna, or San Giovanni, situated in the lower part of the valley of the Pellice, still less any places in the open plain.[1] From 1638,

1638.
Government of the Duchess Christina.

when the Duchess Christina, the sister of Henrietta Maria, became Regent in the name of her son, Charles Emmanuel II., and who virtually governed the country for some years after he reached his nominal majority in 1648, a different spirit prevailed at Turin.   On the one hand missionaries were introduced to convert the inhabitants of the valleys, and these missionaries, indiscreet and presumptuous even by the confession of their supporters, had at their disposal all the temptations, and sometimes the armed force, of the Government.   The Vaudois on their part occasionally allowed their indignation to get the better of their prudence.   In 1650, for instance, they burnt a mission-house at Villar.   This and other similar offences, however, were condoned by the Govern-

1653.
The edict of toleration confirmed.

ment in 1653, when an edict was issued confirming the privileges granted in 1561 to all who lived within the limits then fixed;[2] on which consideration the Vaudois replaced the burnt mission-house.   It was also decreed that mass was to be said and the doctrines of the Roman Catholic Church proclaimed wherever the missionaries took up their quarters.[3]

Though, with certain intermissions, the Duchess had on the

Edict, $\frac{\text{May 26}}{\text{June 5}}$, 1561.   Morland's *History of the Evangelical Churches of the Valleys of Piedmont*, 237.

[2] *Ib.* 291.

[3] Muston, *L'Israël des Alpes*, ii. 261–94; Claretta, *Storia del Regno . . . di Carlo Emanuele II.*, i. 75–91.   The first of these authors is a strong partisan of the Vaudois, the second an equally strong opponent; but they both refer to documents, many of them unpublished, and it is usually, though not always, possible to make out the truth between them.

whole been favourable to the maintenance of the privileges of
the Vaudois within the limits defined in 1561, she had constantly testified her dislike of their extension to the
plain. A sober and industrious race was unlikely to
confine itself to the higher valleys, and the Vaudois,
like most mountaineers, pushed down into the lower
levels, filling the towns as traders and occupying farms in the
open country. Their industrial energy was equalled by their
religious zeal, and by 1650 they had erected no less than eleven
temples—as their places of worship were styled—in places
where they were forbidden even to take up their abode.[1] From
time to time efforts had been made by the Government to put
an end to what it regarded as an insolent defiance of its
authority, but up to 1655 it had in every case recoiled before
the resistance it provoked.

Vaudois settle outside the tolerated limits.

In January 1655, however, the Duchess, egged on by the
fanatics who surrounded her, resolved to enforce the law. In
January the auditor Guastaldo ordered, in the Duke's
name, all families 'of the pretended Reformed religion' to quit Luserna, Lusernetta, San Giovanni,
La Torre, Bibiana, Fenile, Campiglione, Bricherasio, and San
Secondo, within three days, under pain of death and the loss
of their property if they remained outside the tolerated limits,
unless within three days they declared their resolution to become Catholics or to sell their property to Catholics.[2] It was
hardly to be expected that such an order would meet with
prompt obedience. The Vaudois settled in the
places named were for the most part not new-comers.
Their families, their trade, and their possessions
bound them to the soil, and they took the reasonable
course of memorialising the Government, in the hope of obtaining such a permission to remain as had from time to time been
granted them before. There was the more ground for complaint as the upper valleys, to which they were relegated, were
not only covered with snow at the time, but had been impover-

1655. Jan. 13/23. Guastaldo's order.

The Vaudois outside the limits petition for leave to remain.

1 *Muston*, 280.
2 Guastaldo's Order, Jan. 15/24, 1655, *Morland*, 303.

ished by the action of the Government in quartering on the inhabitants a large number of French troops on their passage to or from the war which was at that time raging in North Italy. Their petitions, however, were waived aside, on the plea that their representatives were not empowered to tender a complete submission—the meaning of these words being, as they imagined, that they were expected to assent to the complete suppression of the liberty of their religion, even within the limits of the Edict of 1561.[1]

The Duchess was resolved to enforce obedience, and on April 6 the Marquis of Pianezza was despatched from Turin

April ₆/₁₆. Pianezza leaves Turin. with a small force, which it would be easy for him to convert into a large one by the accession of troops already quartered in the neighbouring valleys. On

April ₇/₁₇. He attacks La Torre, the following day he found most of the villages in the plain deserted, and only late in the evening, as he approached La Torre, did he become aware that it was held by a considerable party of Vaudois. Sending forward a messenger to demand quarters for his men, he was answered that, in obedience to the late edict, those now in the place had removed their domiciles to the upper part of the valley, and that as they no longer possessed houses in La Torre they were unable to give quarters to his soldiers. Dissatisfied with so halting an explanation, Pianezza pushed on to the attack. The Vaudois within were desperate men, whose livelihood was at stake as well as their religion. Throwing up barricades, they defended

April ₈/₁₈. and takes it. themselves to the uttermost, and it was only in the early morning that, finding their position turned, they

---

[1] Much has been said about the murder of the parish priest of Fenile. *Claretta* (i. 94) throws the blame on Leger, the minister who took the foremost part amongst the Vaudois. Leger, on the other hand, throws it, not very probably, on a Catholic official, *Morland*, 310. The priest had made enemies by insisting on the duty of evacuating Fenile, and in the excited state of feeling which existed these persons are likely to have been at the bottom of the murder. The evidence as it stands hardly permits of a strong opinion on the subject. The important thing is that the Duchess, as will be seen, did not rest her case on the murder.

cut their way through their assailants and took refuge in the surrounding hills.[1]

The affair of La Torre necessarily made a different impression on the two parties concerned.   To the Vaudois the attempt

Different views of the affair.

April $\frac{8}{18}$.
Pianezza attacks the fugitives.

to force soldiers on their villages was but the commencement of systematic persecution.   To the authorities at Turin the resistance to the troops was an act of avowed rebellion.   Pianezza and his men held themselves at liberty to follow up their victory by an attack on the fugitives who had taken refuge amongst the hills.   Whomsoever they lighted on they killed, setting fire to the houses and cottages.[2]   For the next two days the advantage was not on the side of the assailants.   Occupying well-chosen positions, with numbers increased from the neighbouring valley,

April $\frac{11}{21}$.
A negotiation.

the peasants repulsed all attacks till, on the 11th, the Piedmontese general invited to a conference the men whose defences he was unable to storm, and required

---

[1] The story as given above is taken from *Muston* (303–310), who is here much fuller than *Claretta*.   His narrative, he tells us, is founded on that of a Piedmontese officer preserved in the archives of Turin.   He gives the number of the defendants as three or four hundred.   Morland tells us that Pianezza 'fell into the Burgh of La Torre, where they met with not so much as one soul of the Protestants, save only a little company of eight or ten persons, who, not at all thinking that the enemy was there, were seeking up and down for something to satisfy their hunger ; but so soon as ever they approached the convent they were immediately descried by the monks and the troopers, who had been there concealed several days before for that very purpose, who, to show the kindness they had for them, saluted them with a great volley of shot, whereby they slew upon the place one Giovanni Combe of Villaro, and hurt Pietro Rostain of La Torre ; thereupon the rest, who saw themselves thus encompassed on every side, immediately fled for their lives.'   Those who place implicit confidence on Morland—or rather in Leger, who supplied the materials for his book—should examine carefully this extraordinary misstatement.   No doubt reports of the wildest description were flying about, many of which he swallowed without discrimination.

[2] " Andarono scarmucciando per quelle montagnuole rentrezzando gli eretici, ammazzando molti ed abruciando qui sue case o cassine che possono prendere." *Muston*, ii. 312, note 1, quoting the Piedmontese officer.

them to receive garrisons into their respective villages. Lulling them to sleep by his apparent friendliness, he held back from suggesting to them any terms likely to be accepted, in the hope that their rejection of his demand for unqualified submission would enable him to make an example of them without com-

April 12/22.
The massacre.

punction.[1] He had his wish. On the 12th he pushed his troops up the valleys of Pellice and Angrogna. The peasants, taken unawares, were speedily over-powered. Then began a massacre, accompanied with such deeds of cruelty as befitted a rude and exasperated soldiery in whose ranks released criminals were to be found. In many cases, it is true, prisoners were taken and children were saved and sent to Piedmont, that they might there be educated in Catholic families.

It is indeed also possible that some of the tales spread abroad of hideous and unmentionable tortures were unfounded or exaggerated.[2] Yet, after all is said, the account of an eye-

---

[1] Muston says that the Vaudois agreed to the occupation of their villages, and that they were thereby tricked into letting him pass. Claretta thinks the Vaudois were in fault for refusing complete obedience. It is better to suspend judgment till the documents in the Turin archives are published. In the meanwhile, it may be remarked that an extract from a letter of April 12/22 from Pianezza to the Duchess, printed by *Claretta* (i. 99), tells against the view that Pianezza was straightforward in the matter. He distinctly says that he did not wish to propose to the Vaudois the terms of their submission 'dubitando se le proponeva cose mediocri che l'accettassero essi ed io mi legassi le mani, sicche non potessi poi tirar le cose a quell' alto segno del servizio di S.A.R. che io pretendevo, ed io per contro le scoprivo cosi sulla fine tutto il rigore non venisse a mettergli in total disperazione avante il tempo.' He says he had sent them back with orders to bring a better answer next morning, but when they came they only expressed in general terms their readiness to submit.

[2] Dr. Melia, in *The Origin, Persecutions, and Doctrines of the Waldenses*, 73–83, publishes a number of depositions taken in 1673–74, in which many of the most horrible cases which Morland derived from Leger are denied, and persons said by the same author to have been killed in 1655 are alleged to have died before that date, or to have been subsequently alive. The time in which the depositions were taken was too late for extreme accuracy, and though many of the witnesses were Vaudois,

witness, Captain du Petit Bourg, a Huguenot officer, who threw
up his commission in a French regiment rather than
take a part in such villainy, goes far enough to
justify the resentment of the Protestant populations
of Europe. Petit Bourg had been authorised by Servien to offer
his mediation between Pianezza and the Vaudois. Though his
intervention was refused, he remained with the army, and subsequently gave an account of its proceedings. "I was witness," he wrote, " to many great violences and extreme cruelties
exercised by the Piedmontese outlaws and soldiers on persons
of all sorts and conditions, and of both sexes. I saw them
massacred, dismembered, hanged, burnt and violated, with
many frightful conflagrations.[1] . . . It is certain that, without
any distinction of those who made resistance from those who
made none, they were used with every sort of inhumanity, their
houses burnt, their goods plundered, and when prisoners were
brought before the Marquis of Pianezza, he gave, in my sight,
order to kill them all, because his Highness wished to have
none of the religion in his dominions. And as for what he
protests . . . that there was no damage done to any except
during the fight, and that not the least outrage was committed
upon any persons unfit to bear arms, I do assert and will

Petit Bourg's account.

they may have spoken under pressure. Still, I think that the exception
to Morland's account is in the main justified. A letter from the Vaudois
written on April $\frac{17}{27}$ speaks of the soldiers as having ' cruelly tormented no
less than 150 women and children, and afterwards chopped off the heads
of some and dashed the brains of others against the rocks.' Of prisoners
who refused to go to mass, they ' hanged some, and nailed the feet of
others to trees, with their heads hanging towards the ground.' This is
bad enough, and possibly some abatement must be made on the score of
the excitement in the midst of which the writers were living ; but at least
there is no specific mention here of the worst of the unmentionable horrors
detailed by Morland. It does not of course follow that some of them did
not occur.

[1] ' Plusieurs effroyables incendies.' This probably means that houses
were burnt. Morland translates ' with many horrid confusions.' According to the *Relation véritable de Piedmont*, many persons were burnt with
the houses. The worst horrors in Morland's list are to be found in this
book, published at Villafranca in 1655.

maintain that it is not so, as, having seen with my eyes several
men killed in cold blood, as also women, aged persons and
young children miserably slain." [1]   The inclemency of the
weather came to the aid of the persecutors.   A heavy fall of
snow blocked the passes, and many of the fugitives were
either swept away by avalanches or perished of cold and
hunger.

According to an official calculation made about three weeks
after the massacre, out of 884 persons in the two communes of
An official   Villar and Bobbio alone, there were 55 refugees in
calculation.   France or in the mountains, whilst 75 were prisoners
or scattered in Piedmont.   Of the remaining 759, 36 had
perished in an avalanche, 274 had been killed, whilst no less
than 449 had renounced their religion and professed themselves
to have adopted the faith of their persecutors.   The number of
this last class is the surest measure of the terror that had fallen
on the valleys. [2]

Such was the news, exaggerated, it may be, like that of the
Irish massacre in 1641, which reached the Protector towards
May 24.   the middle of May.   On the 25th he despatched
The   Samuel Morland, who had been attached to White-
Protector
writes to   locke in his Swedish embassy, as the bearer of a
European   letter composed by Milton, in the hope of rousing
Powers.   the Duke of Savoy to a sense of his iniquity.   It was supported
by another written on the same day to the King of France,
diplomatically assuring him that it was scarcely credible that
any of his troops had taken part in the massacre, and asking
him to use his influence with the Duke to obtain what reparation was still possible.   In another letter he reminded Mazarin
of his own tolerant practice, and hinted that the all but successful close of the negotiation in England was an argument
for yielding to his wishes in this matter.   To Protestant rulers
Oliver wrote in another style.   He had long had it on his mind
to gather round him a league in defence of the Protestant
interest, and he now urged the Kings of Sweden and Denmark,

[1] Petit Bourg's Declaration, Nov. 27, 1655, *Morland*, 333.
[2] *Muston*, ii. 306, note 1.

the States General, and the Prince of Transylvania, to join him in obtaining redress for so unparalleled a wrong.[1]

In the letters to France and Piedmont not the shadow of a threat was to be found. The Protector's earnestness in the

May 16.
The nego-
tiation with
Bordeaux. matter was clearly, though delicately, shown in his negotiation with Bordeaux. On the 16th the English commissioners were allowed to exhibit every sign of eagerness to complete the treaty. On the

May 24.
Nothing to
be signed
till an
answer is
received
from France. 24th, however, Thurloe informed the ambassador that the Protector would sign nothing till an answer had been received to the missive which he was about to despatch.[2] That nothing on his part might be left undone, Oliver on the day on which his letters

May 25.
A collection
ordered, were sent off issued a Declaration appointing June 14 as a day of humiliation, and inviting English Protestants, as being under safe protection, to contribute out of their means to the help of the miserable survivors of the

June 1.
and a
house-to-
house
visitation. massacre.[3] On second thoughts it appeared better to reinforce this appeal by a house-to-house visitation by the minister and churchwardens of each

July 12.
A fresh
proclama-
tion. parish. Six weeks later, when it was found that many parishes had contributed nothing, a proclamation called on these laggards to fulfil their duty, and enjoined upon those parishes in which a collection had been made to send in the proceeds without delay.[4] The Protector's own name headed the list of subscribers with a magnificent donation of 2,000*l*., and in the end the collection amounted to

Large sums
collected. 38,232*l*. The amount was so large that, after meeting all the necessities of the case, no less than

---

[1] Milton's *Prose Works*, ed. Symmons, vi. 25–28 ; Hamilton, *Original Papers Illustrative of the Life . . . of John Milton*, p. 2 ; *Masson*, v. 184–190.

[2] Bordeaux to Mazarin, $\frac{\text{May 24}}{\text{June 3}}$, Bordeaux to Brienne, $\frac{\text{May 24}}{\text{June 3}}$, *French Transcripts, R.O.*

[3] Declaration, May 25, *S. P. Dom.* xcvii. 82.

[4] Instructions by the Protector, June 1, *S. P. Dom.* xcviii. 4; Proclamation, July 12, Council Order Book, *Interr.* I, 76a, p. 75.

17,872*l.* remained in the hands of the treasurers, who, with the assistance of an influential committee, had been appointed to guard the fund. This sum was put out at interest, the dividends being destined to provide pensions for sufferers and to meet any fresh needs that might arise. So long as the Protectorate lasted this source of revenue continued intact.[1]

In the meanwhile the Protector's diplomatic intervention had not been without result. Morland, the bearer of the letters, reached the French Court at La Fère on June 1. On the next day Louis's answer was placed in his hands. In it the French King gave assurances that his troops had been employed without his knowledge, adding that he had already signified his dissatisfaction with the use to which they had been put, and had given orders that such of the fugitives as had taken refuge in French territory should be kindly treated. He would continue to entreat the Duke to re-establish the unfortunate sufferers within the limits assigned them by his predecessors.[2] Two results may be deduced from these phrases. In the first place, France would intercede but would not threaten. Oliver, indeed, had asked for no more than this ; and, in fact, the doctrine that each prince was responsible to no external Power for his treatment of religious questions arising in his own dominions had not only been consecrated by the recent Treaties of Westphalia, but was firmly rooted in the conscience of Europe, being even accepted by Oliver himself, who would not have hesitated to give a sharp answer to

Marginal notes: June 1/11. Morland at the French Court. — June 2/12. The French reply.

---

[1] The original accounts, as well as the minutes of the committee, are in the Record Office. A useful summary of the former is given by Mr. W. A. Shaw in the *Hist. Rev.* (Oct. 1894), ix. 662. This may be compared with an abstract given in *Morland*, 586. On July 9, 1659, Parliament misappropriated some of the capital, but this was after the fall of Richard Cromwell.

[2] " Je continuerai mes instances envers ce prince pour leur soulagement et pour qu'il consente qu'ils puissent rétablir leurs demeures aux lieux de ses états esquels il leur avait été concédé par les ducs de Savoie ses prédécesseurs." Louis XIV. to the Protector, June 2/12, *Guizot,* ii. 522.

any foreign ambassador who ventured to question his right to deal at his own pleasure with the Irish Catholics. In the second place, Louis did not propose even to ask the Duke of Savoy to repatriate the exiles outside the limits fixed by the edicts of his ancestors. The Protector, who was himself acting much on the same principle when he transplanted Irishmen to Connaught, must be content if the system established in 1561 were reverted to, and all Vaudois refusing conversion to the religion of the State required to fix their domicile within the assigned limits.

The French Government had already acted in accordance with the spirit of the King's engagement. It is true that in the letters sent to Servien at Turin, before Morland's arrival at

May.
Pressure put by Mazarin on the Duchess.

La Fère, no pretence had been made of showing pity for the sufferers. The ambassador was to found his case on merely political considerations. The Duchess was to be urged to consider that her own States would suffer if the hostility of England and the Protestant cantons of Switzerland were roused against her at a time when all her energies should have been devoted to the war against Spain.[1] From this argument Mazarin never varied. On the other hand, the Duchess defended the rectitude of her conduct, and at first declined to concede anything. Her position was simply that the Vaudois, by refusing to obey legal orders to depart from the places in which the edicts had forbidden them to settle, had committed an act of rebellion, which had been legitimately punished.[2] The Duchess held out for some

---

[1] Le Tellier to Servien, $\frac{\text{May } 23}{\text{June } 2}$, Brienne to Servien, $\frac{\text{May } 25}{\text{June } 4}$, *Arch. des Aff. Étrangères, Savoie*, xlix. foll. 299, 301.

[2] " S. A. R. Monsieur mon filz ayant essayé inutilement par la voye de la douceur et de la négotiation de ramener à leur devoir les hérétiques des vallées de Luzern, ses sujets, qui en estoient écartez par la désobéissance à ses ordres, et par le mespris de son auctorité, accompagné d'une manifeste rebellion ; elle a esté contrainte d'y employer la force de ses armes, qui ont eu par tout l'heureux succez." The Duchess of Savoy to Mazarin, $\frac{\text{April } 27}{\text{May } 7}$, *Arch. des Aff. Étrangères, Savoie*, xlix. fol. 234. There is not a word here of any special misbehaviour of the Vaudois. Everything is charged to their disobedience.

time, and, when Morland appeared and remonstrated in strong
language, she contented herself with expressing her
regret that the Protector had been deceived by false
reports of what was in reality a fatherlike and tender
chastisement.[1] To Servien she confided her opinion
that the English Government might have been less
trenchant in their criticism, considering the measure they
were dealing out to their own Catholics. Her real feelings
were further exhibited in the assertions of her representatives
that there was no evidence that the Edict of 1561 had been
actually signed by the Duke of that day ; and that, even if his
signature could be proved, he had no power to bind his suc-
cessors. It was precisely the suspicion that such arguments as
these would be broached, and that their religious existence was
at stake, even within the limits assigned to them, that had
roused the Vaudois to the resistance now qualified as rebellion.[2]

On July 19 Morland left Turin, after receiving a formal
memorandum in which, after the case for the Piedmontese
Government had been duly set forth, the Duke
ended by expressing his intention to pardon his
rebellious subjects at the intercession of His Highness.[3] As a matter of fact, it was not to His
Highness that the Court of Turin made this concession. Mazarin had been doing his utmost to
trample out a fire so dangerous to his own schemes.
Having rejected a proposal, made through Pianezza,
that the King of France should take over the heretic
valleys in exchange for some other territory, he urged the
Duke and Duchess to give way with a good grace. There was
the more reason for him to require haste as voices had already
been raised in Paris to object to the way in which he was
employing his influence, on the ground that England, however
powerful, could not send an army or a fleet into a Piedmontese

Side notes:
June ¾¼. Morland's remonstrance.

Explana-tions of the Duchess.

July 1⁹/₉. Morland leaves Turin.

July 1⁹/₉. Pardon offered by the Duke.

Pressure put on him by Mazarin.

---

[1] *Morland*, 568, 575.
[2] Servien to Brienne, June 30/July 10, *Arch. des Aff. Étrangères, Savoie*, xlix. fol. 392 ; *Morland*, 579.
[3] *Morland*, 580.

valley. It was quite true, wrote Brienne to Servien ; but it was also true that English money could raise troops in Switzerland, and that English influence might stir up the French Huguenots to give assistance to their brethren on the other side of the Alps.[1]

Mazarin's intervention had the greater weight as there were signs that Oliver had part, at least, of the Protestant world Interven-   behind him. The Swiss Protestant cantons and tion of the   the United Provinces were sending envoys ; whilst Swiss and the Dutch.   before the end of July he not only directed Pell, his agent in Switzerland, to support Morland, who was by that time at Geneva, but despatched a third agent—George Downing[2]—to encourage them both. In order to give an air of spontaneity to the concessions he was compelled to make the Aug. ⁸⁄₁₈   Duke summoned representatives of the Vaudois to The Duke   Pinerolo, where on August 8 he issued a pardon to issues a   all concerned in the rebellion, even enlarging the pardon.   limits of toleration so as to include La Torre and part of the commune of San Giovanni ; whilst he prolonged to November 1 the time within which those whose property lay outside the new limits were required to dispose of it.[3] It had originally been intended that the French and Swiss ambassadors should sign the Duke's pardon in the character of mediators. Servien, however, purposely absented himself, with the intention of making it impossible for the Swiss to append their signatures, hoping by this means to strengthen the presumption that the pardon was a free act of grace on the part of the Duke.[4]

[1] Brienne to Servien, July ⁸⁄₁₈ ; Servien to Brienne, July ¹⁴⁄₂₄ ; Brienne to Chauvelin, $\frac{\text{July 23}}{\text{Aug. 2}}$; Brienne to Servien, $\frac{\text{July 24}}{\text{Aug. 5}}$, Arch. des Aff. Étrangères, Savoie, xlix. foll. 410, 446, 471, 479.

[2] Morland, 601–612.   [3] Ib. 652.

[4] Servien to Brienne, Aug. ¹¹⁄₂₁, Arch. des Aff. Étrangères, xlix. fol. 531. It has been often said that the Protector intended Blake to attack Nice and Villafranca, and it is indeed probable that Oliver had the design of seizing the two ports—not, indeed, for the purpose of sending an army across the mountains to Turin, but as a blow to the Duke. On Aug. ¹⁶⁄₂₆ Bordeaux wrote that the Protector had mentioned to him these two places as suitable for the landing of troops ; and in a brief narrative, written

Though Oliver had to some extent got his way, he was far from satisfied either with the extent of the concessions or with the way in which they had been made. On September 10 he ordered Downing to return home to give an account of the situation, resolving at the same time to hold back from the negotiation with Bordeaux till this matter had been cleared up.[1] A little further consideration, however, convinced him that it was useless to protest further against a settlement which had been accepted by the Vaudois themselves, and to which the Protestant Swiss had raised no objection.[2] His abandonment of any intention to make further demands upon the Duke led to the resumption of the negotiation with Bordeaux. Already on July 12 the Protector had signified his acceptance of the French offer of mediation by recalling all letters of marque issued against French subjects.[3] On September 19, three days after the resolution to drop the question of the Vaudois had been taken, Bordeaux was informed that though the Council disliked the idea of requesting him to resume the discussion of the treaty so soon after their disaster in the Indies, they would not object to take it up if he asked them so to do. On this hint Bordeaux made the required demand, and the negotiation entrusted to him was once more in full swing.[4]

Difficulties removed.

A treaty drawn up.

Under these circumstances difficulties which some months before had hampered the negotiation were speedily dispelled. There was, of course, no mention in the treaty now drawn up of any active co-operation

shortly after the time of these events, Morland speaks of the Protector's intention of sending ships for this purpose, *Clarendon MSS*. liii. fol. 132. I fancy that, if it had been necessary, ships would have been sent, but not under Blake, who was at that time employed in looking out for the Plate Fleet, an occupation from which the Protector was hardly likely to recall him.

[1] Thurloe to Pell, Sept. 10; Thurloe to Morland, Sept. 10, Vaughan's *Protectorate*, i. 259–65.

[2] Thurloe to Downing, Pell, and Morland, *ib*. i. 268.

[3] Proclamation, July 12, Council Order Book, *Interr*. I, 76a, p. 76.

[4] Bordeaux to Brienne, Sept. $\frac{20}{30}$, *French Transcripts, R.O.*

against Spain, as England was still formally at peace with that Power. All that was now aimed at was the restoration of friendly relations with France. The disputed clause about the renunciation by each Power of any claim to protect the rebels of the other [1] was modified into a perfectly harmless phrase forbidding assistance to be given to rebels ' now declared,' thus leaving the possibility that Oliver might wish to assist some future rising of the Huguenots entirely unnoticed. After a succession of articles tending to facilitate commercial intercourse, the question of recouping the merchants and shipowners on either side for their losses was met by an engagement to appoint arbitrators to assess the damages—an engagement which was never carried out, because the French Government preferred in the end to leave the profits on both sides in the hands of those who had already secured them. Equally ineffectual was an article referring the question of the restoration of the Acadian forts to the same arbitrators. As no such arbitrators were appointed, these forts remained in English hands as long as the Protectorate lasted. [2]

A secret article gave satisfaction to the Protector on a point of no little importance. A list of persons no longer to be

Banishment of the Stuarts and their adherents from France. harboured in France included Charles, eldest son of the late king, James, Duke of York, and seventeen of the principal adherents of the Stuart cause, many of whom, however, were no longer residing in Louis's dominions. Henrietta Maria, as the daughter, sister, and aunt of three kings of France, was permitted to remain in the refuge she had chosen. In return Oliver willingly consented to send away Barrière and nine other persons who were or had been agents, either of Condé or of the rebellious community of

Oct. 24.
Nov. 3.
Signature of the treaty. Bordeaux. The treaty was at last signed on October 24, three days before Cardenas left London. [3] Though it did no more than remove the obstacles

[1] See *supra*, p. 160.

[2] Acadia was not restored to France till 1667. Lucas, *Colonial Geography*: *Canada*, i. 180.

[3] Treaty, $\frac{\text{Oct. 24}}{\text{Nov. 3}}$, *Dumont*, VI., ii. 121.

standing in the way of a good understanding between the
nations, it could hardly fail to pave the way for a closer alliance
between Governments now threatened by a common enemy.
No doubt the victory for humanity which Oliver had achieved
with the help of France was but a halting victory. For the
victims who had been slain or tortured by the brutal soldiery
of the Duke of Savoy no vengeance had been taken and no

Milton's
sonnet. justice had been exacted, and Milton's appeal to
Heaven was in itself a confession of earthly failure :—

> Avenge, O Lord, thy slaughter'd saints, whose bones
>   Lie scatter'd on the Alpine mountains cold ;
>   Ev'n them who kept Thy truth so pure of old,
> When all our fathers worshipp'd stocks and stones,
> Forget not ; in Thy Book record their groans
>   Who were Thy sheep, and in their ancient fold
>   Slain by the bloody Piedmontese, that roll'd
> Mother with infant down the rocks. Their moans
>   The vales redoubled to the hills, and they
> To Heav'n. Their martyr'd blood and ashes sow
>   O'er all th' Italian fields, where still doth sway
> The triple Tyrant ; that from these may grow
>   A hundredfold, who, having learn'd Thy way
> Early may fly the Babylonian woe.

The poet's prayer was but a pious aspiration. In Oliver's
mind it was the leading thought, which gave energy to a foreign
Waller's
panegyric. policy nobly conceived, but too complex to be carried
out in successful action. Waller, writing about the
time when Milton's sonnet was penned, and certainly before
the bad news from Hispaniola had reached England, had
celebrated in his facile verse, not the spiritual hopes and fears,
but the earthly glory of the Protector :—

> The sea's our own, and now all nations greet
> With bending sails each vessel of our fleet ;
> Your power extends as far as winds can blow,
> Or swelling sails upon the globe may go.

> Heaven, that hath placed this island to give law,
> To balance Europe, and her States to awe—

In this conjunction doth on Britain smile,
The greatest leader, and the greatest isle !

.   .   .   .   .

Hither the oppressed shall henceforth resort,
Justice to crave and succour at your Court ;
And then His Highness, not for ours alone,
But for the world's Protector, shall be known.

This thought of being the world's protector lay at the bottom of Oliver's suggested league for the defence of the Protestant interest. As he himself had put it a year earlier, "God had brought them where they were, in order that they might consider the work they had to do in the world as well as at home." [1] It was a noble and inspiriting thought, needing even for its partial realisation not merely a political self-abnegation rarely, if ever, to be found, but also the fullest and most accurate knowledge of the character and aims of the Governments and peoples of other nations, a knowledge never completely attained to by any statesman, and in which Oliver was himself singularly deficient.

Oliver to be the ' world's protector.'

Of all the Continental rulers, none had attracted Oliver's sympathies more strongly than the new King of Sweden, Charles X. ; and when, in the spring of 1655, the nephew and successor of the great Gustavus was threatening an attack on Poland, he was regarded at Whitehall as a champion of Protestant truth against a Popish nation. In reality Charles was incited to war by very different motives. " Other nations," a Swedish diplomatist had confessed, " make war because they are rich ; Sweden because she is poor." [2]

Charles X. of Sweden.

When Christina abdicated in 1654, she had left the Swedish Crown even more impoverished than when that remark was made. Between her own lavish expenditure and the encroachments of the nobility it was hard for her successor to provide for the bare necessities of govern-

His position at his accession.

[1] *Clarke Papers*, iii. 207.

[2] Erdmannsdörffer, *Deutsche Geschichte vom westphälischen Frieden*, i. 212.

ment. Yet he found himself at the head of a well-disciplined army out of proportion to the number of his subjects, of whom there were little more than a million in Sweden itself, and perhaps a somewhat larger number in the subject lands.[1] Like Oliver himself when he planned the war with Spain, and like Frederick the Great when he planned the invasion of Silesia, he was carried away by the temptation to seek for war. The temptation was the stronger as Charles was what Frederick was not at the time of his accession, a tried warrior, who had already commanded armies in the field.

If war there was to be, there was much to determine the King to fix on Poland as the chosen enemy. Poland was weak Charles X. through the insubordination of her nobles, and was and Poland. at this time, much to her disadvantage, at war with the Cossack outlaws within her own borders and their Russian allies, the troops of the Tsar Alexis. There was, moreover, a hereditary dispute between Charles and John Casimir, the Polish king, relating to the succession to the crown of Sweden, which made it easy to pick a quarrel.

The real cause of war must, however, be sought elsewhere. When Charles X. mounted the throne, Sweden held, beyond Swedish the Gulf of Bothnia and the Baltic, lands which gave possessions her almost every point of vantage on the further beyond the Baltic. shore of the sea. Hers were — before Gustavus Adolphus landed in Germany — Finland, Esthonia, Ingria, Livonia. To these she had added at the Peace of Westphalia Western Pomerania, Wismar and the Duchies—formerly the bishoprics—of Bremen and Verden, and had established a garrison at Warnemünde, which commanded the port of Rostock. Though her occupation of the coast to the west of the Courland frontier was not continuous, she at least held positions of the greatest importance from a commercial point of view, planting herself on the mouths of the Weser, the Elbe, and the Oder. It was but natural that a King of Sweden should desire

---

[1] Carlson, *Carl X. Gustaf*, 14, says the population of Sweden proper was about 1,000,000. Philippson, *Der grosse Kurfürst*, i. 176, puts it at 1,200,000.

to lay his hands on the Vistula as well—the great river which, flowing through Polish territory from its source to its mouth, brought down the wood, the hemp, and the pitch which were the chief of Poland's products. Such an acquisition would be of exceeding value to Charles in the exhausted state of the finances of Sweden, now that the Crown had been robbed of the greater part of its revenue. His eye was set, not so much on territorial acquisition as upon the tolls which would arise from the possession of the ports beyond the sea. War must be waged, not for the legitimate interests of Sweden, but to replenish the empty exchequer of the nation.

Sooner or later the attempt of any State to hold strips of land beyond the sea for the sake of revenue alone is doomed to failure. It rouses too many interests in opposition amongst the inland inhabitants, whose way to the sea is blocked and whose material interests are detrimentally affected. The position inherited by Charles, and still more the position he coveted, could only be held by the strong hand. Some day another Swedish king would be compelled to defend against a Tsar the lands by which Russia was cut off from an approach to the Baltic. The future enmity of Brandenburg was no less assured. The Elector's territories stretched from west to east — intermittingly, like the Swedish possessions on the coast—in a line from beyond the Rhine to the further limits of East Prussia, for the most part to the landward of the Swedish possessions. A glance at the map is sufficient to show that the Elector was urged by the geographical position of his States to drive the Swedes into the sea ; to say nothing of the fact that, but for the weight which the Swedish sword had thrown into the balance when the treaties of Westphalia were under discussion, he would have put forward an unanswerable claim to the possession of Western Pomerania, which had been appropriated by the Swedes.

It is true that the want of geographical coherence in these territories was an element of weakness ; but it was an element which might be turned into strength by a great ruler mingling

vigour with caution, and ready to seize opportunities as they
rose, whilst turning away from impossible ideals.

Frederick William and his States.

Such a ruler was Frederick William, who was one
day to gain the title of the Great Elector. Geography,
indeed, forbade him to be the author of a persistent policy
carried out to the end in spite of obstacles. His aims were as
many as the fragments of his territory, and it was incumbent
on him to change them from time to time as circumstances
allowed. Yet, shifty as his policy necessarily was, he was in
no sense a trickster or a flatterer. As an ally he could
thoroughly be depended on for to-day, though it would be
folly to depend on him for to-morrow. His chief merit is to
have thoroughly grasped, in the first place, the fact that the
Empire was virtually dissolved, and that his duty to his own
territorially complex State must take precedence of all personal
interests of his own ; and, in the second place, that, considering
that men and not frontiers constitute the State, it was his duty
to keep on foot, in lands guarded by no deep rivers or lofty
mountains, as well-disciplined and well-equipped an army as
possible, and thereby to establish his own absolute power at
the expense of the local oligarchies, which represented the
special interests of certain classes in the several fragments of
his dominions.

So far as the impending war was concerned the Elector's
interests drew him in two directions. What principally concerned him was to take care that the Swedes, by

The Elector's course uncertain.

seizing West Prussia from the Poles, did not cut him
off from his own outlying duchy of East Prussia. If,
however, it proved too dangerous to oppose the King of Sweden,
there was always a chance of gaining with his help the conversion into absolute sovereignty of the feudal tenure by which he
held East Prussia from the Crown of Poland. It was therefore
impossible to foretell what the Elector's course would be—at
least in the immediate present.

From other quarters hostility to the Swedish plans was
more surely to be counted on. Denmark, indeed,

Position of Denmark,

established as she was on both shores of the Sound,

was an ancient enemy, only waiting for an opportunity to recover the losses she had suffered at the Peace of Bromsebro in 1645. The ill-will of the United Provinces was just as certain. Swedish acquisition of seaports to the south of the Baltic would be injurious to the trade of other nations, and no nation had so firm a hold upon the commerce of the Baltic as the Dutch. In 1634 they employed 6,000 ships in the Baltic trade, and only 1,500 in that of the rest of the world.[1] A state so circumstanced, to which commerce was as its life-blood, could not submit to the seizure by Sweden of the mouths of such a river as the Vistula.

and of the United Provinces.

With this calamity in prospect it was natural that the States General and the Elector of Brandenburg should draw closer together. On July 17 a defensive alliance was signed between them, directed against any attempt of Sweden to increase the existing tolls.[2]

July $\frac{1}{27}$. Alliance between Brandenburg and the United Provinces.

For some time before the signature of this treaty the States General and the King of Sweden had been bidding against one another for the alliance of the Protector. On March 17 Coyet had landed in England, charged by Charles X. with the duty of announcing the speedy arrival of an ambassador whose work it would be to lay the foundations of an alliance between the two States. His own business was to exchange the ratifications of the Treaty of 1654,[3] to obtain an agreement settling in detail the points relating to commerce which that treaty had laid down in general terms, and to procure leave for the levy of six or eight thousand Highlanders for the Swedish service. Coyet was received with the utmost friendliness by Oliver himself, and he was able to report that the popular feeling ran strongly against Poland. Yet, for some reason or other, his negotiation dragged. Leven, who was now in London, had sufficiently remembered his ancient ties to

March 17. Arrival of Coyet in England.

April 11. His reception.

---

[1] Vreede, *Inleiding tot eene Geschiedenis der Nederlandsche Diplomatie*, Gedeelte ii., Stuk 2, Bylage xxviii.

[2] *Erdmannsdörffer*, i. 227.   [3] Vol. iii. 76.

Sweden to promise to raise 2,000 men in Scotland, who were
Question of
allowing
Sweden to
levy High-
landers,
to be commanded by his son-in-law, Lord Cranston,
one of the prisoners taken at Worcester, and still in
custody.   Month after month, however, rolled away,
and the required permission was still held back,
possibly because the English Government remembered too
well how Leven had himself invaded England in command of
Scottish soldiers, many of whom had been trained in the service
of Gustavus Adolphus, an example which might be repeated
by the Highlanders who had lately been in arms under Glencairn if they were sent abroad under the command of a Royalist
and of a
commercial
treaty.
colonel.[1]   The progress of the commercial negotiations was quite as slow.   The commissioners had
always excuses to make for being unable to meet.
The Council was, as they truly said, overwhelmed with business,
or some of their most important members were in ill-health.
In any case, the month of July was at an end before a single
forward step had been taken.

The truth was that such questions as these were subordinate to the greater question whether England and Sweden
Oliver's
ideal view
of the
situation.
should enter into a fighting alliance.   It is beyond
doubt that Oliver yearned for such an outcome of
Coyet's mission.   On June 15, after assuring Coyet
that the permission to levy men in Scotland was only delayed
till the fleet in the West Indies returned with the good tidings
which he then expected in two or three weeks, he burst forth
into a eulogy of the great Gustavus Adolphus, relating how he
had welcomed the news of his successes with tears of joy in his
eyes, and how he had mourned for his death as if he had been
himself a Swede.   He now hoped that Charles would follow
his example.   He, for his part, was ready to help in the good
work, though he acknowleged that in former days England had
failed to do her duty.[2]

[1] This is suggested by Coyet in his letter of May 18, *Stockholm
Transcripts* ; compare Carlbom, *Sverige och England*, 17.
[2] Coyet to Charles X., June 22 ; compare *Sverige och England*, 25.

So far as can be judged from incidental remarks dropped by Coyet, the greater number of the councillors, with Lawrence,

View taken by the Council.

Fiennes, and Strickland at their head,[1] took a more practical view of the situation. Nieupoort, the

Arguments of Nieupoort.

Dutch ambassador, had left no stone unturned to convince them of the danger which English commerce would run, together with that of his own countrymen, if the mouths of the Vistula were allowed to fall into Swedish hands. Was it really for the interest of England, he asked, that the whole of the Baltic coast should be under one dominion? Nieupoort had reason to believe that this view of the case found acceptance even with the Protector, whose good sense was never entirely at the mercy of senti-

May 9. A conversation with Thurloe.

mental considerations. On May 9 Thurloe assured the Dutch ambassador that he concurred with his views, and told him that they were about to despatch an emissary to the King of Sweden—Rolt, a gentleman of the Protector's bedchamber, who was ostensibly to carry the ratifi-

June. Thurloe's explanations.

cation of the last treaty—to examine the question on the spot.[2] A month later Thurloe explained to Nieupoort that the levy of men had been refused to Coyet merely to please the States General, though it was to the Protector's interest to clear the Highlands of every single Highlander.[3] It is unnecessary to take these diplomatic revelations too literally, but they at least testify to the energy of the struggle between the two ambassadors. About the same time

The dominion of the Baltic.

Coyet, alarmed at the news that the Dutch were about to send armed vessels through the Sound as a convoy to their merchant fleet, took care that Nieupoort should hear of his boast that the dominion of the Baltic rested with his master, and that any men-of-war, save those of Sweden

---

[1] Coyet speaks distinctly of Lawrence's tendencies, and hints as much of Fiennes. Strickland's Dutch propensities are subsequently mentioned by Bonde.

[2] Nieupoort to the States General, May $\frac{10}{20}$, *Add. MSS.* 17,677 LLI., fol. 208.

[3] Nieupoort to De Witt, June $\frac{8}{18}$, De Witt's *Brieven*, iii. 71.

and Denmark, attempting to sail in that sea would meet with forcible resistance. Charles had already supported his minister by ordering him to appeal to the Protector's supposed jealousy of his Dutch neighbours, and to assure him that, if only he would side with the Swedes against them, privileges should be granted to English traders which would place them at a distinct advantage over their rivals.[1]

As an appeal to English commercial interests the proposal was not attractive, as there was no security that, when once the Swedes had made themselves masters of the Baltic ports for the present outside their sphere of domination, they would not take away those privileges which they were ready to grant in a time of conflict. The Dutch policy of hindering any one Power from securing a monopoly in the trade seemed to be the more advantageous for England as well as for the Netherlands. Oliver was thus dragged asunder by conflicting policies. His determination to forward the interests of English trade drew him to the side of the United Provinces ; his ideal hopes of being able to do something for oppressed Protestants drew him to the side of Sweden. He would not have been the man that he was if he had not persisted in attempting to conciliate opposing factors long after it had been possible to do so.

English trade interests on the side of the Dutch.

The difficulty became greater when the promised ambassador—Christer Bonde, one of the most prominent of Charles's Swedish councillors — landed at Gravesend on July 18.[2] In the course of the following month he was received with exuberant delight by Oliver. At one of his audiences the new ambassador, knowing, as he explained to his master, that ' discourses about religion pleased him much,' took care to recall to the mind of the Protector that the Pope had condemned the treaties of Westphalia, and that the Poles, against whom he craved the Protector's help, were a Popish nation. The bait took. Oliver repeated, almost word for word, the language he had

July 18. Bonde's arrival.

Aug. His reception by the Protector.

[1] Instructions to Coyet, May 15, Carlbom, *Sverige och England*, 35.
[2] Bonde to Charles X., July 20, *Stockholm Transcripts*.

used in speaking to Coyet about his veneration for the great
Gustavus and his admiration of his successor. Admitting that
many thought the war with Poland unnecessary, he declared
that he was under no obligation to that State. It was, however,
otherwise with the Dutch, who were of the same religion with
himself, and had borne themselves nobly in throwing off the
yoke of the Papacy. In face of such a complication he must
take some time to consider the proposal of an alliance between
England and Sweden. Then followed an outburst against the
Catholic Powers. The Pope, he said, was eager to make peace
between all Governments of his own religion, and to direct
their energies against the Protestants. It was, therefore, much
to be desired that the design which the Most High God had
only begun to accomplish in Germany through Gustavus of
glorious memory might be completed by the great King Charles.
To such a consummation he would gladly lend a hand.[1]

Oliver's reference to Gustavus Adolphus was a clear indication of his hope that Charles X. would engage in war, not with
Poland alone, but with the Emperor as well, whom he believed
to be threatening the rights of Protestants at the bidding of the
Pope. So far, indeed, as concerned Pope Alexander
VII., who had succeeded Innocent X. in the preceding April, Oliver's fears were undoubtedly well

Policy of
Alexander
VII.

---

[1] [The Protector] "upreppade hwadh fahra som wår Religion hafwer
sigh af the Påweske att wänta, att jag wäll om denne Påwenz protest
hade påmint thet wara een saak utaf öfvermåttan stoor importance, och
kunde han migh thet seya sig wetta therom godh skedh at thenne Påwen
medh all macht arbetar uppå att göra fredh emellan the Catholiske Konun-
gar, och sedhan wända all theraz macht emoot oss. Hanzock the Catho-
liskez actioner emoot the fattige reformerade i Savoyen som öfwer 100 åhr
ther sin Religion oturberade exercerat hafwe, så wäll som i Tyskland,
uthyder nogsambt theraz intention. Han . . . sadhe sigh wisserligen
troo att K¹ M⁴ widh thenne närwarende intention icke skall stadna utan
hoppaz att then nyttige dessein som den högste Gudh syntez igenom
K. Gustaf höglofligst i aminnelse i Tyskland ärna att uthrätta, och likwäll
af honom ey annat än begynt bleef, skall af thenne stoore K. Carl blifwa
fulbordat, och sin önskelige effect till Gudz ähraz högste befordran, nå
och erhålla, hwartill han hwadh han kunde contribuera wille." Bonde to
Charles X., Aug. 23, *Stockholm Transcripts.*

founded. From the beginning of his reign he had set his
heart on concluding a peace between France and Spain, and,
whatever his precise designs may have been, he may safely be
credited with a desire to induce these two Powers, as well as
the German branch of the House of Austria, to co-operate for
unacceptable to the Catholic Powers. the weakening of Protestantism. What Oliver did
not understand was that the material interests which
divided France and Spain would never allow them to
work together for a common object, and that the Emperor
Ferdinand III. was in reality the most peace-loving sovereign
in Europe. Prematurely aged, and saddened by the death of
his eldest son, whose election as King of the Romans he had
with some difficulty secured, he was too conscious of the
hideous sufferings inflicted on his subjects in the course of the
late war to be desirous to embark on another in the guise of an
anti-Protestant crusade.[1]

Oliver's mistake in believing that a general attack on
Protestants was imminent was closely connected with his mis-
Cujus regio, ejus religio. apprehension of German feeling on the relations
between rulers and subjects in matters of religion.
As every German knew, an attempt to interfere with
the internal government of any single State would bring back
the horrors of the Thirty Years' War, and such a recurrence of
evil was the one thing which every German, from prince to
peasant, was determined to avoid. Though it was perfectly
true that Ferdinand was persecuting his own Protestant subjects in Bohemia and Silesia, it did not follow either that he
was dreaming of suppressing Protestantism in Brandenburg or
Saxony, or that the Electors of Brandenburg and Saxony were
dreaming of intervening to stop his cruelties in his own
dominions. As often happens, an opinion based on political
convenience took shape in men's minds as a conviction of

---

[1] For Mazarin's treatment of the Pope's scheme see Valfrey, *H. de
Lionne, ses ambassades en Italie*, pp. 347–51. Pribram's *Freiherr von
Lisola*, and Carlbom's *Sveriges Förhallande till Österrike*, give full proof
of the constancy with which Ferdinand III. attached himself to the
maintenance of peace.

absolute justice, and neither the Emperor nor any other
German prince being prepared to interfere in matters of
religion outside their own territories, they held that such an
action would be not merely replete with danger, but also positively unjust.

Neither Bonde nor Charles was therefore likely to be hood-
winked by so preposterous a policy as that which dazzled the
eyes of Oliver. In replying to the Protector the
ambassador had some difficulty in using expressions
warm enough to conceal his real feelings. In conferring subsequently with the commissioners appointed to negotiate with him he let slip a few words which
should have convinced them how little he realised the phantom
of a religious war. Although, he said, the general Protestant
interest appeared to be in some danger, yet peace still prevailed, and up to the present time the Catholics had attempted
little except in the case of the Savoyard Protestants.[1] What
Bonde sought was, not an alliance against the Catholic Powers
in general, but twenty English ships in the Baltic to assist in
keeping off the Dutch ; in return for which aid the King of
Sweden would assist the Protector with the like number of
ships in the North Sea whenever he needed them. Virtually
the request was one for an alliance against the United
Provinces.[2] At the same time Nieupoort was urging
Oliver to enter into an alliance with the States
General, Brandenburg and Denmark against the
Swedish attempt to monopolise the Baltic trade.[3]

Bonde's feelings about a Protestant crusade.

Nieupoort's diplomacy.

[1] Mr. Guernsey Jones (*Cromwell and Charles Gustavus*, 35, note 2)
follows an exaggerated rendering of this passage by Kalling (*Chr.
Bondes Ambassad*, 17). The words of the original despatch are :
" Utförde så att huru almenne Protestantiske wäsende syntez någon fahra
hafwa att förwänta, så woro likwäll ännu fredh, och föga annat af the
Catholiske, än hooz the Savoiske Protestanter in till thenna dagh atten-
terat," *Stockholm Transcripts*.

[2] *Ib.*

[3] Nieupoort to De Witt, Aug. $\frac{17}{27}$, $\frac{Aug. 24}{Sept. 3}$, De Witt's *Brieven*, iii. 111,
114.

Oliver's hesitation to accept the overtures on either side may perhaps, to some extent, be accounted for by the failure of his
The Pro-   expectation of the inflow of wealth, which was to
tector in   have resulted from the expected reduction of His-
financial
straits.   paniola by Venables, and from the no less expected
capture of the Plate Fleet by Blake. Another motive for hanging back was undoubtedly his reluctance to abandon the hope of bringing about a harmonious co-operation between the Dutch and the Swedes. On the other hand, as the summer drew to a close, the military sympathies of the Protector were enlisted on behalf of the Swedish King, whose brilliant achievements in the field took all Europe by surprise, and could hardly fail to stir to the depths the heart of the soldier who now held the reins of power in England. Having sent his
Aug.-Oct.   lieutenant, Wittenberg, across the Polish frontier on
The vic-   July 11, he followed in person on August 4. On the
torious
caree˜ of   23rd he defeated John Casimir's army at Sobota,
Charles X.   and occupied Warsaw on the 30th. After another
victory won at Czarnova on September 16, he advanced against Cracow, compelling it to surrender on October 8.[1] The Polish Republic, to all appearance, lay bleeding at the feet of the conqueror. Polish nobles, jealous of one another, and still more jealous of their elected King, flocked in crowds to the headquarters of the intruder, whom they welcomed as their lawful sovereign. The towns on the Vistula, German by origin and institutions, dreading the strong hand of the Swede, con-tinued to hold out for Poland, whose yoke in matters of trade had been an easy one. The rapid return of Charles, however,
Surrender   threatened to bring them to reason. Thorn and
of Thorn   Elbing surrendered on November 24. On Decem-
and Elbing.   ber 11 Danzig alone—the queen of Baltic commerce
—persisted in setting him at defiance.[2]

The successes of Charles X. gained him one favour at the hands of the Protector. George Fleetwood, a brother of the

[1] Carlson, *Sveriges Historia under Konungarne af Pfalziska Huset*, i. 232–49.

[2] *Ib.* i. 252, 253.

Lord Deputy, who had been in the Swedish service since 1629, had been for some time in England, soliciting the Protector to give permission for the levy of troops in Scotland. On

Oct. 12.
A levy of
1,000 men
allowed in
Scotland.

October 12 leave was given to Cranston to raise a bare one thousand men in the place of the six or eight thousand for which Coyet had asked.[1] It was not much to Bonde's taste that so little was accorded, and still less was he satisfied when Oliver's congratulations

Sept. 21.
A proposed
Swedish
alliance.

took the shape of a fervent hope that when all was over the Swedish monarchy might have the Caspian for a boundary, whilst no progress was made with the proposal of sending an English fleet to support its claims in the Baltic.[2] On the other hand, it might be argued that there was no immediate need of such assistance, as the Dutch had by this time relinquished the idea of sending armed ships through the Sound.[3]

It was the fault of Oliver's diplomacy that he did his best to ignore the deep-seated commercial opposition between Sweden and the United Provinces, as well as the worldli-

Sept. 28.
A scheme
for settling
the Baltic
difficulty.

ness of the aims of Charles X. On September 28 he directed Thurloe to announce to Nieupoort a scheme for the settlement of the Baltic difficulty. Sweden, he thought, might be asked to enter a general alliance with England, Denmark, the United Provinces, and the Elector of Brandenburg. Such a plan was hardly suited to meet the demands of a sinful world. All that can be said for it as a contribution to practical politics is that it paved the way to a better understanding between England and

Oct.
The Pro-
tector and
the Elector
of Bran-
denburg.

Brandenburg. The Protector had for some time had good reason to regard Frederick William with the gravest distrust. The Elector was not merely allied to the Stuarts by his marriage with a sister of the last Prince of Orange, but had thrown himself warmly into the cause of the exiled family, having contributed to Charles's

---

[1] See *supra*, p. 198.

[2] Bonde to Charles X., Sept. 28, *Stockholm Transcripts*.

[3] De Witt to Nieupoort, Sept. $\frac{7}{17}$, De Witt's *Brieven*, iii. 120.

support more largely than any other German prince.[1] The
Elector, however, was too anxious for the support of England
to hesitate in sacrificing a family alliance to the needs of the
State ; whilst Oliver was, on his part, inclined to look favour-

Oct. 20/30.
Schlezer
to be the
Branden-
burg agent
in England.

ably on the friendship of a Protestant ruler. On
October 20 the Elector was able to issue instructions
to one of his subjects who bore the name of Schlezer
to act as his representative at Whitehall, with the
knowledge that his reception would meet with no obstacle in
England.[2]

Oliver, in short, was gradually coming round to the belief
that the Swedes intended to establish over the Baltic tolls a sole
proprietorship which could not but be injurious to English

Oct. 17.
The
Protector's
assurances
to Nieu-
poort.

trade. On October 17 he assured Nieupoort that
he would accept no offers from Sweden without the
concurrence of the United Provinces. He continued,
however, to harp on the necessity of union between
all Protestant Powers in the face of the mischievous designs of

Nov. 15.

the new Pope.[3] About a month later he returned to
the subject, and expressed his readiness to mediate
between the Swedes and the Dutch without regard to his own

Dec. 11.
A conver-
sation with
Schlezer.

interests.[4] Later, on December 11, the Protector
appears to have opened his mind to Schlezer, who,
like Bonde, had the advantage of being able to con-
verse in English. Ever since he had taken up the government, he declared, he had done his utmost to keep all Protestant States in friendship with one another, a friendship which
was the more necessary in view of the dealings of the Papists
with the Vaudois. What, therefore, could be said for those—
the King of Sweden was evidently intended—who misused this

---

[1] *Urkunden und Aktenstücke*, vii. 706–12.

[2] Instruction to Schlezer, Oct. 20/30, *ib.* vii. 721.

[3] Nieupoort to De Witt, Oct 19/29, De Witt's *Brieven*, iii. 135. Nieupoort to the Greffier of the States General, Oct. 19/29, *Add. MSS.* 17,677
W, fol. 168.

[4] Nieupoort to the Greffier of the States General, Nov. 16/26, *ib.* fol.
225.

conjuncture of affairs to extend their own territory or to draw commerce to themselves.   His own first thought on assuming the Protectorate had been to place himself on good terms with the Dutch.   If only he could have had the same consideration from the King of Spain he would never have gone to war with him, and he regarded his inability to keep the peace in that quarter as a sore burden imposed on him by God.   If, in the end, he had preferred an understanding with France, it was because the French Government was comparatively tolerant as contrasted with Spain.   Schlezer sought to bring the Protector back to the consideration of the Baltic question, which pressed the harder on the Elector as Charles X. was requiring him to place the two ports of East Prussia, Memel and Pillau, in Swedish hands.   As Schlezer had not yet received a cipher, he omitted to record the Protector's answer.[1]

There can be little doubt what was the nature of that reply. Diplomatists engaged in a negotiation with Oliver could run into no more fatal error than by imagining that his devotion to the Protestant cause made him oblivious to commercial interests.   On November 1, a few weeks before his interview with Schlezer, he had enlarged the Committee for Trade, originally named in July, by adding to its numbers, besides his own son Richard, the

Nov. 1.
The Committee for Trade enlarged.

two Commissioners of the Treasury, and three judges, a considerable number of persons actually engaged in commerce in the chief ports of the country.[2]   The man who thus sought for the advice of experts was unlikely to belittle the subject of their inquiries.   At his next interview with Bonde he besought the Swedish ambassador to remove the material causes of disagreement.   Bonde, however, pleaded that he had as yet no precise instructions, and the question of trade was therefore held over

Dec. 14.
Oliver urges Bonde to give satisfaction about trade.

for the present.   The Swede, however, took the opportunity of magnifying so convincingly his master's zeal for religion as to

---

[1] Schlezer to the Elector, Dec. $\frac{14}{24}$, *Urkunden und Aktenstücke*, vii. 727.

[2] Council Order Book, *Interr.* I, 76, p. 357.

draw from the Protector the exclamation, " I wish your instruc-

1656.
His
Jan. 1.
language to
Nieupoort.
tions were as wide as your heart." [1]   Yet on New
Year's Day Oliver took an opportunity of assuring
Nieupoort once more that he would never come to
an agreement with Sweden apart from the United
Provinces. At the same time he showed himself not altogether
satisfied with the course taken by Charles.   He would have
been better pleased, he said, if that King 'had struck towards
those territories'—Bohemia and Silesia were evidently in his
mind—'where large numbers of Protestants had for many
years been exposed to persecution.' As for himself, he was in
duty bound not only to hinder a rupture between Protestant
States, but to unite them in a league against the inhuman
cruelties of the Papacy. [2]

By this time Oliver had a fresh grievance against the Pope.
In Switzerland the Papal canton of Schwytz had expelled its
Troubles in Protestants and had stripped them of their property.
Switzerland. Remonstrances from the Protestant cantons, in
which the refugees had found shelter, had been answered with
an assertion that Schwytz was a sovereign State, and as such
had a right to treat its own subjects as it pleased.   The
principle of *Cujus regio ejus religio* was thus asserted by a
Swiss canton as boldly as by any German prince.   Truly or
falsely, Oliver believed that the peasants of Schwytz had a
whole confederacy behind them, and his partial success in
relieving the Vaudois—due in reality to special circumstances
in his diplomatic relations with France, which were most
unlikely to recur—led him to imagine that similar results
could be obtained in this instance.   For him it was a short step
from a protest against the policy of a single Government to
a protest against the policy of every Catholic Power in Europe.

Jan. 7.
A complaint
to Bonde.
On the 7th he complained to Bonde that Spain,
Bavaria, and the Pope were ready to support the
tyrannical canton.   After this he proposed more
clearly than he had as yet done that his alliance with Sweden

---

[1] Bonde to Charles X., Dec. 21, *Stockholm Transcripts*.
[2] Nieupoort to De Witt, Jan. $\frac{4}{14}$, *Add. MSS.* 17,677 LLL, fol. 239.

must be directed against the Catholic Powers,[1] and more especially against the House of Austria. A merely defensive alliance would be of little use. The enemy was so powerful that it would be necessary for all Protestant States to combine together against him. In other words, Sweden would have to begin by renouncing all claims to the East Prussian tolls, and by satisfying the Dutch in the matter of the commercial independence of Danzig. Bonde, being still without instructions, took care to humour the Protector, and suggested—no doubt ironically—that if any Protestant States refused to join the league it would be reasonable to coerce them.[2]

With plans so enlarged the Protector was resolved to have a clear understanding on the trade dispute. On January 31 Bonde had an interview with the commissioners appointed to treat with him on the subject. He was surprised and disgusted at what he considered to be the harshness of the terms proposed. An appeal to the Protector produced no effect. It was necessary, replied Oliver, to take the Dutch into consideration.[3]

Jan. 31.
Bonde dissatisfied with the commercial proposals.

Feb. 4.
He appeals to the Protector.

In one quarter the risk of war between two Protestant States had been at least temporarily averted. The Elector of Brandenburg had every reason to deprecate the establishment of a strong military monarchy on the ruins of anarchical Poland ; but the army of Charles X. was very near, and neither England nor the United Provinces was prepared to assist him. Bowing, therefore, to necessity, he accepted from the King of Sweden such terms as were offered him. By a treaty signed at Königsberg [4] he received, indeed, Ermeland as an

Brandenburg and Sweden.

Jan. 17.
The Treaty of Königsberg.

---

[1] France, in the Protector's eyes, must certainly not be included among these.

[2] Bonde to Charles X., Jan. 11, *Stockholm Transcripts.*

[3] Bonde to Charles X., Feb. 1, 8, *ib.* ; Carlbom, *Sverige och England*, 59, 62.

[4] Sometimes known as the Treaty of Welau, where it was signed by Charles.

accretion to East Prussia, but, on the other hand, he exchanged, so far as that duchy was concerned, the light overlordship of the Polish King for the heavy feudal superiority of Charles X. Moreover, he consented to abandon to Sweden half the tolls of Memel and Pillau, and to admit Swedish men-of-war into his harbours. The march of Charles to commercial supremacy in the Baltic was proceeding apace.[1]

Such a treaty, so one-sided in its effects, was made only to be broken ; but in the meanwhile, so far as Brandenburg

Feb. 1.
The treaty known in England.

was concerned, it removed the danger of an immediate outbreak of hostilities between two Protestant Powers. The arrangement, the news of which reached England on February 1,[2] appeared so satisfactory in the eyes of the Protector that he omitted to consider the

Feb. 7.
The Protector's letter to Charles X.

bearing of the agreement on the commercial question in which he was interested. On February 7 he took the opportunity of the news that a son and heir had been born to Charles to despatch to the King a letter, drawn up by Milton, congratulating him on his political as well as on his domestic fortune, and dwelling on the service he had done by wresting Poland 'as a horn from the Papal Empire,' and by making peace with the Elector, ' to the great satisfaction of the pious.' [3]

The day after this letter was written Bonde received the instructions for which he had been waiting. He was to offer

Feb. 8.
Bonde receives instructions.

to the Protector a defensive alliance on the one hand against all enemies of either party, and on the other hand against all who infringed the Treaty of Osnabrück.[4] The Protector's overtures received a rebuff on

---

[1] Philippson, *Der grosse Kurfürst*, i. 218-21 ; Carlson, *Sveriges Historia*, i. 251, 265-67.　　　　[2] Carlbom, *Sverige och England*, 62.

[3] The Protector to Charles X., Feb. 7, Milton's *Prose Works*, ed. Symmons, vi. 21. The date of the letter is given by Carlbom from the original document at Stockholm, *Sverige och England*, 62, note 4.

[4] *Ib.* 64. The instructions were dated January 6, the day before the signature of the Treaty of Königsberg (Carlbom, *Sverige och England*, 64). They were accordingly given in full assurance that Charles had nothing to fear from the side of Brandenburg.

every point.   A defensive alliance against all enemies [1] might easily lead him in the course of the summer into a war with the Dutch, whilst the proposal of a joint guarantee of the Treaty of Osnabrück left out of the question any concerted interference with the claim of Catholic States to deal with their own Protestant subjects at their pleasure.   It based itself on a pretended acceptance of Oliver's notion that a Papal crusade was impending, and offered no more than an engagement to take arms in defence of the religious independence of the Protestant States of Germany—an independence which, as Charles knew perfectly well—though Oliver did not—was in nowise endangered, and on behalf of which, if there had existed any design against it, all Protestant Germany would have risen as one man, with the willing assistance of a considerable number, if not of the whole, of the Catholic princes.

The Treaty of Osnabrück to be guaranteed.

  Nor was this all.   It was notorious that though Ferdinand III. had no desire to break the peace in Germany, and though he was at this time stubbornly resisting the efforts of his ablest diplomatist, Lisola, to drag him into a war with Sweden on behalf of Poland, he had not been able to resist the temptation of rendering some assistance to his Spanish kinsman in his prolonged struggle with France.   It was not impossible, therefore, that Oliver, now himself at war with Spain, might plead that Sweden was bound to protest against the help given by the Emperor to the enemies of England.   The reference to the Treaty of Osnabrück cut short such expectations.   There had been two treaties which together made up what is usually known as the Peace of Westphalia.   Of the two, that of Münster concluded between the Emperor and France, contained the obligation of those two Powers to take no hostile measures against one another.   Charles X, by confining his proposed guarantee to the Treaty of Osnabrück, which, having been concluded between the Emperor and the Protestant States

The Emperor and Spain.

[1] Bonde to Charles X., Feb. 16, March 27.   The Swedish proposals, as ultimately presented on March 17, are printed in *Thurloe*, iv. 623.

in and out of Germany, naturally kept silence on the future relations between the Emperor and France, virtually refused to interfere in such a case. Oliver had to learn the bitter truth that if he was to do anything against the House of Austria on the Continent, he must not expect the co-operation of the King of Sweden. His aims had been high and his wish to benefit the world had been undoubted. The lesson taught him, if he had ears to hear, was that no beneficence of intention could avail him aught in this direction so long as his mind was steeped in ignorance of Continental modes of thought and of the intentions of Continental statesmen.

Oliver's diplomatic failure.

CHAPTER XLVIII

COLONISATION AND DIPLOMACY

THE financial condition of the Protectorate being what it was, the King of Sweden must have known that, if he had accepted Oliver's scheme of an aggressive war against the House of Austria, the burden of the proposed war against the German branch of that House would have fallen exclusively upon himself; whilst the fight against the Spanish branch, with its chances of booty to be acquired if only the Plate Fleet could be captured, would have fallen to the share of the Protector. When he was not dazzled by the glitter of his imagined championship of the Protestant interest, Oliver was well aware that the work he had already undertaken was sufficient for his own shoulders to bear. In September 1655, the Venetian ambassador Sagredo[1] having urged upon the Protector the advantages of an alliance against the Turks, soon discovered that he was but beating the air. He was told that if he had arrived a year earlier, at the time when Blake's expedition to the Mediterranean was in contemplation, he might have prevailed on the English Government to give precedence to a Turkish war, but that it was useless to make such a proposal at a time when a war with Spain was unavoidable. Sagredo, though by orders from the Senate he remained in England till February, soon discovered that his mission was fruitless. When he was preparing for his departure, the Senate contented itself with

1655.
The war with Spain.

Sept. Sagredo's mission.

[1] See p. 18.

directing him to leave behind him his secretary, Giavarina, as agent for the Republic. No Venetian ambassador again landed in England till after the Restoration.[1]

The war with Spain was undoubtedly unpopular with English merchants. Those of them who traded with that country had to lament the loss of their property sequestered in Spanish ports, and complained that the issue of letters of marque to make reprisals on Spanish vessels was no adequate compensation for the interruption of so lucrative a trade. The French markets now opened to them promised little in comparison with that which they had lost.[2]

The war with Spain unpopular.

On one point at least the Protector had made up his mind. Whatever might happen in Europe, he would maintain his hold upon Jamaica. On June 11, 1655, before the disaster in Hispaniola was known in England, he had sent out a fresh regiment, under Colonel Humphries, to keep up the numbers of the army, and Humphries was accompanied by Major Sedgwick, who was empowered to act as an additional commissioner. When, on October 1, the party reached Jamaica, Sedgwick found himself without a colleague. Winslow had died on the voyage from Hispaniola, Searle had never left Barbados, and Butler, following the example of Penn and Venables, had taken ship for England. Under these discouraging circumstances Sedgwick made an informal agreement with Goodson, to whom Penn had handed over the command of the fleet, and with Fortescue, who was at the head of the military forces, to act as commissioners with himself. A month later he sent over a melancholy report to the Protector. "For the army," he wrote, "I found them in as sad and deplorable and distracted condition as can be thought of, and indeed think, as never poor Englishmen were in : the commanders—some dead, some sick, and some in indifferent health : the soldiery—many dead, their carcasses

June 11. Humphries and Sedgwick sent to Jamaica.

Oct. 1. Their arrival.

Nov. 5. Sedgwick's report.

---

[1] Sagredo's despatches, Sept. $\frac{14}{24}$, Feb. $\frac{8}{18}$, *Venetian Transcripts, R.O.*

[2] Bordeaux to Brienne, Nov. $\frac{5}{15}$, *French Transcripts, R.O.*

lying unburied in the highways and among bushes . . . many of them that were alive walked like ghosts or dead men, who, as I went through the town, lay groaning and crying out, ' Bread, for the Lord's sake ! ' The truth is, when I set my foot first on land, I saw nothing but symptoms of necessity and desolation. I found the shore thereabout filled with variety of several casks and hogsheads, puncheons, butts, barrels, chests, and the like, and several dry goods of the State's, as linen shirts and drawers, shoes, stockings, hats, armour, arms and nails, with divers other things lying without any shelter, exposed to all the damage that either rain or sun could do to them, and to the theft and rapine of either soldiers or strangers who, without question embezzled much of them. All the little bread they had, which was about thirty thousand, only kept in casks without doors, and much of it damnified by weather, which bread was kept to distribute a little to the soldiers—and most when sent upon parties. The people here were in daily expectation of a supply of provisions, yet made not the least preparation for the receiving of them. It is a wonder to consider so many wise men that had been here should leave the State's goods so exposed to rain that were so absolutely necessary for the well-being of the army ; when, in a few days, a few men might have made a house to have secured them all ; but so things lay, as if men had run away in a strange, distracted, affrighted condition, as leaving all to the spoil, and never once looking back."

Once more it devolved on the seamen to make good the deficiency of the soldiers. A party of Goodson's sailors ran up a storehouse in six or eight days. Yet the provisions thus secured from the effects of the weather could not be counted on to last longer than six months at the utmost, even if the men were put on short allowance. The comparative vigour of the sailors was undoubtedly due to their living on board ship under healthier conditions than those to which the men belonging to the land service were exposed. The soldiers owed the dysentery and fever from which they were suffering not only to the tropical heat striking on bodies enfeebled by a low diet, but to the

absolute neglect of all sanitary precautions.[1]   Fortescue himself
fell a victim ; and after his death his authority passed into the
hands of a council of officers, Colonel Doyley being ultimately
appointed   President   and   Commander-in-Chief.   Yet the
ravages of disease were not stayed.   The regiment brought
over by Humphries landed with a strength of 831 'lusty, health-
ful, gallant men.'   In a few weeks fifty of them were dead,
'whereof two captains, a lieutenant, and two ensigns.'   The
Colonel himself was 'very weak, the Lieutenant-Colonel at
death's door.'   All the surviving captains were ill ; no more
than four commissioned officers were fit to march, and the
men, for the most part, were suffering to a greater or less
extent.   "Soldiers," continued Sedgwick, "die daily. . . . It is
strange to see young lusty men, in appearance well, and in
three or four days in the grave, snatched away in a moment
with fevers, agues, fluxes and dropsies—a confluence of many
diseases."   The island itself was 'desirable, capable of producing any kind of merchandise that other islands do ; full of
several sorts of cattle.'   Yet of these cattle the disorderly mob
which called itself an army had recklessly slaughtered at least
20,000, and had rendered the remainder so wild that there was
little chance of capturing more.   Though the soldiers were
ready to claim allotments of land, not one of them would
cultivate his lot under that burning sun, and there were no
negroes available to undertake a burden beyond the white
man's powers.   "Dig or plant," complained Sedgwick, "they
neither can nor will, but do rather starve than work."   No
wonder officers and men with one accord cried out to be led
back to the fleshpots of England.[2]

[1] This is Dr. C. Creighton's opinion. He holds that the disease from
which the force suffered was 'certainly not yellow fever,' but 'was probably allied to it in type.' "Dysentery," he adds, "had been almost
universal ; there was no care of the sick, and, so far as one hears, no
medical attendance, no hospitals, no scavenging, no security taken to keep
the water supply pure—nothing, in short, of what is now called sanitation."
A History of the Epidemics in Britain, i. 643, 644.

[2] Sedgwick to the Protector, Nov. 5, *Thurloe*, iv. 151.   Goodson, on
Jan. 24, 1656, writes in as melancholy a strain, *ib.* iv. 451.   In a joint

Before this miserable account was written it had naturally occurred to Thurloe that a supply of other, than military colonists would be likely to improve the position, and requests were accordingly sent to those in authority in Scotland and Ireland to make provision by sending young persons of both sexes to Jamaica. The reply from Scotland was somewhat discouraging. " If I do not mistake," wrote Thurloe's correspondent, " there are three sorts of persons to be exported, viz., such men as are to be recruits ; such as are to be planters ; and such women as will go over with their husbands, or will adventure to seek husbands there." To send men as soldiers, unless voluntarily, would ' put the country in a flame.' Planters might perhaps be secured if good conditions were offered. As for ' women and maids, there were not many likely to consent, and it was probable that more might be got out of Ireland than here.' [1] In Ireland the transplantation had taught the authorities to deal with such matters with a high hand. " Concerning the young women," wrote Henry Cromwell, " although we must use force in taking them up, yet, it being so much for their own good,[2] and likely to be of so great advantage to the public, it is not in the least doubted that you may have such number of them as you shall think fit to make use of upon this account." A few weeks later it was resolved in England that 1,000 boys and 1,000 girls should be shipped at Galway in December, the age fixed in both cases being under fourteen.[3] From time to time, however, Thurloe wrote that the Council was too busy to attend to

1655.
Sept. 4.
Proposal to send non-military colonists.

Scotch colonists wanted.

Irish girls to be sent from Ireland.

report of the same day Goodson and Sedgwick write that ' it is our desire to attend your Highness's command, in keeping up love, unity, and amity between army and fleet, which through mercy we have attained to in a good measure.' Goodson and Sedgwick to the Protector, Jan. 24, 1656, *Thurloe,* iv. 455.

[1] Broghill to Thurloe, Sept. 18, *ib.* iv. 41.

[2] These words imply Henry Cromwell's intention that, as Broghill said of Scotland, they were to be wives to colonists, military or otherwise.

[3] Order in Council, Oct. 3, Penn's *Mem. of Sir W. Penn,* ii. 585.

the affair. In the end it dropped out of sight, and not a single
Irish boy or girl was despatched across the Atlantic in consequence of this resolution.[1] It was well that the scheme was not carried out. In its existing state of disorder Jamaica was no place for the inrush of a couple of thousand lads and lasses, especially as the matrons already in the colony were too few in number to afford fit guardianship for a large importation of young girls. So deplorable did the situation appear about this time on the spot that widows of soldiers preferred to sell themselves into temporary servitude in other islands rather than keep their freedom on the accursed soil of Jamaica.[2]

Alleged transportation of Irish boys and girls.

1656. Jan. Widows sell themselves into servitude.

In the spring of 1656 a proposal still more reprehensible in modern eyes was said to have been made. Full of his great design of establishing morality in London, Barkstead made a raid on the houses of ill fame, and committed some four hundred of their inmates to the Tower. It was at once rumoured that these women were to be sent to Jamaica—as the Dutch ambassador quaintly put it—to nurse the sick.[3] Such immigrants were not unknown in Barbados,[4] and it is not unlikely that Barkstead may have been eager to rid himself of his unruly charges, whose own moral position might be improved if they could be induced to settle in Jamaica as soldiers' wives. His plan, however, pro-

Reported proposal to send out loose women to Jamaica.

---

[1] Not only can no such transportation be traced in the records, either in London or in Dublin, but there is the negative evidence of the absence of any mention of the arrival of so numerous a body by the writers of the voluminous letters which chronicle the position of affairs in Jamaica. So careful are the writers to tell everything that concerns the colony that it is incredible that they should have closed their eyes to such an importation, if it had ever taken place.

[2] Sedgwick to Thurloe, Jan. 24, *Thurloe*, iv. 454.

[3] Nieupoort to the States General, $\frac{\text{Feb. 29}}{\text{March 10}}$, *Add. MSS.* 17,677 W, fol. 235. The translation in *Thurloe*, iv. 567, is less plainspoken as to the character of the women.

[4] See *supra*, p. 112, note 1.

bably did not commend itself to the Protector and Council, as it appears to have been definitely abandoned.[1]

The Protector, indeed, was doing his best to induce settlers of a different stamp to throw in their lot with the military colonists in Jamaica. In September 1655 he despatched Daniel Gookin, a cousin of the Vincent Gookin whose advice on the affairs of Ireland he had gladly taken, to urge on the people of New England the advantage of transferring themselves to a more productive soil;[2] whilst, about the same time, he appealed to the Governors of the West India islands to induce their surplus population to seek fresh homes in Jamaica.[3] Gookin, on his arrival, had to report that the miserable condition of the Jamaica colony was sufficiently well known to deter the New Englanders from embarking on the proposed transfer of their homes.[4] As for the West India colonies, it was only from Luke Stokes, the Governor of Nevis, whom the Protector at once named to one of the vacant commissionerships,[5] that a favourable response was returned. From Jamaica itself the news which continued to reach England was indeed deplorable. A resolution was taken by the Protector to confer the title of Governor on Sedgwick, but when the news of his appointment reached him he took to his bed and died from sheer hopelessness, as was alleged, of being able to

Marginal notes:
1655. Sept. An invitation to the New Englanders,

Oct. and to West India colonists.

1656. Refusal of the New Englanders.

In the West Indies, Nevis alone accepts.

May 24. Death of Sedgwick.

---

[1] The story is told, with variations, by most of the foreign ambassadors, as well as by Royalist letter-writers. On $\frac{\text{March } 31}{\text{April } 10}$, however, Bordeaux states that the women were not yet sent, and as in the case of the Irish girls, the silence of the letter-writers in Jamaica must be held to be conclusive that they never were sent.

[2] Instructions to Gookin, Sept. 26, Penn's *Mem. of Sir W. Penn*, ii. 585.

[3] The Protector to Goodson, Oct. ?, *Thurloe*, iv. 449, v. 6.

[4] Goodson to Thurloe, Jan. 24, May 10, *ib.* iv. 449, v. 6.

[5] The Protector to Stokes, Oct., *Carlyle*, Letter CCV., where, as Mrs. Lomas has pointed out to me, the letter is incorrectly said to have been addressed to Searle. For Stokes's commissionership, see Brayne to the Protector, March 12, 1657, *Thurloe*, vi. 110.

accomplish any good.[1] Nor were the prospects of winning spoil from the enemy—on which Oliver had counted as a means of recouping his expenses—any brighter. In 1655, after Penn's departure, a squadron of the fleet under Goodson had sacked and burnt Santa Marta. The whole of the plunder, however, amounted to no more than 471*l*.[2] In 1656 Goodson burnt Rio de la Hacha, carrying off nothing but four brass guns, a cargo of wine, and another of cacao, which latter he sent over to England, in consequence of its value in producing the beverage known as chocolate, recently introduced into Europe as a medicament to be used under the advice of physicians.[3] The products of these two enterprises went but a little way towards defraying the expenses of the fleet.

Burning of Santa Marta,

and of Rio de la Hacha.

Sedgwick was succeeded in the command in Jamaica by Doyley, the senior officer in the island, an active and energetic soldier. Having no commission from the Protector, he found it difficult to maintain order. The great body of the officers, bent on returning to England, threw every possible difficulty in the way of plantation by the soldiers under their authority. The machinery of a court-martial was even brought to bear against those who attempted to fulfil the object which they had been sent to accomplish. By this means Colonel Holdip was cashiered on a charge of malversation in respect to the regimental chest, though Goodson believed that his real offence was that he had been more forward in the encouragement of plantation than was approved of by his brother-officers, who wished the private soldiers to be as discontented as themselves.[4] It was known, too, that these very officers had freely threatened the men that, if they planted at all, it must be as compulsory servants, and not as owners of the soil assigned to them as their

Doyley in command in Jamaica.

Misconduct of the officers.

Holdip unjustly cashiered.

---

[1] Aylesbury to Thurloe, June 25, *Thurloe*, v. 154.

[2] Goodson to the Council, Nov. 7, 1655, *ib.* iv. 159.

[3] Goodson to Thurloe, Jan. 7, 25, *ib.* v. 96, 151. The use of chocolate is illustrated by many letters amongst the *Verney MSS.*

[4] Holdip was however disliked by more reputable persons on other grounds.

property.   The true remedy for the evil was to cut the mischief-makers adrift, and Doyley went so far as to send home one of the
Humphries sent home. most seditious, Colonel Humphries.   One example, however, was far from being enough.[1]   It was left to
Dec. Arrival of Brayne. Brayne, who arrived in December at the head of a considerable force, with a commission from the Pro-
Officers allowed to return. tector establishing him as Governor, to find a remedy by informing the dissatisfied officers that they were at liberty to return to England as soon as they pleased.[2]
Those who remained after the exodus which resulted from this permission threw themselves into the work of planting, now that the principal influences working for evil had been removed, and though hard times were still in store for Jamaica, the neck of its difficulties was broken.

The growing progress of the colony was not, however, entirely owing to Brayne's firmness and good sense.   The nego-
Nov. Settlement of families from Nevis. tiation with Luke Stokes [3] resulted in November in his removal to Jamaica at the head of no less than 1,600 of the poorer inhabitants of his island.   Their number was the least part of the advantage they brought to their new homes.   They came in whole families—men, women, children and servants—to introduce those domesticities of home life which had been wanting to the military settlers.

It was quite as much to the purpose that by Goodson's advice they avoided the pestilential district round Santiago de la Vega, and established themselves at Port Morant, near the eastern extremity of the island.[4]   In fresh ground these family settlements, accustomed as they had long been to West Indian life, might be expected to pay some regard to the laws of health, so far, at least, as they were recognised in the seventeenth century.   Yet, even with these advantages, the settlers from Nevis lost two-thirds of their numbers, including Stokes

[1] Goodson to Thurloe, June 25 ; Doyley to Thurloe, Oct. 6, *Thurloe,* v. 151, 476.   [2] Brayne to the Protector, Jan. 9, 1657, *ib.* v. 770.

[3] See *supra,* p. 220.

[4] Goodson and Stokes to the Protector, Oct. 18, 1656 ; Stokes to the Protector, Jan. 7, 1657, *Thurloe,* v. 500, 769.

himself, before they had been three months in their new homes.[1]

1657.
State of the
settlers from
Nevis.
In the spring of 1657 the remaining third were in good health, and established themselves without further check. Whatever may have been the proximate causes of this turn of events, the retention of Jamaica is primarily due to the dogged persistency with which the Protector refused to admit the possibility of failure after the disaster of 1655—a disaster which had been mainly caused by his inability to grasp the conditions of military success under circumstances outside of his personal experience.

Nearer home the position of the Stuart princes could not fail to be affected by the outbreak of hostilities with Spain.

1655.
Spain and
the Stuart
princes.
Even before that event had actually taken place overtures had been made to Charles at Cologne to put his trust in a combination in which the Levellers in England were to play a leading part in connection with the Spanish monarchy. Of this strange coalition the protagonist

May.
Sexby at
Antwerp.
was Sexby, who after his escape from Portland[2] reached Antwerp in May 1655, where he at once sought out the leading Royalists in the Low Countries, assuring them that both king and kingdom would be the better if they relied on the assistance that he was able to secure among

June.
His views on
a restora-
tion.
his own friends. In June he was more explicit, explaining that the English Levellers would gladly see the King restored, on condition that he would accept the system of constantly recurring Parliaments, and would content himself with exercising the executive power only when Parliament was not in session. Personally, he added, he would gladly see the King in possession of his legal rights, if only the liberties and the property of his subjects could be secured. The chief difficulty, he added, would be to satisfy the purchasers of the lands of ecclesiastical dignitaries, who would be certain to oppose a restoration unless their claims could be secured.[3] At the same time he pressed Fuensaldaña,

---

[1] Brayne to the Protector, March 12, 1657, *Thurloe*, vi. 110.

[2] See vol. iii. p. 270.

[3] Phelips to Nicholas, May $\frac{11}{21}$, June $\frac{5}{15}$, *Nicholas Papers*, ii. 299, 340.

who, as commander of the army, was next in authority to
the Viceroy himself, to support the cause of the exiled
King against the usurper who was dragging England
into a war with Spain.

He urges
Fuensaldaña
to support
Charles.

Fuensaldaña, knowing as he did that Sexby's advocacy of a
friendly understanding between England and Spain was not
of recent growth, was inclined to listen favourably to this self-
appointed negotiator.   The intermediary between the two
was Peter Talbot, an Irish Jesuit, whose brother
Richard was afterwards notorious as the Tyrconnel
of the reign of James II.   Sexby, magniloquent
and unscrupulous, had in his conversations with the English
Royalists laid stress on the advantages of a democratic
parliamentary monarchy.   In his conversations with the Irish
priest he set forth the desire of his friends to establish in
England complete liberty of religion, including even the
Catholics.   He even went a step further, and contrived to per-
suade the Jesuit that he was himself a Catholic at heart.[1] Sexby's
resolution to gain his ends was, in fact, seldom checked by
any consideration for veracity, and before he left England he
had induced Cardenas to receive him as the spokesman, not
only of the Levellers, but of the Cavaliers and the moderate
Presbyterians as well.   In the Low Countries he produced
letters, probably genuine, from Grey of Groby, Wildman
and Lawson.   One which he also showed, as having been
written by Lawrence, the President of the Council, can hardly
have contained any approval of designs hostile to the Protectorate.[2]

Employ-
ment of
Peter
Talbot.

Sexby's rodomontades in magnifying his own importance

---

[1] P. Talbot to Charles, $\frac{April\ 30}{May\ 10}$, $\frac{May\ 24}{June\ 3}$, June $\frac{7}{17}$, *Clarendon MSS.* l. fol.
273, *Clar. St. P.* iii. 271, 272.

[2] Talbot's statement, that these writers placed themselves in Sexby's
hands 'in tutto che tratasse col Papa e col Rè di Spagna,' may probably
be true of the first three, but cannot be accepted of Lawrence.   Sexby,
however, may have shown an old letter written to him when he was
in the Protector's confidence, and merely expressing sentiments of goodwill.

went beyond all reasonable limits. He persuaded Talbot that
Sexby's rodomon-tades. his popularity amongst the soldiers outweighed that
of the Protector, and to induce belief in this ex-
travagant assertion recounted an incident which he
alleged to have occurred on the march preceding the battle of
Preston in 1648. Cromwell, he said, had then thrown himself
on his knees before him, and had even promised to give him
his daughter in marriage to induce him to take service in his
army. So great, he affirmed, was his own influence with the
soldiers at that time, that out of 1,500 men of which Cromwell's regiment was composed, all but seventeen deserted their
commander to serve under himself.[1]

Fuensaldaña, carried away by this torrent of lies, despatched
Sexby to Spain to plead his cause in person with Philip and
His mission to Spain. his ministers. Upon his arrival at Madrid Sexby
proposed to establish in England under the restored
monarchy a Constitution in accordance with that
Lilburnian *Agreement of the People*, which he had formerly
flashed before the eyes of Condé's faction at Bordeaux,[2] under
which complete liberty of religion was offered even to the
Catholics ; though he now admitted that, at least for a time,
it would be impracticable to grant them liberty of worship in
churches open to the public. He also offered that, as a
security that he and his friends would stand by their engagements, some of them should give themselves up to be held as
hostages at Dunkirk ; that when the expected insurrection took
place in England Irish troops should be placed as garrisons in
fortified towns ; and that part of the fleet—doubtless so much
of it as was under Lawson's influence [3]—which was expected to

---

[1] This story is a fiction founded on the fact that Sexby brought to
Cromwell a letter from Lilburne, the effect of which was to reconcile the
Levellers in the army to service under Cromwell as their commander.
Sexby had no position in that army. See *Great Civil War*, iv. 178.

[2] See vol. ii. 157.

[3] "Scrive il mio amico che habita in le Dune, questo è il generale
de la flotta che adesso resta in Inghilterra." Sexby to P. Talbot, *Nunziatura di Bruselas*, *Vatican Archives*. This points unmistakably to
Lawson.

join the insurgents, should be brought across the Straits, and be anchored under the guns of Dunkirk. As soon as the movement had attained success Charles was to be asked to receive the Crown as the people's gift, and on assenting to these terms, and on repudiating any claim to hold England by right of conquest, was to be permitted to remount the throne. As the Spanish Treasury had little to spare for the support of so costly an enterprise, Sexby proposed to invite the Pope to contribute 100,000*l.* towards an undertaking likely to prove advantageous to his Church.[1]

If Philip had accepted this verbiage as a solid basis of action, he would have shown himself even more ignorant of England than the Protector was showing himself of Austria and Sweden. As it was, Sexby had to content himself with a promise of pecuniary support, only to be given after the insurrection was in full swing.[2] Nor was Sexby, upon his return to the Low Countries towards the end of October, any more successful with the English Royalists, who, ready as they were to receive any assistance that might offer itself, were as profoundly suspicious of the proposal to erect a democratic monarchy as they were of Sexby himself. Meanwhile some of the Royalists were hoping to obtain their ends by the shorter course of assassination, and about the middle of November Richard Talbot and James Halsall were arrested in England on suspicion of being concerned in an attempt to murder the Protector. It was a conspiracy which has the peculiarity that, while the English Government failed to secure satisfactory evidence against the conspirators, the fact that they were employed in a murder-plot is established upon the evidence of Royalists; whilst it is placed beyond doubt that the respectable Ormond, and other Royalists of equal respectability, sympathised with those who were contriving murder.[3]

Marginal notes:
A dilatory answer.

Oct. 27 / Nov. 6.
Sexby returns to Antwerp.

Nov. 16.
Richard Talbot and Halsall arrested.

---

[1] Sexby to P. Talbot, *Nunziatura di Bruselas, Vatican Archives.*

[2] Talbot to Charles II., Nov. 29 / Dec. 9, *Clarendon MSS.* l. fol. 213.

[3] It is true that Talbot in writing avoids such an unpleasant word as murder, and only talks of 'an attempt upon the Protector's person,' and

In the eyes of the exiles the Protector was himself a murderer of the blackest dye, and might be done to death without compunction by all true-hearted subjects. Both Talbot and Halsall succeeded in effecting their escape to the Continent, after baffling the interrogatories to which they had been subjected.[1]

The Protector's failure to produce sufficient evidence to convict these two men may perhaps be accounted for by the loss of his principal spy at Charles's Court. Suspicions having

Nov. 25. Manning arrested and executed. been roused by Manning's frequent correspondence with England, he was arrested and his papers seized. It was found that he had drawn up an account of a discussion in the Council on a plan for the seizure of Plymouth. In vain Manning pleaded that he had never given any but useless information to Thurloe, and also that he had made up his mind to break off the connection as soon as possible. Nicholas and Culpepper, who conducted the inquiry into his conduct, were not to be blinded.[2] The only question was in what way he could be executed as a traitor to a king who had not a foot of land over which to exercise sovereignty The Elector of Cologne refused to permit so anomalous a jurisdiction within his territory. The Count Palatine of Neuburg, however, authorised the execution in his Duchy of Juliers, and the unfortunate man was accordingly taken across

so forth. But it is impossible after reading the correspondence to feel any doubt as to what was intended. R. Talbot to Ormond, $\frac{Jan. 22}{Feb. 1}$, Carte's *Orig. Letters*, ii. 69.

[1] Peter Talbot writes that nothing made him laugh more 'than that Cromwell should ask of my brother why he should think of killing him . . . seeing he had never prejudiced him in his life ; as if to murder the King and the nobility and gentry of three nations were nothing.' P. Talbot to Harding, $\frac{Dec. 25}{Jan. 5}$, *Clarendon MSS.* li. fol. 10.

[2] *Nicholas Papers*, iii. 149–87. Mr. Warner expresses a doubt as to the trustworthiness of Manning's information about the deliberation on the seizure of Plymouth. Manning's denial of its truth is worthless, and it chimes in with what we know of Sexby's projects at this time. Clarendon's account of the affair (xiv. 142–45) cannot be relied on for details.

the border and shot in a wood by Armorer and Sir James Hamilton.[1]

Little as was to be expected from a combination with the Levellers, the exiled Court was all but driven into their arms by the credulity of the Government at Brussels. Having vainly tempted Charles to change his religion by dangling before his eyes the offer of a Papal grant large enough to set Sexby in motion, Fuensaldaña next pressed him to assent to the projected insurrection of the Levellers. Charles, however, who had rejected the plan of conversion from prudential motives, took care to indicate that though he had no objection to the Levellers assisting the English Royalists, he would not assent to a republican movement in which his own friends would be swamped.[2] The difficulty of giving to Sexby's scheme a plausible form lay principally in the obvious fact that no insurrection was likely to be successful unless the Royalists could gain the command of the sea, as in no other case would it be possible to support it with Spanish regiments. For the attainment of this object Sexby was necessarily dependent on his confederate, Lawson, who, however, was no longer, as he had been in the summer and autumn, in possession of an independent command.

Dec. $\frac{18}{10}$.
Charles asked to change his religion.

The command of the sea necessary to the Royalists.

During the winter months a fleet was preparing for service on the coast of Spain, with the ulterior object of watching for the Plate Fleet, which might be expected to arrive at the end of the summer of 1656. Blake was, as a matter of course, to accompany it as admiral ; but this time he was to receive a colleague in the person of one of

A fleet preparing.

Blake and Montague to command.

---

[1] *The Public Intelligencer*, E, 491, 10 ; Sagredo to the Doge, Jan. $\frac{18}{28}$, *Venetian Transcripts*, *R.O.* The Count Palatine was the Elector of Brandenburg's opponent, Philip William. Sagredo erroneously calls him the Count Palatine, Duke of Brandenburg. In Hyde's correspondence he is invariably styled Duke of Neuburg—a non-existent title.

[2] P. Talbot to Charles II., Dec. $\frac{14}{24}$, Jan. $\frac{7}{17}$; the King's answer to the proposals of Mr. S[exby], *Clar. St. P.*, iii. 280, 284 ; *Clarendon MSS.* li., fol. 55.

the Protector's most attached friends, Edward Montague. To Lawson was given the position of vice-admiral. As it is hardly possible that Montague's nomination by the Protector proceeded from any distrust of Blake as a commander, it may reasonably be accounted for by Oliver's wish to have someone in command of the fleet on whom he could rely to keep an eye on Lawson, and who was sufficiently acquainted with the political currents to know where the danger lay.[1]

Probable object of Montague's appointment.

The truth was, that though Lawson was known to be in the secrets of the Levellers, he was, as the author of the seamen's petition, too popular among the sailors to be easily dismissed, and it may well have seemed to the Protector that, if he were removed from the command of the Channel fleet, he would be safer under Montague's eyes on the coast of Spain than in any other position. The risk from Lawson's hostility to the Government was, indeed, not to be treated lightly. The difficulty of manning the fleet was great, as the destination of the expedition was kept secret and the sailors suspected it to be destined for the West Indies. Moreover, the financial straits into which the Government had fallen stood in the way of the prompt payment of wages. Officers directed to press seamen into the service of the State met with organised opposition. Yet in the end their object was attained, partly by seizing sailors on shore, partly by compelling outward-bound merchantmen to surrender the most efficient seamen.[2] That the

Lawson to go as vice-admiral.

1656. Difficulty of manning the fleet.

---

[1] Clarendon says (xv. 26) that Montague was appointed at Blake's request, on the ground of his state of health. It is not unlikely that Clarendon heard this from Montague himself. It does not follow that the statement was true. A Royalist agent distinctly named the person to whom Blake oomplained that the Protector had 'joined him to a very worthless fellow.' Ross to Nicholas, July $\frac{11}{21}$, *S. P. Dom.* cxxix. 32. Giavarina, too, after making some inquiry, declares that Blake and Montague were not on good terms during the voyage.

[2] Weald to Peters, Jan. 22 ; Hatsell to the Admiralty Commissioners, Feb. 1 ; Hatsell to Blackborne, Feb. 5, *S. P. Dom.* xxiii. 59, cxxiv. 9–24, with other letters in the same collection.

sailors were not without justification for their unwillingness to
serve the State is shown not merely by the fact
that, in accordance with existing regulations, the
crews of Blake's fleet of 1654–55 received no pay during the
twenty months of their service at sea,[1] but that not a penny of
the money due to them had been made over to their wives and
families, a grievance which had found its place in the seamen's
petition of 1654.[2] As for prize goods, they were apt to remain
in the hands of officials, or to be detained for the use of the
State, instead of being distributed amongst the captors.[3]

Sailors' grievances. (margin)

With such a feeling of discontent prevailing amongst the
crews it is no wonder that Lawson's presence in their midst
was regarded by the Government as a danger. It is
at least certain that Charles was looking hopefully
in this direction, and that on February 1 he instructed an agent to assure Fuensaldaña that, if he
were openly received in Flanders, 'some of those
ships may come in before they pass the Channel, at least that
they will drop into the ports of Spain as they pass that coast
and the Mediterranean.'[4] It may be suspected that Charles
failed to realise the disinclination of the English sailor to
desert his flag in the presence of the enemy.
Lawson, who can have been under no delusion on
this score, suddenly threw up his command, either
because he despaired of being able to satisfy the expectations
he had raised at Cologne, or because he discovered that his
secret had been betrayed.[5] His own explanation was that he

Lawson regarded dangerous. (margin)
Feb. 1. Charles's hopes from the fleet. (margin)
Lawson resigns his command. (margin)

---

[1] The fleet had been lying at Portsmouth long before it sailed for the
Mediterranean.

[2] The Admiralty Commissioners to the Protector and Council, Oct. 12,
1655, *Thurloe*, iv. 79.

[3] Oppenheim's *Administration of the Navy*, i. 315–19. On the other
hand, Goodson sold the plunder of Santa Marta 'at each ship's mast.'
Though he does not say the price was divided, according to rule, amongst
the crews, there can be little doubt that it was so. Goodson to the
Council, Nov. 7, 1655, *ib.* iv. 159.

[4] Instructions to De Vic, Feb. $\frac{1}{11}$, *Clar. St. P.* iii. 286.

[5] The Protector informed Bordeaux somewhat later that he had had

would not go to sea till he knew the design of the voyage.[1]

March 1.
His example
followed by
three
captains.
About a fortnight later Captain Lyons resigned, testifying his discontent at ' the neglect of due care for both commanders and seamen and their families in case of death or long absence at sea,' adding that ' he was not satisfied in the design . . . neither against whom we should go, nor where.' On the following day Captain Hill followed his example. Hill's objections to serve were still more explicit than those of Lyons. Englishmen, he alleged, and not Spaniards, had been the cause of the trouble in the Indies, and he consequently disapproved of the orders given to Blake the year before to attack the Plate Fleet. His conscience, he averred, would not ' suffer him to fight the Spaniards either in the West Indies or southerly,' though he was ready to defend his own country if

March 2.

---

information of Sexby's design ' d'exciter un soulevement dans la flotte,' Bordeaux to Mazarin, $\frac{\text{March 31}}{\text{April 10}}$, *French Transcripts, R.O.*

[1] "I cannot but admire at Captain Lawson's actings, seeing he went so far ; and thus to retreat renders him not the person I took him for. Ingenuity would have prompt[ed] him to have done otherwise, but I fear he is so strongly biassed by those that wish not well to the present public transactions that he consulted not his own reason as he ought on the best of accounts." Hatsell to the Admiralty Commissioners, Feb. 15, *S. P. Dom.* cxxiv. 34. Hatsell's statement to that effect is also corroborated by the statement of the Dutch ambassador that Lawson ' seyne comissie heeft nedergelegt.' Nieupoort to the States General, Feb. $\frac{15}{25}$, *Add. MSS.* 17,677 W, fol. 229. Also, in a letter of Jan. 1, 1657, John Thompson writes (*S. P. Dom.* cliii. 6) to Robert Thompson, the Navy Commissioner, that his friend, Vice-Admiral Lawson, had laid down his commission. It is, if possible, even more conclusive that the official warrant of the Navy Commissioners issued on August 28, 1656, for Lawson's pay (*ib.* cxliv. 111) directs that it is to be reckoned up to Feb. 11, the day he laid down his commission. On the other hand a royalist puts it otherwise. " Your most admired Lawson, the Vice-Admiral, is cashiered for refusing to go to sea till he knew the design." Pile to Whitley, Feb. 21, *ib.* cxxiv. 90. The epithet ' most admired,' occurring in a letter from one Royalist to another, indicates the expectations formed in that quarter, but the term ' cashiered ' cannot be accepted in view of the preponderating evidence that Lawson resigned.

attacked by an enemy in the Channel. A few days later

March 7. Captain Abelson also laid down his commission on the plea of his wife's ill health. A lieutenant who declared that if he had been in Lawson's place he would have acted in the same way as the Vice-Admiral was promptly cashiered.[1] At Whitehall, where Sexby's projects were well known, the whole trouble was attributed to Spanish intrigue.[2]

Feb. 14.
Badiley
suceeeds
Lawson.

Lawson's place had been filled without delay by Badiley,[3] whose conduct against the Dutch in the Mediterranean had left nothing to be desired.

Though Lawson's defection put the Government on its guard against the Levellers, he had no connection with the

Lawson not
connected
with the
Fifth Mon-
archy Men.

Fifth Monarchists, and, with characteristic hopefulness, the Protector seized the opportunity to make one more attempt to conciliate the latter, who, whatever other reasons for dissatisfaction they might have, were at least unlikely to object to an attack on Papal Spaniards. On February 19 the Council took into consideration the release of Harrison and his fellow-sufferers, Carew, Courtney, and

March.
Liberation
of Harrison
and Rich.

Rich.[4] Their liberation was, however, postponed for a little time ; but on March 22 Harrison, in spite of his asseveration that he preferred imprisonment to liberty, was forced to accept the freedom which he deprecated, and is heard of before the end of the month in his house at Highgate.[5] Rich appears to have been set free, voluntarily or involuntarily, about the same time, though Carew and Courtney remained in durance. The delay was probably owing

A meeting of
Anabaptists
and Fifth
Monarchy
Men.

to information which reached the Government of the intention of the Anabaptists and Fifth Monarchy Men to meet in London to discuss the question of taking arms. Such a meeting was actually held

[1] Montague to Thurloe, March 2, 7, 10, *Thurloe*, iv. 570, 590, 594.

[2] Thurloe to Montague, March 4, Carte's *Orig. Letters*, ii. 87.

[3] *The Public Intelligencer*, E, 492, 6.

[4] See vol. iii. p. 268.

[5] Council Order Book, *Interr.* I, 76, pp. 554, 586 ; Rogers, *Jegar Sahadutha*, 133 ; *The Public Intelligencer*, E, 493, 2.

about the middle of March. With his usual dislike of unnecessary bloodshed, the Protector, instead of sending soldiers
to disperse it, invited some of his own Baptist supporters to
argue the matter out with their more extreme co-religionists,
with the result that the gathering dispersed in a more peaceable
frame of mind than had been expected.[1] It was, no doubt,
less with the object of defending the Protector against movements of this kind, which might properly be dealt with by the
regular forces, than to preserve him against a renewal of assas-
sination-plots such as that with which Halsall and Talbot had
been charged, that a new lifeguard, composed of
picked and highly paid men who had served with
credit in the army, and no less than 160 strong, was
instituted as a security for his person.[2]

Feb. 20.
A new life-
guard.

With Lawson's resignation all chance of a successful issue
to Sexby's schemes came to an end for the present.[3]
It was, perhaps, a tardy conviction that Sexby was no
better than a braggart that induced Fuensaldaña

Sexby's
chance of
success at an
end.

---

[1] Thurloe to H. Cromwell, March 18, *Thurloe*, iv. 629. The officers
sent to liberate Harrison reached Carisbrooke on the 20th ; they must
therefore have left London about the 17th or 18th, soon after this affair took
place, thus justifying the suspicion that it had something to do with the
postponement of a decision in the Council on Harrison's liberation. Rich
must have been freed—though we have no statement to that effect—as
he was re-imprisoned in August. Carew and Courtney were still in
confinement in October.

[2] Council Order Book, *Interr.* I, 76, p. 556.

[3] Dyer, Sexby's servant, when examined on Feb. 27, 1658 (*Thurloe*,
vi. 829), said that 800*l.* had been given to Sexby in Spain ; whilst
Thurloe, on April 15, 1656, mentions that precise sum as having come
into his hands (*ib.* iv. 698). In another examination Dyer (*ib.* vi. 832)
speaks of two sheepskins full of pistoles being sent over by Richard
Overton. If so, it looks as if Overton was the person who betrayed
Sexby's plans to the Government. It is known that on Sept. 6, 1654
(*ib.* ii. 590), he offered his services to Thurloe, and he appears on
Thurloe's list of payments out of the secret service money as having
already received 20*l.* for his services on Dec. 13, 1653. *S. P. Dom.* xcv.
90, xcviii. Dyer in his information confuses the two Overtons, and
generally mixes up his dates. .

to seek a more direct understanding with Charles. Before the

April $\frac{2}{12}$.
A treaty
between
Charles and
Spain.

end of March Charles visited Brussels in strict incognito, and on April 2 a treaty was signed between his representatives and those of the King of Spain. By it Philip engaged to lend 6,000 soldiers to the Stuart prince as the nucleus of a larger army of Royalists.[1] The sole condition was that a port of disembarkation should be secured in England. Subsequently, after Charles had by this means recovered his throne, he was to assist Philip to regain Portugal. On the burning question of the West Indies, Charles was to retain all that his father had held at the time of the Treaty of 1630, that is to say, Barbados, St. Kitts and Nevis. He was, however, not merely to abandon territory acquired since that date—in other words, Antigua, Montserrat, and Jamaica—but was to engage never to allow his subjects to make any fresh settlement either in the islands or on the mainland—a stipulation which is mainly interesting as showing the limits of Spanish

April $\frac{3}{13}$.
A separate
article on
religion.

concession. In a separate article, added on the following day, Charles engaged to execute the Irish treaty to which Ormond had consented in 1646,[2] and to suspend the penal laws against the Catholics in all parts of his dominions, as well as to do everything in his power to bring about their total repeal.[3] Though the whole treaty was intended to be veiled in profound secrecy, it was well known to the Protector before six weeks were out.[4]

Neither at Brussels nor at Madrid did Spanish statesmen lay much stress on this agreement. Without Lawson's aid

The
Spaniards
not enthu-
siastic on
Charles's
behalf.

there was no chance of obtaining the services of any part of the English fleet, and unless the command of the Channel could be secured it was useless to think of sending a Spanish force into England.

---

[1] Spain was to provide 4,000 foot and 2,000 horse, *Cal. Clarendon State Papers*, iii. 110, 136.

[2] *Great Civil War*, iii. 55.

[3] Abreu y Bertolano, *Colleccion de los Tratados de Paz . . . de España*, viii. 305.

[4] Bordeaux to Brienne, May $\frac{12}{22}$, *French Transcripts, R.O.*

When Philip ratified the treaty, he did so only on the ground that it might be useful to him at some future time, whilst it bound him to nothing for the present. Charles's request to be allowed to take up his abode in the Low Countries was granted with extreme reluctance. After the signature of the treaty, however, it was difficult to refuse his reiterated demand, and he was permitted to take up his quarters at Bruges, where for some time he spun out an idle existence with the help of a pension accorded to him by the Spanish Government.[1]

Charles at Bruges.

Now that Charles was brought into so close a connection with the enemy it was but natural that Oliver should seize with avidity on any opportunity of discrediting him in the eyes of Englishmen. Such a chance was at this time thrown in his way. In 1648, one Lucy Walter, the daughter of a Welsh gentleman, was living at The Hague as the mistress of Colonel Robert Sidney. When Charles returned from his expedition to the Thames, Sidney passed her on to his sovereign, whose infatuation went so far as to induce him to acknowledge as his own a son—the future Duke of Monmouth —to whom she gave birth seven months after he landed in Holland. So openly, indeed, did he display his affection that even his sister, the Princess of Orange, referred some years later to Lucy as his wife. When, however, Charles came back in 1651 from his long absence in Scotland, and found her again about to become a mother, he permanently discarded her. In June 1656, after various discreditable adventures, she made her way to London, this time in company with Thomas Howard, a Gentleman of the Horse to the Princess of Orange. Living at a great expense, with no avowable source of income, she became an object of suspicion to the guardians of order. Being lodged in the Tower, she was found in possession of a warrant from Charles for a pension of 5,000 livres, and she openly boasted that her boy was the son

Career of Lucy Walter.

June. Her arrival in England.

---

[1] Cardenas to Philip IV., March $\frac{15}{25}$; the Archduke Leopold to Philip IV., $\frac{\text{March } 29}{\text{April } 8}$; Committee of the Council of State, $\frac{\text{April } 27}{\text{May } 7}$; Cardenas to Philip IV., July $\frac{19}{29}$, *Guizot*, ii. 562–72.

of the King.[1] On July 1 the Council ordered that she should

July 1.
Ordered
back to
Flanders.

be sent back to Flanders.[2] The courtly *Mercurius Politicus* printed Charles's warrant, and then proceeded to draw an inference :—"Those that hanker

Remarks of
Mercurius
Politicus.

after him may see they are furnished already with an heir apparent, and what a pious, charitable prince
they have for their master, and how well he disposeth of the collections and contributions which they make for him here towards the maintenance of his concubines and royal issue. "[3]

For immediate purposes, however, the enemy was not Charles, but Spain. On March 28 the fleet, which had long

March 28.
Sailing of
the fleet.

been preparing in the Channel ports, at last sailed from Torbay.[4] Its delay, caused either by internal dis-
sensions or by contrary winds, enabled two galleons and two smaller vessels from the belated Plate Fleet of the last season to reach Cadiz unmolested,[5] though their consorts had been wrecked in the Indies. When Blake and Montague

April 20.
It arrives in
Cadiz Bay.

reached Cadiz Bay, they found that the Spanish ships of war had taken refuge in the narrow and tortuous
Carraca channel,[6] at the entrance of which had been placed vessels ready to be sunk on the approach of an enemy, and that the entrances to the harbour itself had been strongly fortified since Cecil's appearance in 1625, rendering an attack hazardous in the extreme. An attempt on Gibraltar was next thought of, but Montague declared that the enterprise would be hopeless without at least 4,000 soldiers to blockade the rock on the land side, holding that seamen were 'not for land service, unless it be a sudden plunder.'[7] For some weeks, there-

---

[1] The evidence is collected in Steinman's *Althorp Memoirs*, 77–92.

[2] Council Order Book, *Interr.* I, 77, p. 218. She would be transported under the clause of the Instructions to the Major-Generals authorising them to send abroad persons without ostensible means of subsistence.

[3] *Merc. Pol.*, E, 494, 13.

[4] Weale's Journal, *Sloane MSS.* 1431, fol. 43b.

[5] *Merc. Pol.*, E, 493, 8, 13.

[6] See map prefixed to *Hist. of Engl.*, 1603–1642, vol. vi.

[7] Montague to Thurloe, Apr. 20–May 29, *Thurloe*, v. 67 ; Weale's

fore, the fleet continued cruising off Cadiz, occasionally exchanging shots with galleys creeping out when the sea was calm,

May 20.
The gene-
rals sail for
Lisbon.

but it neither suffered nor inflicted damage worthy
of mention. On May 20, leaving sixteen frigates to
keep up the blockade, the generals, with the more
powerful ships, sailed for Lisbon.[1]

The presence of the fleet in Portuguese waters was required
to compel the reluctant King to ratify the treaty negotiated

The
Portuguese
treaty still
unratified.

with Peneguiaõ in 1654.[2] The main objection taken
by John IV. was to the article conceding to English
merchants and seamen the free exercise of worship in
their ships and houses.[3] An article which had been repelled
at Madrid was not likely to be favourably regarded in Portugal.

Determined to have his way, the Protector despatched
Philip Meadowe to Lisbon to demand that the treaty should be

March 11.
Meadowe's
mission to
Portugal.

ratified without the alteration of a syllable.[4] Meadowe
had some acquaintance with the foreign policy of the
Government, having for some time discharged the
duties of Latin secretary, from which Milton had been incapa-
citated by his blindness, and he might therefore be trusted to
carry out his instructions with dexterity. His first interview

The King's
reluctance
to give way.

with the King was, from his own point of view, un-
satisfactory. "I am King," said John, "of Portugal,
not of the Church."[5] A few days later an intimation

Journal, *Sloane MSS.* 1431, foll. 44-45. It is probable that the Protector had suggested an attempt on Gibraltar before the expedition sailed.
In a letter of April 28 (*Carlyle*, Letter CCIX.) he took up the subject,
but so far as we can gather from Montague's letter this did not reach the
fleet till after the question had been discussed.

[1] Montague to Thurloe, Apr. 20–May 29, *Thurloe*, v. 67.

[2] See vol. iii. 81.

[3] Pile to Ross, $\frac{\text{Feb. 29}}{\text{March 10}}$, *S. P. Dom.* cxxiv. 110. The statement contained in this letter is confirmed by the course of the subsequent negotia-
tions.

[4] Nieupoort to the States General, March $\frac{7}{17}$, *Thurloe*, iv. 587.

[5] Giavarina to the Doge, May $\frac{2}{12}$, *Venetian Transcripts*, R.O. The
Venetian fancied that the treaty demanded a public church for Englishmen
in Lisbon, which was not the case.

that the fleet, then on its way to Cadiz, might look in at Lisbon
with the kindliest intentions was not without effect, and the
King was ultimately induced to make what he probably regarded

as a considerable concession.   He would consent to
grant the religious liberty demanded, if only the
article were approved of by the Pope ;[1] unless, indeed, the Protector would revert to the Treaty of 1641, giving
liberty to Englishmen only so long as they gave no scandal.

When the Protector, on May 3, heard of this offer, he
treated the proposed reference to the Pope as an in-
sult to himself,[2] and ordered Blake and Montague to
leave Cadiz and sail for Lisbon, where a homeward-
bound fleet from Brazil was expected shortly to arrive.[3]
It was this order which brought about the relinquish-
ment of the station off Cadiz by the larger portion of the ships
under the command of the English generals.   At the same time
Meadowe was ordered to obtain ratification within five days of
the reception of these new instructions or to come away.

A few days before this despatch was sent away an event
occurred which, if the English diplomatist had been less public-
spirited than he was, might easily have served to
embitter the relations between the two countries.
As Meadowe was returning from an audience he was
wounded in the hand by a shot from an arquebus.
The King, in his anxiety to shield himself from English
vengeance, did his utmost, or appeared to do his utmost, to discover the criminal ; but though it was a matter of common belief
in Lisbon that the shot was fired either by Peneguiaõ himself or
by his orders, with the intention of avenging his brother,[4] no
arrests were made.[5]   It is probable, indeed, that the Protector's

Side notes:
April 21. A useless concession.

May 3. The Protector hears of it, and

May 5. orders the fleet to sail for Lisbon.

May 1. An attempt to assassinate Meadowe.

---

[1] Meadowe to Blake and Montague, May $\frac{3}{13}$, *Thurloe*, iv. 759.

[2] Bordeaux to Brienne, May $\frac{12}{22}$, *French Transcripts*, R.O.

[3] Thurloe to Montague, May 6, Carte's *Orig. Letters*, ii. 106.

[4] See vol. iii. 80.

[5] John IV. to the Protector, May $\frac{16}{26}$; Montague to Thurloe, June 17,
Thurloe, v. 28, 124 ; Giavarina to the Doge, July $\frac{4}{14}$, *Venetian Transcripts*, R.O.

demands had so irritated public opinion in the country [1] that no other result was to be expected. All the more was King John desirous of showing personal courtesy to the wounded man, even going so far as to send no fewer than ten of the best physicians and ten of the best surgeons in Portugal to attend him when his wound was dressed.[2] In spite, however, of this multitude of advisers, Meadowe's wound proved not to be dangerous, and though, when the five days to which his negotiation was limited were expired the King had shown no signs of yielding, the

May 31. Ratifications exchanged.

envoy was able to announce on May 31 that the ratifications had been at last exchanged.[3] Praiseworthy as was the conduct of Meadowe in refusing to aggravate the situation on account of his personal grievance, it cannot be said that his diplomatic success was the consequence of his own efforts. His most powerful argument was the approach of the fleet, which was off Cape Espichel on the 27th, fully prepared to cope with the expected convoy from Brazil.

The differences of opinion between the two admirals were becoming a matter of public notoriety in London ;[4] and causes

The differences of opinion between Blake and Montague.

for misunderstanding were not wanting on this occasion. Montague, with the fiery zeal of a landsman, was burning for the fray, and would have been glad to see Meadowe disavowed on the grounds of the expiration of the five days before the King yielded, and of the failure to punish the authors of the attempted assassination. Blake prudently supported Meadowe, as having effected the

---

[1] Bordeaux remarks that France could not support the Protector's demand for religious liberty 'dans un pays dont les loix interdisent la diversité de religions, où le clergé a grand pouvoir, et le Roy ne jouit que d'une autorité précaire.' Bordeaux to Brienne, June $\frac{2}{12}$, *French Transcripts, R.O.*

[2] Giavarina to the Doge, July $\frac{18}{28}$, *Venetian Transcripts, R.O.* ; *The Public Intelligencer*, E, 494, 11.

[3] Meadowe to Blake and Montague, May 31, *Thurloe*, v. 79.

[4] See p. 229, note 1. Compare Giavarina to the Doge, June $\frac{20}{30}$, *Venetian Transcripts, R.O.*

object of his negotiation in substance ; [1] and Blake's view was shared by the Protector, who was not the man to take excep-

Blake and Meadowe supported by the Protector.

tion to mere points of form. Meadowe was, more-over, able to advance a potent argument in favour of his views by shipping off to England the 50,000*l.*[2]

50,000*l.* sent home.

which the King had engaged to pay to the English merchants in compensation for losses suffered by them during Rupert's visit in 1649,[3] but which now found its way, at least for a time, into the Protector's Treasury.[4] After this there was no longer any reason to detain the fleet in Portuguese

June 28. The fleet returns to Cadiz Bay.

waters, and on June 28 the generals returned to Cadiz Bay,[5] whence they sent out squadrons from time to time to harass what little of Spanish commerce was in existence, whilst they trusted to Providence to send, sooner or later, a Plate Fleet within their reach.

The seizure of the Plate Fleet, if it were ever realised, would do much to fill the empty treasury of the Government.

Spanish privateers.

English merchants might be pardoned for looking nearer home, where the mariners of Ostend and Dunkirk, as well as those of the Biscay ports, were now actively employed in matching their quick-sailing privateers against the mercantile navy of England. Having little trade of their own to protect, these hornets of the sea were freed from the necessity of guarding their own waters, and it would go hard with them if they did not find a lucrative occupation in the capture of a fair number of the 3,000 English merchantmen, who were, on an average, constantly exposed to danger.[6] In

---

[1] Meadowe to Thurloe, June 16 ; Montague to Thurloe, June 17, *Thurloe*, v. 123, 124.

[2] *Ib.* v. 286. This was reckoned as the value of the coin sent home. It ultimately produced only 48,058*l. Receipt Books of the Exchequer*, Aug., Sept. 12, 16, 20 ; Council Order Book, *Interr.* I, 77, p. 601.

[3] See vol. iii. 81.

[4] The division of the money among the merchants was to be settled by arbitration. I have not yet been able to discover when this took place.

[5] Montague to Thurloe, June 30, *Thurloe*, v. 170.

[6] Sagredo to the Doge, Nov. $\frac{2}{12}$, 1655, *Venetian Transcripts, R.O.*

February some of these privateers had anticipated the issue

Feb.
Their
activity
in the
Channel. of Spanish commissions, and by the middle of March forty sail, leaving the ports of Dunkirk and Ostend, had secured some thirty prizes in the Channel and the North Sea.[1]   The Newcastle colliers, especially, fell an easy prey, and the price of coals began, in

March–
June
Losses of
English
shipping. consequence, to rise in London.[2]   In the Channel matters were quite as bad.   Even when merchant-men were sailing under convoy it was easy for a nimble frigate to slip in amongst them and carry off

its prey.   The Dunkirkers were not only built for speed, but they were kept scrupulously clean, and frequently returned to port to be re-tallowed, whereas English men-of-war were often allowed to stream with seaweed.   The complaints of those who lost their goods or their kinsmen were loudly raised, and the blame would naturally be thrown on the Government which had entered on a war for which there was no national demand.[3]

The question of the possession of Dunkirk thus passed from the region of diplomatic possibility to that of urgent

Question
of the pos-
session of
Dunkirk
revived. political necessity.   The Protector, at least, had made up his mind that the offending port must be transferred to his own guardianship, and as Mazarin had offered to comply with his wishes in 1654, he

can hardly have expected much difficulty in attaining his object ; and he therefore found great cause for dissatisfaction when Bordeaux, returning from his leave of absence, had but

March 29
April 8 .
Bordeaux's
audience. little to say, at his first audience on March 29, about that closer alliance for military purposes which was so much in the Protector's mind, especially now that

the much-talked-of conjunction with Sweden had proved elusive.   Another source of dissatisfaction with France was the knowledge that, just as the Protector had made up his

[1] Intelligence from Dunkirk, March 11, *S. P. Dom.* cxxv. 27 ; Cardenas to Philip IV., March $\frac{15}{25}$, *Guizot*, ii. 562.

[2] Giavarina to the Doge, March $\frac{14}{24}$, *Venetian Transcripts, R.O.*

[3] The documents amongst the State Papers are too numerous to be quoted separately.

mind to offer 20,000*l.* to support the resistance of the Swiss

End of
the Swiss
troubles.

Protestant cantons to the claim of Catholic Schwytz to persecute its own Protestants,[1] a peace had been concluded under French mediation in which each canton was acknowledged to have the right of dealing as it pleased with its subjects.[2] The result was none the less disliked at Whitehall because it was a counterpart to the appeal by Charles X. to the Treaty of Osnabrück.

Oliver was the more anxious because the rumours of a mediation on the part of the Pope between France and Spain

Rumours of
a mediation
of the Pope
between
France and
Spain.

had lately been acquiring consistency. When, therefore, Bordeaux's silence confirmed the impression that the friendship with France was less solid than he had hoped, Oliver resolved to despatch a special ambassador to the French Court to discover from Mazarin in person what his intentions really were.[3] For this purpose he selected Sir William Lockhart, a Scot who, after an adventurous

Lockhart
named am-
bassador to
France.

His career.

career, in the course of which he had served as a soldier in the armies of France and of the United Provinces, had returned home to fight under the standard of his own country in the Civil War. He was knighted by Charles I. after his surrender at Newark, and subsequently fought under Hamilton at Preston ; but, considering himself slighted by Argyle, he threw up his commission before the battle of Dunbar, and, perhaps for that reason, saw his offer of service refused by Charles on the march to Worcester. In his anger he transferred his services to the English Parliament, and in May 1652 took his seat at Edinburgh as a member of the Commission for the Execution of Justice. In 1653 he represented Scotland in the Nominated Parliament, and in the first Protectorate Parliament he sat for his native

---

[1] See *supra*, p. 209.

[2] Pell's correspondence (Vaughan's *Protectorate*, i. 282–429) gives the salient features of the struggle.

[3] Bordeaux to Brienne, $\frac{\text{March 31}}{\text{April 10}}$, *Guizot*, ii. 582 ; Bordeaux to Mazarin, $\frac{\text{March 31}}{\text{April 10}}$, *French Transcripts*, *R.O.* Only a portion of the latter is printed by *Guizot*, ii. 584.

county of Lanark. In July 1654, before that Parliament was chosen, he sealed his devotion to the Protector by marrying his widowed niece, Robina Sewster.

All that Mazarin and Bordeaux could do to avert this unwelcome mission was attempted in vain. Mazarin protested

Mazarin tries to avert Lockhart's mission.

that the life of any representative of the Protector would be in danger from the English Royalists.[1] All that he effected was a resolution to provide Lockhart with a guard of twelve soldiers, disguised as his domestic servants, besides a certain number of officers, who would

Mazarin's peace projects.

appear as the gentlemen of his chamber.[2] Mazarin had, indeed, more cause to deprecate any step which might bind him to an active alliance with England than Oliver was aware of, even though a rumour that the French had proposed to open a peace conference at Savona had reached his ears.[3] Such a frame of mind, once known to the Spanish ministers, could not fail to produce overtures on their part, now that they had to dread the fleets of England as well as the armies of France. Accordingly, in the course of

Feb. 19/29. Mission of Bonifaz.

February the Archduke Leopold had despatched a Spaniard named Gaspar Bonifaz to Madrid to adjure Philip to come to terms with France, at the same time emphasising his request by tendering his own resignation of the viceroyalty, on the plea that he could no longer hope to

Feb. 14/24. Bonifaz assured of the concurrence of France.

resist the enemy with credit. Bonifaz was directed to pass through Paris in order to obtain, if possible, the consent of Mazarin to the opening of a negotiation. Mazarin, who wished for nothing better than a peace which would secure her conquests to France, was highly delighted. Even Louis XIV. was brought on the scene. "Tell the King of Spain," he said, "that I desire his friendship more than anything else. No," he corrected himself, "there is something I desire still more, and it is that we should make peace and put our two crowns into a condition to defend

---

[1] Mazarin to Bordeaux, Apr. 16/26, *Guizot*, ii. 587.

[2] Schlezer to Jena [?], *Urkunden und Aktenstücke*, vii. 749.

[3] Intercepted letter from Boreel, Jan. 4/14, *Thurloe*, iv. 386.

religion, which is dangerously threatened." Such words betrayed the Frenchman's true feeling in the face of that Protestant alliance which was never long absent from the Protector's mind. Before the end of March Bonifaz brought back from Madrid the reply that Philip was as anxious for peace as Louis.[1]

At his first audience, on May 8, Lockhart was received with every show of courtesy by the King, in the presence of the
May $\frac{8}{18}$.
Lockhart's
first
audience. Cardinal,[2] but was unable to obtain an interview with the latter till he met him at Compiègne on the 19th. In the conversation which ensued the French
May $\frac{19}{29}$.
Mazarin
proposes an
attack on
Mardyk. minister suggested the smaller fort of Mardyk as the place to be attacked and surrendered to England after its capture, but put certain questions which, as they must necessarily be referred to England, would take some time to answer.[3] Before the reply could arrive Mazarin casually mentioned that he could not be ready
May 23.
June 2.
A date fixed
for co-
operation. to commence operations before July 20.[4] It is obvious that the date was fixed, not on account of military exigencies, but because Lionne, the ablest of the French diplomatists, was to start on May 31
May 31.
June 10.
Lionne
starts for
Madrid. for Madrid to treat for peace, and that time must be afforded for knowing whether his mission proved a success or a failure.[5] A discussion on such points as whether France should or should not pay the English troops
June.
State of the
negotiation. to be used in the siege kept the ball rolling till June 20.[6] By that time Mazarin knew that the negotiation at Madrid was less promising than he had hoped, as, whilst Lionne considered the restoration of any

---

[1] Valfrey, *Hugues de Lionne, ses ambassades en Espagne et Allemagne,* 1–8.

[2] Letter to Bampfield, May $\frac{10}{20}$, *Thurloe,* v. 8.

[3] Lockhart to Thurloe, May $\frac{19}{29}$, *ib.* v. 41. Lockhart's chief despatch of this date is missing; but compare the despatch of $\frac{\text{May 23}}{\text{June 2}}$, *ib.* v. 52.

[4] Misprinted June in *ib.* v. 53.   [5] *Valfrey,* 13.

[6] Lockhart to Thurloe, June $\frac{20}{30}$, *Thurloe,* v. 142.

one of the fortified places secured by France as a favour to Spain, Don Luis de Haro considered it to be a favour to France if she were allowed to keep a single one of the fortresses she had conquered.[1] Yet for all that Mazarin was not without hope of a better answer. The French army was laying siege to Valenciennes, and if, as there seemed every probability, the town fell into its hands, Spain might possibly be brought to acknowledge her helplessness. The siege also enabled him to delay a final answer to Lockhart, as it was obvious that the army was insufficient to master Valenciennes and a Flemish

July 5/15.
Valenciennes relieved.

port at the same time.[2] The day, however, arrived when this excuse ceased to be available. On July 5 the French besieging army was broken up by

Aug. 8/18.
Condé taken.

the Spaniards, who followed up their success by the capture of Condé on August 8.

The failure to take Valenciennes affected both negotiations. Mazarin assured Lockhart, with little regard for truth, that

July 12/22.
An interview with Mazarin.

Lionne had been sent to Madrid merely to satisfy the Pope and the clergy, and then, with more convenient truthfulness, unrolled the exorbitant demands

of Spain before the Englishman's ears as an argument to show that France was driven to carry on the war at all costs. He did not mention, indeed, that Lionne had not yet been recalled, but he urged a demand for the loan of 4,000 English soldiers, to be employed, not in the siege of Dunkirk or Mardyk, but in

July 29.
Aug. 8.
Dunkirk to be besieged in the next spring.

that of some inland place.[3] A fortnight later, when he was pressed to join in an attack on Dunkirk, with the object of placing it after its surrender in English occupation, he for some time positively refused to

agree. To besiege Dunkirk, he said, would enable the Spaniards to gain some other fortress, and to deliver up Dunkirk to his Highness, whilst this other place was, at the same time, lost to France, would render him so odious to the whole country that

---

[1] *Valfrey*, 14–22.
[2] Lockhart to Thurloe, $\frac{\text{June 27, 30}}{\text{July 7, 10}}$, July $\frac{4}{14}$, *Thurloe*, v. 164, 172.
[3] Lockhart to Thurloe, July $\frac{16}{26}$, *ib.* v. 217.

he durst not venture upon so dangerous a policy. Yet before the interview was at an end the Cardinal so far yielded as to engage to join in an attack on Dunkirk, if only the execution of the plan could be deferred to the following spring.[1] Evidently what he was really aiming at was to postpone any irrevocable engagement with England till he was absolutely certain of Lionne's failure. With this answer the Protector was obliged to be content.

At the time when this communication was made Lionne's mission was by no means at an end. Early in September Don

Sept. $\frac{8}{18}$.
Breach of
the nego-
tiations.

Luis de Haro gave way so far as to abandon all claim to the lost territories of Spain. On one point only was he obdurate. Condé must be restored, not only to his property in France, but to those governments and other offices which had gone far to enable him to dictate terms to the Crown. Philip, in point of fact, had engaged to Condé in 1650 to make no peace with France without safe-guarding these claims, and he was now ready to plunge his country once more into a hopeless war, rather than break his word. On this point of honour the long negotiation reached its term.[2]

Mazarin's failure was Oliver's opportunity. In the war before her France stood in need of an ally, and that ally could

Mazarin
turns to the
English
alliance.

be no other than England. As the friendship of England could only be secured by the delivery of Dunkirk, the Cardinal had no longer a choice. On

Nov. $\frac{8}{18}$.
An agree-
ment about
Dunkirk.

November 8 he and Lockhart came to an agreement. "A levy of 3,000 men," wrote the ambassador to Thurloe, "is expected on your part. The mainte-nance of the whole land forces and all the charges of the land seized is to be theirs, and whether Dunkirk or Gravelines shall be begun at is referred to Marshal Turenne. The first of them that shall be taken is to be put into your hands ; if Gravelines, it's to be put into your hands as a pledge for

[1] Lockhart to Thurloe, $\frac{\text{July } 29}{\text{Aug. } 8}$, *Thurloe*, v. 252.

[2] *Valfrey*, 33-63.

Dunkirk; if Dunkirk first, it's to be put into your hands absolutely, and the Protector is to dispose of the 3,000 men as he shall judge fit." [1]

In coming to this decision, the French Government knew perfectly well that though the Protector was driven to wrest Dunkirk from Spain on account of the ravages of the privateers which issued from that port, it was jealousy of France which determined his resolution to bring it under his own rule, as it was doubtless jealousy of France which had made him cling to the hope of a Spanish alliance up to the autumn of 1654. [2] The future he believed himself able to confide to the strength of the English fleet and army. It is most unlikely that he was unaware that he could not hold the place without irritating a nation which, strong already, was about to grow stronger by his aid. Yet he seems hardly to have reckoned on the anger which his general policy raised beyond the Channel. "All persons here," Lockhart had written a few days before the completion of his task, "that pretend to be good Catholics express a passionate zeal for an accommodation between France and Spain upon any terms. The clergy press the necessity of it upon their auditories at all occasions." [3] If the Protector could have been informed of the language used by Louis himself to Bonifaz earlier in the year, [4] he would have had matter to give him pause. To claim to be the champion of the Protestant interest in Europe, and in so doing to hold lightly

The Protector jealous of France.

Opposition of the French clergy.

---

[1] Lockhart to Thurloe, Nov. $\frac{8}{18}$, *Thurloe*, v. 574.

[2] " M. le Protecteur ayant au temps du Parlement le plus contribué à la prise du secours de Dunkerque sur ce fondement que, si tous les portz de costé tomboient entre nos mains, l'Angleterre ne joueroit point de la liberté de commerce dans la Manche sans nostre consentement." Bordeaux to Brienne, May $\frac{12}{22}$, *French Transcripts, R.O.* This is, I believe, the only authority for supposing that Cromwell played a leading part in sending Blake to seize the French relieving ships. The account is, however, intrinsically probable, and, if true, shows how consistent Cromwell was in his dealings about Dunkirk.

[3] Lockhart to Thurloe, $\frac{\text{Oct. 29}}{\text{Nov. 8}}$, *Thurloe*, v. 532.

[4] See *supra*, p. 243.

the rights of kings and rulers over their subjects in matters of religion, was the very policy to provoke such a youth as Louis, who had no mind to see his own Protestant subjects supported against him by a foreign Power, and was perfectly aware that Oliver, in the course of the recent negotiations, had refused to renounce his assumed right to take up the cause of the Huguenots. The seeds, which were ultimately to come to an evil fruitage in the Revocation of the Edict of Nantes, were being unwittingly sown by the self-constituted Protector of the Protestant world.

CHAPTER XLIX

PARLIAMENTARY ELECTIONS

WHATEVER might be said, from a political point of view, of the Protector's gigantic schemes of foreign and domestic policy,

1656.
Nov.-Dec.
Insuffi-
ciency of
the means
assigned to
the Major-
Generals.

there could be but one opinion as to the inadequacy of his financial resources to meet their cost. Even the Major-Generals had not been many days at work before they discovered that the product of the decimation would be insufficient to meet the expenses of the militia under their orders, a discovery which led to the demand that the limit of property below which there was to be

They ask
that the
limit may
be lowered.

no taxation should be considerably lowered. As might be expected, there was considerable difference of opinion as to the new limit, but the greater number—so far as their reports have reached us—asked that the tax might fall upon income derived from landed property down to 50*l.* a year, and upon personal property valued at 500*l.*, or even at 300*l.*[1] Whalley, writing from Nottingham, stood alone in objecting to a change, on the ground that 'it would discontent many, and ruinate some in this country.' He was, moreover, persuaded that the change would 'bring very little into the treasury, the middling sort of men being almost all for the Parliament or neuters.' It is

The pro-
posal re-
jected.

possible that this last objection may have been of purely local concernment, but, at all events, when the Council early in January took the question into considera-

---

[1] Their reports, running from Nov. 1656 to Jan. 1657, are printed in *Thurloe*, iv. 215–391 *passim*.

tion, it came to the resolution that no alteration should be made.[1]

The determination left the burden on the shoulders of the Major-Generals unlightened. When January drew to an end they were expected to find six months' pay for troops levied in the preceding June, and cast about in vain for the means *Complaints* of fulfilling their obligations. Goffe, writing on *of the diffi-* February 2, was the first to cry out. "The truth *culty of* *paying the* is," he wrote, "the money raised in this association *militia* *troops.* will not . . . amount to above three months' pay; for though I am not prepared to send an exact account, yet I do clearly find that Sussex will not amount to above 1,500*l.* per annum, Hampshire 1,000*l.* per annum, and Berks will, I hope, rise to 1,000*l.* per annum, which for the two first counties is but just half as much as will pay the troops."[2] Butler again wrote that he needed 1,080*l.* for Northampton-shire alone, whereas the decimations in that county produced no more than 800*l.* in the half year.[3] The reports from poorer districts were not likely to be even so favourable as these. A proposal of Goffe's that all the money collected should be paid into a common treasury having been set aside,[4] the *A reduc-* Council resolved on February 27 to reduce the *tion in the* number of the men in each troop in eleven counties *number of* *men* from 100 to 80. It was not, however, till March 20 *ordered.* that this recommendation was accepted by the Pro-tector.[5] About three weeks later, on April 11, the Council, feeling no doubt that the eleven counties selected were better

[1] Desborough to Thurloe, January 12 ; Worsley to Thurloe, January 24 ; *Thurloe,* iv. 413, 449.

[2] Goffe to Thurloe, Feb. 2, *ib.* iv. 497.

[3] Butler to Thurloe, Feb. 7, *ib.* iv. 511.

[4] Goffe to Thurloe, Feb. 2, *ib.* iv. 497.

[5] Council Order Book, *Interr.* I, 76, p. 565. The counties were Oxford, Berks, Bucks, Herts, Hants, Sussex, Kent, Cambridge, Suffolk, Norfolk and Rutland ; that is to say, all Fleetwood's district except Essex, the whole of Goffe's, and the whole of Kelsey's except Surrey, Rutland being relieved out of Butler's. Essex and Surrey may have been omitted as rich enough to pay the full amount.

able to bear the burden than many others, determined, this time with the immediate approbation of the Protector, to make the reduction universal. The result was a diminution of expenditure from 80,067*l.* to 67,010*l.*[1]

The reduction, however, had no retrospective effect, and the delay of payment of any kind was certain to give rise to dissatisfaction. When on March 19 Goffe reduced the troops in Sussex,[2] paying them in full for the first half year, he was met with a demand for payment for another quarter as well. He was told by the officer in command that 'he could not hire servants at such a rate, to hire them for a year and put them off at three quarters' end with half a year's pay.' So angry were the soldiers that they at first refused to touch the money, crying out that they would have all or none. It was only on Goffe's representation that the third quarter was not yet at an end that they quieted down. In his letter to Thurloe Goffe acknowledged that their grumbling was not unreasonable, as many of them had spent more than they demanded 'in furnishing themselves with horse and arms.'[3] So compassionate was Berry at Worcester that he paid the men dismissed as though they had been under arms for a whole year, asking that, if he had done wrong, the overplus might be deducted from his own salary.[4]

March 19. Goffe reduces the Sussex troops.

April 7. Berry at Worcester.

To avoid for the future any risk of bringing the Major-Generals into personal collision with their militia, the responsibility for the payment of the men was on April 11 transferred from them to the Army Committee of the Council which had hitherto been employed in making arrangements for the financial needs of the regular

Financial arrangements left to the Army Committee.

[1] Council Order Book, *Interr.* I, 76, p. 861. Mrs. Everett Green, in the *Calendar* for 1655–56, has made an unfortunate slip in speaking of the old establishment beginning on June 24, 1655, as if it was to begin in June 1656. *Cal.* pp. 263–372.

[2] This was the day before the Protector's assent was formally given.

[3] Goffe to Thurloe, March 22, *Thurloe,* iv. 642.

[4] Berry to Thurloe, April 26, *ib.* iv. 742.

forces.[1]   Whatever might be the result of the reduction effected
in the militia, the Government—so far as the general national
expenditure was concerned—had already reached the length of
its tether.   By the middle of May the Council was earnestly
directing its attention to the almost insoluble problem of
meeting, out of a strictly limited income, the expenditure required to carry out a spirited foreign policy.   In 1654 the
Protector had looked forward to the war with Spain as a lucrative enterprise.   In 1656 its cost was more evident than its
gains.   Jamaica had not hitherto shown itself a profitable acquisition, whilst the Plate fleet had not as yet been captured.

So far as it is possible to recover a trustworthy balance sheet
from a few imperfect and disconnected accounts, it may be
Dec. 1655.   gathered that at the close of 1655 the national finances
A deficit.   showed a deficit of somewhat more than 230,000*l.*,
though every care had been taken to economise in the home
government by lopping off expenses with a severe hand.[2]   It
might be found possible in the course of 1656 to make some
slight diminution in the expense of the navy, and to find some
relief in the results of the disbandment and plantation in Ireland.   Such favourable prospects were, however, more than
counterbalanced by the increasing load of debt, which there
was no visible means of lightening or even of maintaining at a
stationary level.[3]   Yet, in all this, no account was taken of the

---

[1] Council Order Book, *Interr.* I, 77, p. 41.

[2] See *Carte MSS.* lxxiv. fol. 7, 18 ; *Rawlinson MSS.* A, 195, fol. 241.

Expenditure				Revenue			
	£	s.	d.		£	s.	d.
Army	1,057,819	12	0	Assessments	919,478	4	0
Navy	768,538	8	3¾	Customs and Excise	700 000	0	0
Miscellaneous	124,220	15	10	Miscellaneous	101,000	0	0
Total	1,950,578	16	1¾		1,720,478	4	0

I am inclined to think that the miscellaneous expenditure is under-
estimated, but whether the miscellaneous revenue is also I cannot say.
At all events the deficit may have been greater and cannot have been less
than is shown above.

[3] The debt on the navy alone was estimated in August 1655 as
200,000*l.*, in addition to 38,000*l.* due for the freight of ships formerly
hired.   *Carte MSS.* lxxiv. fol. 29.

sums needed for the operations which the Protector was proposing to conduct against Dunkirk in co-operation with France, still less of those which would be required if the Protector's magnificent scheme of a war against the whole House of Austria in defence of the Protestant interest was to be reduced to practice. Whatever differences of opinion may be entertained as to the wisdom of Oliver's foreign policy, there can be no doubt that, in the spring of 1656, it threatened to land him in financial ruin.

Before the end of May it had become evident that the meddlesome proceedings of the Major-Generals combined with the pressure of taxation were giving strength to a demand, heard at least in London and its neighbourhood, for the assembly of another Parliament.[1] The Council having been unable to come to a conclusion on the financial difficulty, the Major-Generals were summoned to London to give advice on a subject which threatened to undermine the system of which they were the representatives most prominent in the eyes of the world.[2] So unusual a stir in the regions of government gave rise to the belief that important changes were at hand, and it is noteworthy that this belief took the form of a premature rumour that it had been decided to summon Parliament—not, as in the preceding year, that the Protector was about to change his title or assume the legislative power.[3]

*May.
A cry for a Parliament.*

Meeting of Councillors and Major-Generals.

Nor were the Protector's difficulties lightened by a demand, coming from a military quarter, that he would pass the command of the army to a soldier who would be able to attend

---

[1] Giavarina to the Doge, $\frac{\text{May 23}}{\text{June 2}}$, *Venetian Transcripts, R.O.* The Venetian Resident speaks of the discontent as raised solely by the burden of taxation, and describes the cry for a Parliament as universal. It is safe to add the discontent caused by the action of the Major-Generals, and equally unsafe to suppose that any foreign diplomatist could give evidence worth having on the state of feeling in the country districts.

[2] For this meeting of the Major-Generals see also Carte, *Original Letters*, ii. 109.

[3] Giavarina to the Doge, $\frac{\text{May 30}}{\text{June 9}}$, *Venetian Transcripts, R.O.*

exclusively to the needs of the soldiers. The position became

A demand for a new general. still more strained when the Protector, having agreed to give up the generalship provided that it might be filled by his son-in-law Fleetwood, was answered with a request that Lambert might rather be selected. That the appointment of Lambert would place the army in the hands of a man to whom Oliver's idealisms were the vainest of follies could be no secret, and it is no matter of surprise that the Protector refused his consent to what was practically a summons to abandon that part of his policy which lay nearest to his heart.[1]

It would be interesting to know who were the officers who stood by Lambert on this occasion, and still more to know

Opposition between Oliver and Lambert. whether, as there is reason to suspect, they were identical with those who now urged the calling of a Parliament which, whatever else it might do, was certain, if only for financial reasons, to look coldly on the Protector's more far-reaching designs of foreign policy. Though we are reduced to conjecture in this matter, it is not unlikely that the strong opposition of the Protector to the proposal for calling a Parliament was based on something more than a fear lest a new Parliament would take up the ground occupied by the last one, and would strive to establish its own supremacy on the ruins of the Instrument. However this may have been, the attitude of the Protector was one of uncompromising hostility to the very notion of summoning a Parliament, and an equally uncompromising advocacy of a scheme for raising additional taxation by executive authority alone. The only

The Protector's arguments for the extension of the decimation. question with him was what that scheme should be. Of three that were proposed—the doubling of the monthly assessment of 60,000l. ; a recurrence to the system of Privy Seal loans ; and the extension of the decimation to others than Royalists,[2] he unhesitatingly chose the last, which, as it did not touch anyone with an income derived from land under 100l. a year or in possession of

---

[1] Giavarina to the Doge, $\frac{May\ 30}{June\ 9}$, *Venetian Transcripts, R.O.*

[2] Giavarina to the Doge, June $\frac{13}{23}$, July $\frac{4}{14}$, *ib.*

personal property valued at less than 1,500*l.*, had, like the modern income-tax, the advantage, in the eye of a government, that it roused no opposition in that great majority whose circumstances were materially less easy than those of their more well-to-do neighbours.

That the course he now recommended was unconstitutional as well as illegal probably troubled the Protector little, as he was by this time inured to the habit of playing fast and loose with the Instrument whenever he considered that a necessity had arisen. Yet though he was under no obligation to summon Parliament before January 22, 1658, and though if he acted in accordance with his Council he had the right to levy without recurrence to Parliament any sum, however large, that he considered to be needed for the maintenance of 30,000 men and of a convenient number of ships for the guarding of the seas, he was not allowed to raise money in this fashion for the maintenance of 40,000, which was about the number on foot in the three countries, to say nothing of the garrison of Jamaica.

However trenchantly Oliver may have defended the position he had taken, he was not long in discovering that soldiers and Oliver consents to summon a Parliament. civilians were alike against him. Finding his plan generally condemned as impracticable, he gave way with a good grace and consented to the calling of a supplementary Parliament, as authorised by the Instrument— which, indeed, he ought to have summoned when war broke out not many months before.[1] It was not the least of the defects of that constitution that it provided no independent organ for the interpretation and enforcement of its directions. The consequence was that whilst the Protector and Council

---

[1] Article XXIII. ran thus :—" That the Lord Protector with the advice of the major part of the Council, shall at any other time than is before expressed, when the necessities of the State shall require it, summon Parliaments in manner before expressed, which shall not be adjourned, prorogued, or dissolved without their own consent during the first three months of their sitting ; and in case of future war with any foreign State a Parliament shall be forthwith summoned for their advice concerning the same."

assumed the right of compelling others to conform to it, they reserved to themselves the right of explaining its terms in their own fashion, or even of neglecting to fulfil its positive ·directions whenever they thought such a course desirable. The condition on which Oliver gave his consent to the meeting of Parliament, namely, that no member should be allowed to take his seat without a certificate from the Council,[1] was in itself an interpretation in his own favour of what was at the best an ambiguous clause of that Instrument, the express stipulations of which he flagrantly disregarded where he believed them to be in contravention with the national welfare.[2]

On June 26 it was publicly made known that the writs for electing a Parliament would shortly be sent out.[3] It soon

---

[1] Giavarina to the Doge, July $\frac{4}{14}$, *Venetian Transcripts, R.O.*

[2] The 14th and 15th Articles exclude from Parliament and from voting at elections, those who had participated in the war against Parliament, all persons who had taken part in the Irish Rebellion, and all Roman Catholics. The 16th Article declares all votes and elections made contrary or not according to these qualifications to be null and void. The 17th lays down the rule ' That the persons who shall be elected to serve in Parliament shall be such (and no other than such) as are persons of known integrity, fearing God, and of good conversation, and being of the age of 21 years.' When we come to the 21st Article we find that the Clerk of the Commonwealth in Chancery is ' for the next Parliament and the two succeeding triennial Parliaments,' to certify the returns to the Council, ' who shall . . . examine whether the persons so elected and returned be such as is agreeable to the qualifications, and not disabled to be elected.' The reference to the next Parliament and the two succeeding ones shows that the Instrument only provided for the action of Council in controlling the returns for the first three Parliaments out of the four during which Royalists were to be excluded. After that it is to be supposed that Parliament was to regain its own jurisdiction over elections. The only question arising in 1656 was whether the members ' disabled to be elected ' comprised those mentioned in the 17th Article as well as those in the 14th and 15th. On the one side it may be argued that both were disabled ; on the other hand that the words are put in connection with ' qualifications,' and that the word qualifications in the 16th Article appears only to refer to those already mentioned in the 14th and 15th. Of the interpretation subsequently placed on Article 17 I shall speak hereafter.

[3] Thurloe to H. Cromwell, July 1, *Thurloe*, v. 176.

became evident that the issues of 1654 were dead. The writs

June 26. Announcement that a new Parliament will be summoned.

when they appeared directed, as they had done two years before, that the principal electors should seal an indenture obliging their newly elected member not to derogate from the Government as established in a single person and a Parliament, without rousing the faintest opposition. Still less was there any thought of opposing the zealots of the nominated Parliament, whose influence was no longer to be feared. Two tendencies of political thought, each commendable in itself, now divided the field. On the one side were ranged what it was the fashion at Whitehall to style 'the honest party,' who desired to maintain the Protectorate, though they wished, for the most part, to establish it on a civilian or Parliamentary basis ; and on the other side a motley group whose views ranged from concealed Royalism at one extremity to the fanaticism of the Levellers and Fifth Monarchists at the other ; but which was strengthened and sustained by a desire to abate the influence of the army, and to substitute for it the control of Parliament over the executive.

So far as it is possible to gather from the scanty evidence that has reached us, the Protector—at least during this early

The Protector has no intention of interfering in the elections.

stage—had no intention of interfering with the elections, perhaps feeling himself secure in the exercise of the power of exclusion which he had claimed for himself and the Council.[1] On July 16, Haynes, writing from Norwich, the centre of the Fifth Monarchist

Haynes on the situation.

opinions not unmingled with a strong Royalist element, wrote almost despairingly of the situation. No declaration from the Government, he complained,

---

[1] ' Eletti scelti devono esser li membre dalle Communità, e poi approvati da sua Altezza e conseglio.' Giavarina to the Doge, July $\frac{4}{14}$, *Venetian Transcripts, R.O.* "All possible care is to be used that the qualifications in the Government be observed, and the recognition is to be first taken before they sit in the House." Thurloe to H. Cromwell, July 1, *Thurloe,* v. 176.

had accompanied the writs, an omission which was in his opinion the more disastrous 'in regard the newsbook lately proclaimed a free election; which,' he added, 'is made use of in discourse in the worst sense, and feared will be practised accordingly.' "Indeed," he concluded this part of his letter, "I am jealous we shall send you as bad as we dare choose; and, if there be any alteration of the choice, it will be for the worse . . . and if I might not be thought too impertinent, I would again offer to consideration that the militia troops might be paid, and so mustered before that time, as that which might be improved to a good advantage in this affair." [1]   It is to the credit of the Government that they refused to act on this suggestion. Whalley, on the other hand, was more hopeful. "The general temper of men's spirits," he wrote in defiance of grammar, "are to have a settlement. I trust in the Lord, we shall have a good Parliament." [2]

It is by no means unlikely that, if the Protector could have been assured that no opposition but that of argument was to be dreaded, the elections would have been as free from governmental interference in 1656 as they had been in 1654. This was, however, far from being the case. On June 26 Wildman

Wildman released.   had been released on bond for three months, ostensibly to attend to his business concerns. [3]   Yet within a week at the longest his signature was appended to a petition to Charles, [4] promoted by William Howard,

A petition to Charles II.   a younger son of Lord Howard of Escrick. [5]   Howard was himself an Anabaptist, and the demands which accompanied the petition were those likely to be put forward by a coalition of Anabaptists and Levellers. On the one hand complete religious liberty and the substitution for tithes of some new way of supporting the clergy were asked for,

---

[1] Haynes to Thurloe, July 16, *Thurloe*, v. 220.

[2] Whalley to Thurloe, July 21, *ib.* v. 234.

[3] Council Order Book, *Interr.* I, 77, p. 201.

[4] Charles's answer was dated July $\frac{4}{14}$, *Clarendon MSS.* lii. fol. 70.

[5] He succeeded to the title himself in 1678 and became notorious in the State trials at the end of Charles the Second's reign.

together with the relief of the gathered churches from payment thereto ; on the other hand the Long Parliament was to be restored, not as it stood at its dissolution in 1653, but as it stood in its two Houses before the disruption of 1642. The signatories were ready, as Howard declared, ' to redeem that liberty by arms and force which was treacherously stolen from them by deceit and fraud. ' [1] That Wildman carried the secret to the Protector there can be little doubt.

Wildman informs the Protector.

It is hardly likely that he would have been liberated on any other terms, and though, from this time forward, he posed at Bruges as a Royalist, his straightforwardness was suspected by Charles's more prudent ministers, and, what is more to the purpose, not only was he left at liberty after the expiration of his nine months' bail, but special orders were sent on July 3 from the Protector himself, directing the Lancashire Commissioners to surcease any further proceedings against his estates in that county.[2]

However necessary it might be to keep an eye on this design, it was evident, from the mere fact that Howard had asked the impecunious Charles to advance 2,000*l.* to start the political machinery, that no immediate danger was to be apprehended. It was otherwise when news reached Thurloe on July 8 of a meeting of Commonwealth's men, including Lawson and Clement Ireton, a brother of the late Lord Deputy, to consider ' what opportunity they might have from the Parliament's meeting, and whether they were not to endeavour elections of good men.' Okey, who was closely connected with the party, had been travelling about England, and was known to have had interviews with Harrison and Bradshaw. Unless Thurloe was misinformed, another meeting, held by the Fifth Monarchists

July 8.
Meetings of Commonwealth's men and of Fifth Monarchists.

---

[1] The petition and other documents relating to it are printed in Mr. Macray's edition of Clarendon's *History of the Rebellion*, xv. 105–130.

[2] The Lancashire Commissioners to Thurloe, July 23, *Thurloe*, v. 241. For other grounds of suspicion against Wildman see Mr. Firth's life of him in the *D. N. B.*

on the same day, came to still more trenchant resolutions, concluding that the saints must pull down Babylon, ' the time to be now, and the means to be by the sword.'   Five delegates were to be appointed who were to collect information from the members of the different meetings as to ' what readiness they are in . . . what force they have, what arms, what money, and when to be ready ?'[1]

What further information reached Thurloe during the succeeding fortnight is unknown.   On July 25, Barkstead reported that the wife of Colonel Robert Overton had started for Hull, though she had recently obtained leave to share her husband's imprisonment in the Tower,[2] and it is hardly pushing conjecture too far to suppose that her object was to disseminate amongst the soldiers of a garrison which had not long ago been under Overton's command, invitations to separate their cause from that of the Government.[3]   In the same report Barkstead mentions Portman, a Baptist, who held an office under the Navy Commissioners, and Thomas Venner, a cooper by trade, who preached at a meeting-house of his own, as under sus-

July 29.
Lawson,
Portman,
Venner,
and Okey,
sent for.

picion,[4] and on July 29 these two, together with Lawson and Okey,[5] were sent for by the Council. From a letter of Thurloe, written three weeks later, it appears to have been the intention of the Government to take proceedings against them, on the ground that they had endeavoured to raise disturbances ; but as nothing further

[1] The effect of the meeting of the Fifth-Monarchy men, July 8, *Thurloe*, v. 197.

[2] On July 3, Council Order Book, *Interr.* I, 77, p. 224.

[3] Such an invitation is to be found in a broadside addressed ' To the Honest Soldiers of the Garrison of Hull,' of which the B. M. Press Mark is 669, f. 20, No. 31.   This is dated by Thomason Sept. 25, but it is possible that this is the date of a reprint.   The address to the soldiers deals mainly with the case of Mr. John Canne, but concludes with a general attack on the Government.

[4] Barkstead to Thurloe, July 25, *Thurloe*, v. 248.

[5] Warrant Book, *Interr.* I, 114, pp. 21, 24.   One of the names given as ' Verney ' in the Calendar is in shorthand.   Mrs. Lomas tells me that there is no doubt that it should be read ' Vaner,' *i.e.* Venner.

is known of any action against them, except that Portman lost his place, it is to be presumed that they contrived to satisfy the Council that no appeal to force was contemplated on their part. Venner's escape from punishment is the more unintelligible, as on Sunday, August 3, two men were employed at his meeting-house, whilst he was himself engaged in prayer, in distributing amongst his congregation [1] a paper bearing the name of *England's Remembrancers*, which had been scattered about the streets of London two days before, and which was subsequently despatched in bundles for circulation amongst the country constituencies. [2]

Aug. 1
England's
Remem-
brancers.

As an electioneering manifesto on behalf of a composite Opposition it would be difficult to improve on an appeal which embraced at the same time the religious and secular motives which influenced men who were not Royalists but who, nevertheless, detested the Protectorate from the bottom of their hearts. Protesting against the despair which might lead such men to abstain from going to the poll on the ground that resistance was useless, the author argued that in no other way could honest men effectively protest against the existing misgovernment. " How," he asked, " is the profession of holiness . . . blasted with the names of hypocrisy, falseness, ambition, and covetousness ! How is the glory and strength of our nation spoiled and the blood of many thousands poured forth in waste, like water ! How is the treasure exhausted, trade and commerce destroyed ! And how are all our rights, liberties, and properties invaded and subverted by arbitrary powers and force of arms ! Who can say his life or estate is secured for a moment if the jealousy, envy, pride, lust, or covetousness of some in power please to command it ? And how is destruction threatened daily by foreign enemies ! " Whatever might be said to them, the electors must not suffer themselves to be blinded to the paramount importance of laying down the law through their own representatives. If they elected men

Its
character.

---

[1] Information of Morris and others, Aug. 3, 4, *Thurloe*, v. 272.

[2] This paper is reprinted in *Thurloe*, v. 268. The statement that it had been scattered about the streets by night is given by Thomason, E, 884, 885.

who would stand firm against temptation all might yet be well. "Your liberties," they were assured, "will be vindicated, your grievances and burdens eased, the honour of our country—that now lieth in the dust among all nations—will be again restored ; your trade revived, peace and plenty returned. . . . What shall we say more to you ? . . . Do not the tears of the widow and the cries of the fatherless speak ? Do not your infringed rights speak ? Do not your invaded properties speak ? Do not your gasping liberties speak ? Do not your often affronted representatives—which have been trod upon with scorn—speak ? Do not your encumbered estates speak ? Do not the blood of many thousands speak—some slain with the sword, and others killed with hunger ?[1] Do not the cries of your poor brethren, the honest seamen, the wall and bulwark of our nation against foreigners, who have so freely ventured their lives upon all just accounts and calls, and are now most barbarously forced from their wives and children to serve the ambitious and fruitless design of one man : do not all our ruins at home and abroad, by land and sea, speak to you ? Surely they have loud voices ; surely they do daily cry in your ears, Help ! Help ! or England perishes ! "

Undoubtedly there was much in this indictment which, at the time of its appearance, it was hard to deny. Heavy taxation, disorganised finance, the ravages of pestilence in Jamaica, the blows struck at trade by the Biscayans and the Dunkirkers were, up to August 1656, the main visible fruits of the foreign policy of the Protectorate. No wonder a cry was raised for a change of system. The weakness of the challenge lay in the conviction of those from whom it proceeded that the full religious liberty which they advocated was, in their day, inconsistent with the supremacy of Parliament. Such as it was, the Government lost no time in taking up the glove if, as seems far from improbable, Rich and Alured, who were committed on the 14th to custody, the former in Windsor Castle and the latter in the Isle of Man, were charged with being either the

The case for the Opposition.

Aug. 14. Committal of Rich and Alured.

[1] To this is appended a marginal note, ' Witness Jamaica !'

authors or the original disseminators of the manifesto.[1]   Three other men of mark had been summoned before the Council, even before the appearance of *England's Remembrancers*, and on each case the charge was not merely of having opposed the policy of the Government, but of having sought to substitute a basis of authority for that on which the Government purported

Aug. 1.
Bradshaw deprived of his offices. to be established.   Bradshaw, who appeared on August 1, still held the Chief Justiceship of Chester and the justiceship of three Welsh counties; though deprived of those posts on his persistent refusal to acknowledge the legitimacy of the Government under which he served, he was sent home without further punishment.[2]   On the same day

Ludlow before the Council. Ludlow was summoned on the charge of stirring up disaffection in the Irish army.   In vain Oliver urged that the objects of the war had been now obtained. To his question, " What can you desire more than you have ? "

His argument with the Protector. the unbending republican answered : " That which we fought for, that the nation might be governed by its own consent."   " I am as much," replied the Protector, " for a government by consent as any man ; but where shall we find that consent ?   Amongst the Prelatical, Presbyterian, Independent, Anabaptist, or Levelling parties ? " Even Ludlow, in advocating government by consent, had no thought of bowing to the will of the majority.   The majority in which he trusted was, he declared, to be found amongst those of all sorts who had acted with fidelity and affection to the public. On this the Council gave him four days to give security not to act against the peace of the Commonwealth, in default of which he was to stand committed.[3]   Yet, though he persistently re-

---

[1] Council Order Book, *Interr.* I, **77**, p. 329.   Nothing is stated as to the cause of their imprisonment, but the absence of notice of any suggestion that they might escape by giving security not to act against the Government seems to show that they had been guilty of some special offence.

[2] *Ib.* p. 306.   A report of Bradshaw's examination by the Council is amongst Lord Braye's MSS.   On Sept. 29 he was allowed to go circuit, perhaps because his successor had not been appointed.

[3] *Ib.* p. 306.

fused to enter into any such conditions, the Protector could not find it in his heart to imprison him, and in the end he was allowed to retire in peace to the house of his brother-in-law in Essex. His own explanation of his escape was that all that Oliver really wanted was to remove him from his own county of Wilts whilst the election was pending.[1]

He is allowed to retire to Essex.

As a matter of fact, Oliver must have known perfectly well that, though Ludlow would never recognise the Protectorate, it was most unlikely that he would conspire against it. He did not feel so certain of Vane. On May 12, before any resolution to summon Parliament had been taken, Vane had seized the pretext offered by a few vague words in the proclamation in which the Protector had commanded a fast,[2] to set forth his view of the political situation in a pamphlet, to which he gave the title of *A Healing Question*. He defined the good old cause, of which he proclaimed himself to be the champion,[3] as consisting primarily in religious liberty, and secondarily in control of all civil and military authorities by successive Parliaments freely elected, not by the nation at large, but by the adherents of the cause. In no other way, he argued, could a military despotism be averted. If this were conceded, he was ready to meet the Protector half-way. He had no objection to a constitutional impediment to any infringement of the principle of religious liberty, provided that it was established by Parliament ; no objection to a council appointed for life, or even to the predominance in the executive of a single person, provided that council and executive were alike subject to parliamentary

Vane's case.

*May 12.
A Healing Question.*

---

[1] Ludlow's *Memoirs*, ii. 10–15. The Council to Serjeant Dendy, Aug. 6, *S. P. Dom.* cxxix. 105a.

[2] 'That the Lord would pardon the iniquities both of magistrate and people in these lands, wherein the magistrate desires first to take shame to himself and find out his provocations.' *Proclamation*, March 14, B.M. Press Mark, 669, f. 20, No. 25.

[3] In the body of the work he calls it merely 'the good cause.' The phrase which afterwards became famous is employed in the final note.

control.[1] The modern reader, indeed, will have nothing but praise to award to the challenge thrown out by Vane against those who hold that a few can be trusted permanently to deal out benefits to the many. Nothing can be better than the argument : " It is not denied but that the supreme power, when by free consent it is placed in a single person or in some few persons, may be capable also to administer righteous government ; at least, the body that gives this liberty when they need not are to thank themselves if it prove otherwise. But when this free and natural access unto government is interrupted and declined, so as a liberty is taken by any particular member, or number of them . . . to assume and engross the office of sovereign rule and power, and to impose themselves as the competent public judge of the safety and good of the whole, without their free and due consent, and to lay claim unto this as those that find themselves possessed of the sword . . . this is that anarchy that is the first rise and step to tyranny, and lays the grounds of manifest confusion and disorder, exposing the ruling power to the next hand that, on the next opportunity, can lay hold of the sword ; and so, by a kind of necessity, introduces the highest imposition and bondage upon the whole body, in compelling all the parts, though never so much against the true public interest, to serve and obey, as their sovereign rule and supreme authority, the arbitrary will and judgment of those that bring themselves into rule by the power of the sword, in the right only of a part that sets up itself in preference before, or at least in competition with, the whole." [2]

Instinct with truth as the argument is, the passage is the work of a theorist, not of one whose eyes are directed to the world of actual life. To Vane, as to Oliver, religious liberty was a condition of the exaltation of the soul, but it was hardly, as it was to Oliver, a condition of a healthy political life. What answer, moreover, could Vane give to the question how he was to maintain the exclusion from

Vane and religious liberty.

[1] *A Healing Question*, E, 879, 5.   The pamphlet is reprinted in the Somers Tracts.   [2] *Ib.* E, 879, 5, p. 16.

political life of all who had opposed the good old cause, and still less, how he was to prevent those who had adhered to it from drawing up lists of damnable heresies and starting on the career of persecution afresh. Oliver's system no doubt was faulty in itself, and could hardly be expected to maintain itself permanently, but at least he saw all round the political horizon, and erred because the time was not yet ripe to evolve from the bosom of the nation the guarantees for liberty which he sought in vain in his own generation.

For three months Vane's pamphlet circulated without hindrance from those in authority. It had none of the coarse fibre which gave its popularity as a party weapon to *England's Remembrancers*. In August it was known that Vane aspired to a seat in the new Parliament. Yet his chance of success was not great. The corporation of Boston and the larger constituency of Lincolnshire received his addresses with coldness. "If anything," wrote Whalley with some shrewdness, "promote and accomplish his desire, I fear it will be his sending for at this juncture of time."[1] It was already too late to take Whalley's advice. Vane had been summoned before the Council on July 29, apparently to show that the Protector had no intention of submitting the Instrument to the judgment of Parliament.[2] On August 20, he announced to the Clerk of the Council that it was contrary to the privilege of an Englishman to obey the summons on compulsion. On the following day he was ordered to give security not to act against the Government or the peace, and on his refusal was sent, on September 4, into confinement at Carisbrooke.[3]

Vane stands for Parliament.

July 29. Vane summoned before the Council,

Sept. 4. and committed to prison.

Reprehensible as was the Protector's treatment of Vane from a constitutional point of view, he was at least practically

[1] Whalley to the Protector, Aug. 11, *Thurloe*, v. 299.

[2] Thurloe to H. Cromwell, *ib.* v. 317.

[3] Vane to the Clerk of the Council, Aug. 20, *ib.* v. 328; Council Order Book, *Interr.* I, 77, p. 373. *The Proceeds of the Protector against Sir H. Vane*, E, 937, 2.

in the right in holding that if the honest party was to be secured in possession of authority, it must be with the support of the army and not, as Vane proposed, solely by manipulating the parliamentary machinery in its interest.   So far as the electors

The Major-Generals and the elections.

were concerned, the Major-Generals did their best to popularise what they regarded as right opinions, and the words of a Major-General could not but carry weight in the district over which he presided.   On the other hand, except that packets of *England's Remembrancers* were seized wherever they were found, there was little done to terrorise the voters by hints of evil to befall them if they gave their voices against the Government.

Of the correspondence which has reached us the fullest is that of Haynes, who, as is known by his treatment of the parties

Haynes in the Eastern Counties.

at Colchester, was by no means wanting in vigour. Writing from Bury St. Edmunds, he regrets that he had received no hint that ' some care will be taken as to the encouragement of honest men in their choice of Parliament men before and after the election.'   Honest men, he added, would do their best in Suffolk, but ' will be compelled to take in with the Presbyterian to keep out the malignant.' [1]   At

Case of Boatman.

Norwich Haynes was much troubled by one Boatman, a Fifth-Monarchy preacher who had a strong hold on a large congregation meeting at St. Peter Mancroft.   Having obtained an order from Thurloe, the Major-General commanded him to present himself in London.   Boatman, however, pleaded a verbal permission from the Protector to remain in the country, and refused to stir.   All that Haynes could do was to inhibit him from preaching in Norwich, with the result that he removed to a church two miles outside the city, where multitudes flocked to hear him.   In vain Haynes begged that the Protector would confirm the order of his secretary, but till the election was over the Protector could not be induced to interfere. [2]   In the end,

---

[1] Haynes to Thurloe, July 19, *Thurloe*, v. 230.

[2] Haynes to Boatman [Aug. 7 ?]; Boatman to Haynes, Aug. 8; Haynes to Thurloe, Aug. 10, 15; Haynes to the Protector, Aug. 15, *ib.* v. 289, 296, 311, 312.

though Fleetwood was elected, the other members returned
for the county were hostile to the Government
either as Royalists, or sectaries, 'by which choice,'
as Haynes mournfully remarked, 'the profane, malignant and disaffected party and scandalous ministry are gratified.'
"If other counties," he added, "should do as this, it would be
a sufficient alarm to stand upon our guard, the spirits of people
being most strangely heightened and moulded into a very great
aptness to take the first hint for an insurrection, and the county
especially so disposed may most probably begin the scene."

The Nor-
folk elec-
tion.

With such a prospect before his eyes Haynes recurred to
the advice which he had tendered a month before. "I most
humbly beg," he continued, "that a speedy order may be taken
for the paying and mustering of militia horse, for as yet they
have not been called together, and so am I not able to assure
you what assistance you may reasonably expect from them. . . .
If something of this nature be not done for encouragement of
your friends, their spirits will in all likelihood despond very
much." [1]   To such counsel the Protector gave no heed.   There
was to be no jingling of the sword which he held in his hands.

Whalley's reports were far more hopeful than those of
Haynes.   In Lincolnshire he declared 'a man would not be
chosen but upon apprehensions that they would not
change the Government.' [2]   Writing from Nottingham
he declared his belief that 'in the mediterranean part of the
nation' the heart was sound.   "The people," he explained,
"generally know there is a present necessity for moneys ; the
parting with it upon a settlement will not trouble them.   They
are no less sensible of the necessity of establishing the present
Government, the wisest of them well knowing that many
changes will prove both chargeable and dangerous to them ;
and I am very confident that not a man from hence would be
chosen to sit in this Parliament in whom they conceived a spirit
of opposition to this present Government." [3]

Whalley's
reports.

---

[1] Haynes to Thurloe, Aug. 20, *Thurloe*, v. 328.
[2] Whalley to Thurloe, Aug. 9, *ib.* v. 296.
[3] Whalley to the Protector, Aug. 11, *ib.* v. 299.

Undoubtedly there was much truth in Whalley's argument that the constituencies, in general, were loath to face the dangers of a new revolution. Yet the Opposition had on its side a feeling stronger than royalism or a craving for the rule of the saints. In Northumberland and Durham—at Hazlerigg's instigation, as Lilburne suspected—the cry was raised that the people would 'have no swordmen, no decimator, or any that receives salary from the State to serve in Parliament.'[1] In far-off Kent, Kelsey made a similar report. "Most of the Cavaliers," he wrote, "falling in with the Presbyterians against all those persons that owned your Highness and the present Government ; and the spirit is generally bitter against swordmen, decimators, courtiers, &c., and most of those chosen to sit in the ensuing Parliament are of the same spirit."[2] So disastrous did the result appear to Kelsey that he recommended that dormant commissions might be granted to certain persons in order that in case of an outbreak the honest party might know to whom to rally, and that when Parliament met the members might be asked to sign a recognition so penned as to keep out the most dangerous, and suggested that seats should be refused to all who would not accept the Instrument as it stood, engaging 'not to meddle with altering any part of it.'

Yet when the elections were completed the result did not appear so threatening to the Government as Haynes and Kelsey had anticipated. The Opposition, indeed, were represented by Cooper, Scot, Hazlerigg, Birch, Grimston, and Herbert Morley, but it would be difficult to find any others possessing any sort of distinction, whilst neither Vane, Bradshaw, nor Ludlow had secured seats in the House. On the other hand, of the eighteen Major-Generals and deputies, every one, except George Fleetwood, had been returned. Of the fifteen members of Council four were Major-Generals, and of the remaining eleven all obtained seats except the Earl of Mulgrave and Lord Lisle, who pro-

Lilburne's and Kelsey's reports.

Result of the elections.

---

[1] Lilburne to Thurloe, Aug. 9, *Thurloe*, v. 296.
[2] Kelsey to the Protector, Aug. 26, *S. P. Dom.* cxxix. 156.

bably did not offer themselves for election. Room, too, was found for Admiral Blake and for such officials as Thurloe, Whitelocke, Lenthall, John Lisle, and Maidstone, besides Richard Cromwell, who was chosen both by Cambridge University and Hants, and his brother-in-law Claypole, who obtained a seat at Carmarthen.

So far as the boroughs were concerned the renewal of charters had not had time to take effect, except at Chipping Wycombe, where Bridge, who had lately succeeded upon Worsley's death to the Major-Generalship of the North-west, was returned in the place of Scot, and in Colchester, where the election was deliberately postponed till September 12, the day on which the new Mayor, Aldermen, and Common Councillors took the oaths under the new charter.[1] The free burgesses being now excluded from the franchise, the election fell upon such staunch supporters of the Protectorate as Lawrence and Maidstone.

Borough elections.

Chipping Wycombe.

Colchester.

Of far greater importance is the question of the effect of the influence exercised by the Major-Generals upon the course of the elections. What evidence has reached us points to its being far less than has generally been supposed,[2] and there can hardly be a doubt that the hostility they aroused counted for more in strengthening the Opposition than any pressure they might exert could avail on behalf of the Government. A further consideration tends in

Influence of the Major-Generals.

---

[1] ' Having till this time forborne to proceed to the electing of persons to serve for this borough in Parliament, yesterday, being Friday, we resolved upon the election.' Letter from Colchester, Sept. 13, *Merc. Pol.*, E, 497, 20. This confirms Mr Round's suggestion in the *Eng. Hist. Rev.*, Oct. 1900, xv. 658.

[2] Goffe's instance is a case in point. In his letter after his election he ascribes it to the influence of Richard Cromwell, whereas Colonel Norton had not only left his name off his list, but advised him to withdraw his candidature on the ground that it would be a disgrace for him to be beaten. This is hardly the language of a hectoring manager of elections. Goffe to Thurloe, Aug. 21, *Thurloe*, v. 329.

the same direction. Of the most determined opponents of the Government returned to this Parliament a very considerable majority represented constituencies in those southern and eastern parts of England which had been the main support of Parliament in its struggle with the King, whilst there were but thirty scattered over those northern and western districts which had been the strength of the Royalist cause. There can hardly be any doubt that the explanation of the phenomenon lies in the fact that in the north-western districts, Puritans who opposed the locally predominant royalism, were ready to grasp any hand held out to save them from a reaction in favour of the King and of all that his name imported ; whereas in the south-east, men who had served under the Puritan and Parliamentary standard felt themselves strong enough to enter into a contest with the military power which held them down, and even in some parts to cast their votes on behalf of their Royalist neighbours rather than for men whom they regarded as the mere satellites of a Major-General.

The battle of the polls had been fought out by two distinct parties attaching themselves to two distinct policies—the policy

Two policies at issue.

of uncompromising hostility to the Protectorate as an arbitrary government ruling by the sword, and the policy of building up a constitutional settlement on the foundations already laid. Yet, diverse as were these opinions, they might easily be welded into one opposing force if Kelsey's advice to tolerate no divergence from the Instrument were adopted. No constitutional settlement was attainable on such lines as these, and any attempt to give permanency to the existing system could only avail to drive the new Parliament as a whole to demand a settlement on some such plan as had commended itself to its predecessor.

INDEX

note 4; issues a manifesto, 185;
sends a message to Queen Christina,
ib.; receives bad news from Ireland,
186; considers the Scottish proposals and asks the Committee of
Estates to agree to a union of all
parties, 187; asks the English Presbyterians to urge the Scots to
moderation, *ib.*; writes a letter to
encourage Montrose, 187, 188; sends
Montrose the Garter, 188; autho-
rises Montrose to publish his letter,
191; leaves Jersey, and meets his
mother at Beauvais, 194; arrives at
Breda, 195; appoints Eythin Montrose's lieutenant-general, 196; seeks
aid from foreigners, *ib.*; receives
the demands of the Scottish Commissioners, 197; thinks of joining
Montrose, 198; gives instructions to
Keane, *ib.*; continues to encourage
Montrose, *ib.*; asks the Commissioners to modify their terms, 199;
thinks of sending a foreign army to
England, and of pledging the Scilly
Isles, 200; receives a suggestion
that his decision may be postponed
till his arrival in Scotland, 201; a
marriage with Argyle's daughter
proposed to, *ib.*; urged to promise
anything, 202; again asks for concessions, *ib.*; gives way on almost
everything, *ib.*; makes a private
engagement on the Irish Treaty, 203;
a draft agreement signed, *ib.*; plays
a double game, 204; his conduct
condemned by the Cavaliers, and by
his mother, 205; believes that he
has secured an indemnity for Montrose, and probably intends to em-
ploy him in England, 206; sends
Fleming with instructions to Montrose, 207; asked to annul the Irish
Treaty, 230; writes a letter to the
Scottish Parliament on Montrose's
defeat, 231; possibly misrepresented
by Argyle, 233; receives the Communion on his knees, 235; hears of
Montrose's execution, arrives at
Honslaerdyck, and hears of the additional demands of the Scots, 236;
sails for Scotland without signing a
treaty, *ib.*; signs a treaty with the
Scots off Heligoland, 237; swears to
the Covenants, *ib.*; progress of,
from Speymouth to Falkland, 237,
239; looks to England to free him

from his engagements to the Scots,
240; expects money from London
and from foreign Governments, 241;
tries to engage Cavaliers, Catholics,
and Presbyterians in his support,
ib.; wishes the Cavaliers to be
stronger than the Presbyterians, *ib.*;
directs Beauchamp to assure the
Catholics of his favour, *ib.*; offers
Fairfax the earldom of Essex, 249;
compromised by the publication of
Meynell's address to the Pope, 268;
rides into Leith, 274; a proclamation issued in the name of, *ib.*;
being foiled in his intention of winning the army, retires to Dunferm-
line, *ib.*; refuses to sign a Declaration sent him by the Kirk, 276, 277;
gives way, and tries in vain to gather
an army at Perth, 278; declares
himself a true Cavalier, 279; gives
a commission to Willoughby of
Parham in the West Indies, 316;
is satisfied with the defeat of the
Scots at Dunbar, 331; makes large
offers to Argyle, 334, 335; tries to
unite all parties, 335; divulges a
plan for his escape to the Royalists,
ib.; pleads against the dismissal of
his servants, 337; rides off to Clova,
ib.; returns to Perth and excuses
himself, 338; publishes an Act of
Indemnity, 339; coronation of, 346;
plays golf, 347; asked to compound
with Cromwell, *ib.*; asks his mother's
opinion on his proposed marriage
with Argyle's daughter, 349; visits
Aberdeen, *ib.*; desires Parliament
to countenance the northern levies,
350; supports the appointment of a
committee for the army, 351; the
command of the new army given to,
ib.; causes of the success of, 353;
approves of the invasion of England,
ii. 32; passes through Lancashire,
35; holds a conference with the Earl
of Derby, and hopes to rouse Lancashire, 37; invites Sir T. Middleton
to join him, *ib.*; summons Mack-
worth to surrender Shrewsbury, 40;
reaches Worcester and issues a
manifesto, *ib.*; takes part in the
battle of Worcester, 44, 45; proclamation for the capture of, 49;
his flight from Worcester, 50; his
reception at Whiteladies, 51; hides
himself in an oak, 52; concealed at

ii. 249 ; their probity questioned in Parliament, 251

Commissioners, for securing the peace of the Commonwealth, the, duties of, iii. 321 ; work harmoniously with the Major-Generals, 341

—— over the West Indian expedition, *see* West Indies

Committee for the Army, the, appointed by the Scottish Parliament, i. 351

—— of Estates, the, asked by Charles to agree to a union of parties in Scotland, i. 187 ; considers their relations with Charles, 192 ; parties in, *ib.* ; despatches commissioners to treat with Charles, *ib.* ; urges Charles to leave the army, 274 ; approves of the Declaration required from Charles, 277 ; orders Leslie to descend from Doon Hill, 285, 286 ; urges Leslie to withdraw his resignation, 332 ; orders the purging of Charles's life-guard, and the dismissal of his servants, 336 ; concurs in the publication of an Act of Indemnity, 339 ; Ker refuses to take orders from, 342 ; condemns the Remonstrance, 343 ; orders the confinement of Guthrie and Bennet, 350 ; penitents allowed by the commission of the Kirk to take a seat in, 351 ; captured at Alyth, ii. 66

—— on Courts of Justice, the, appointment of, ii. 4

—— on Elections to future Parliaments, the, appointed to report on elections, and on the duration of the existing Parliament, i. 57 ; ordered to meet daily, 176 ; Vane makes a report from, in favour of a redistribution of seats, and of partial elections, 242 ; of the whole House holds weekly sittings, 243 ; recommences its sittings after Dunbar, ii. 60 ; the Grand, revived, 174 ; its powers transferred to a select committee, 226 ; the select, empowered to consider the date of a dissolution, *ib.* ; reports the Bill on elections with amendments, 235, 236

—— for the Propagation of the Gospel, the, formed to discuss Owen's scheme, ii. 98 ; Cromwell defends religious liberty in, 100 ;

fifteen fundamentals produced before, 101 ; revived, 227 ; reports Owen's proposals to Parliament, 235

—— on law-reform, appointed by the Nominated Parliament, ii. 290

—— on the debt of the Commonwealth, appointed by the Nominated Parliament, ii. 290

—— on the Engagement, appointed by the Nominated Parliament, ii. 290

—— on the Poor, appointed by the Nominated Parliament, ii. 290

—— on the Treasury, revived, ii. 227 ; appointed by the Nominated Parliament, ii. 290

—— on tithes, appointed by the Nominated Parliament, ii. 290 ; makes its report, 323

Common Prayer Book, read in London churches, i. 173 ; no popular zeal for the revival of, ii. 85 ; increasing use of, 300 ; used at St. Gregory's, iii. 335 ; Usher's admission concerning, *ib.* ; its use confined to private houses, iv. 20, 21 ; recited from memory by Sanderson, 22

Commonwealth, the, virtually established by the abolition of kingship, i. 3 ; financial difficulties of, 40 ; formally established by Act, 57 ; Spain refuses to recognise, 69 ; Cardenas proposes a Spanish alliance with, 82 ; foreign Governments too much occupied to interfere with, 179 ; compared by Marten to Moses, 243 ; hostility of London to, 248 ; attitude of Fairfax towards, 249 ; not universally unpopular, 251 ; recognised by Spain, 308 ; hears and dismisses an ambassador from Portugal, 312 ; Croullé advises Mazarin to recognise, *ib.* ; Croullé's sketch of the statesmen of, 313 ; an attack upon France said to be projected by, *ib.* ; advances of Mazarin to, *ib.* ; dismissal of Croullé and Gentillot by, 314 ; hostility of the Prince of Orange to, 318 ; unfitness for diplomacy of the leaders of, 323 ; the new militia rallies to, ii. 13 ; effect of the victory at Worcester on the establishment of, 48 ; conference on the future constitution of, 75 ; tendency to strengthen the

cillor, 116; lands in Dublin, 117; his reception in Ireland, 118; modification of the transplantation policy by, *ib.*; offers to send Irish girls to Jamaica, 218

Cromwell, Oliver, probably supports a proposal to retain the House of Lords as a consultative body, i. 3; chosen a member of the first Council of State, 5; obtains a revision of the Engagement, 6; gives reasons for hesitating to accept the command in Ireland, 24; gives his opinion on the Irish war, 25; warns the army against internal divisions, *ib.*; objects to see England subjected to Scotland or Ireland, 26; accepts the command in Ireland, 27; his Irish policy, *ib.*; cares little about consistency, 32; accused of ruling the State with Ireton and Harrison, 33; urges the Council of State to take strong measures against the Levellers, 35; difficulty of finding money for the Irish expedition of, 40; urges the City to lend money, *ib.*; takes part in suppressing a mutiny in Whalley's regiment, 45; addresses the soldiers in Hyde Park, 50; orders sea-green colours to be plucked out of the soldiers' hats, 52; marches with Fairfax against the mutineers, and sends them a kindly message, *ib.*; falls on the mutineers at Burford, 53; made a D.C.L. at Oxford, 54; accident to the coach of, 59; receives a present from the City, *ib.*; makes overtures to the Presbyterians, 64; receives a letter from Monk justifying his convention with O'Neill, 78; lays Monk's letter before the Council of State, 83; allegation that he authorised Monk to treat with O'Neill discussed, *ib.*, note 4; is in need of money for his troops, 85; proposes an adjournment of Parliament, 86; appointed Lord Lieutenant of Ireland, *ib.*; attempt to find money for the army of, *ib.*; has to meet the danger of an Irish invasion, 92; is tied to England by financial necessities, *ib.*; sends forces to relieve Jones in Dublin, but proposes to land in Munster, 94; wins over Lord Broghill, 95; is still in need of money,

96; sets out for Bristol, *ib.*; attempts to bribe the Governor of Cork, 97; receives Monk at Milford Haven, 103; his good will secured by Monk, 105; resolves to send Ireton to Munster, *ib.*; lands at Dublin, 106; sends a message to Inchiquin's officers, 109; issues a declaration against plundering, 110; lays siege to Drogheda, 112; summons Drogheda, 115; orders a storm, 116; leads the storming party, 117; orders the slaughter of the defenders of the Mill Mount, 118; orders a massacre of all in arms, 119; orders the burning of the steeple of St. Peter's, 120; spares the lives of a few soldiers, *ib.*; makes excuses for his conduct, 124; examination of the arguments of, 125; resolves to attack Wexford, 126; arrives before Wexford, 127; summons Wexford, 128; Wexford Castle betrayed to, 130; does not interfere on behalf of the garrison and townsmen of, 131; comments on the massacre in Wexford, 133; recommends the settlement of Englishmen in Wexford, 134; marches towards Munster and summons New Ross, *ib.*; declares that he will not tolerate the Mass, 135; receives the capitulation of New Ross, and constructs a bridge over the Barrow, *ib.*; hears of the rising in Cork, 136; sends Broghill to extend the insurrection, 137; asks Blake to take service under him, *ib.*; completes his bridge over the Barrow, 141; appears before Waterford, *ib.*; raises the siege of Waterford, 142; meets Broghill, 143; coast-line held by, *ib.*; ravages of disease in the army of, *ib.*; laments Jones's death, *ib.*; goes into winter quarters, 144; issues a declaration in reply to the manifestoes of the prelate at Clonmacnoise, 147; his conduct in Ireland explained by his declaration, 148; his good intentions towards Ireland, 149; sets out from Youghal on a new campaign, *ib.*; summons Kilkenny, 150; Kilkenny surrenders to, *ib.*; accepts the surrender of English Protestants on favourable terms, 151; wishes to make terms with Ormond and

the disposal of the prisoners from Worcester, 66; urges a dissolution, 69; talks of popular reforms, 71; supports the motion for fixing a day for the dissolution, 72; at the head of the poll for the fourth Council of State, 74; summons a conference to discuss the constitution of the Republic, 75; prefers a settlement with somewhat of monarchical power, 76; a socialist book dedicated to, 78; tries to work with Lilburne, 79; his part in the trial and banishment of Lilburne, 81; the Act of Oblivion passed at the instigation of, *ib.*; music cultivated by, 83; makes Owen his chaplain, 97; defends religious liberty, 100; is ready to tolerate Mahommedanism, *ib.*; votes on the enforcement of tithes, 102; opposes the Fifteen Fundamentals, 103; Milton's sonnet to, *ib.*; is the national hero of the nineteenth century, 151; his ignorance of continental feeling, *ib.*; ignores the significance of the treaties of Westphalia, *ib.*; rejects Condé's overtures, 154; sends Vane to De Retz, 155; hankers after a war against France, 158; makes overtures to Estrades for the cession of Dunkirk, 160; favours an alliance with France, 161; informs the Council of State of his plans about Dunkirk, 162; hints that the French government would do well to outbid Condé, 163; sends troops to Dover to be ready to occupy Dunkirk, but is opposed in the Council of State, 166; overruled on the negotiation for Dunkirk, 168, 169; joins the Presbyterians in opposing a war with the Dutch, 172, 173; probably advocates partial elections, 173; sent to inquire into the fight off Folkestone, 179; reconciled to the Dutch war, 181; supports Gerbier's mission to the Netherlands, 188; elected at head of poll to the Fifth Council of State, 202; ceases to be Lord Lieutenant of Ireland, 222; remits his arrears, *ib.*; condoles with Lambert, 223; stands aloof from the army petition, and assumes the office of a mediator, 225; proposes a compromise, *ib.*; complains of cliques in Parliament, 228; said to

have proposed to make the Duke of Gloucester king, 229; attacks Parliament in a conversation with Whitelocke, *ib.*; asks 'What if a man should take upon him to be King?' 230; is displeased with Whitelocke, 231; wishes for a new representative, 233; shrinks from a violent dissolution of Parliament, 236; forms a party in Parliament, 237; gains time for a Dutch negotiation, 238; his probable influence in the framing of the draft of a treaty with Spain, 239; said to desire a general peace, 243; restrains the Council of Officers from dissolving Parliament by force, 245; refuses to see Fairfax and Lambert, and absents himself from Parliament, 246; questions Vavasor Powell, 250; is interested in the propagation of the Gospel in Wales, *ib.*; gives a conditional support to Parliament, 251, 252; dissatisfied with the scheme for filling up vacancies in Parliament, 255; his resignation demanded, *ib.*; his resignation offered and refused, 256; supports a compromise, *ib.*; proposes the appointment of a small governing body, 257; summons a conference, 258; remains at home after the meeting of the House, 259; appears in the House, 261; interrupts the Speaker, 262; orders in the soldiers, 263; dissolves the Long Parliament, 264; dissolves the Council of State, 265; destructive work of, 266; temporary popularity of, 269; pardons criminals, *ib.*; gives a declaration, 271; accepts Harrison's principle of governing by a select body, 273; offers Fairfax a seat in the Nominated Parliament, *ib.*; Harrison's triumph over, 274; tolerant policy of, 275; compared to Moses, *ib.*; invites congregational churches to name members for the new representative, 276; attacked by the Fifth Monarchists, 276, 277; Royalists hope to be assisted by, 278; expected to make himself a king, 279; receives a petition for the restoration of the Parliament, 281; issues writs for the Nominated Parliament, 282; appears as a constructive

Danzig, holds out against Charles X., iv. 205

Daugnon, Louis Foucault, Comte du, invites Cromwell to Rochelle, ii. 155; sends Cugnac to England, 163; deserts Condé, iii. 29

Davenant, William, gives an entertainment at Rutland House, iv. 25

Dawkins, Rowland, Deputy Major-General in South Wales, iii. 340

Day, Wentworth, Cornet, imprisoned for reading Vavasor Powell's manifesto at Allhallows, iv. 42

Day, Robert, Clerk of the Passage at Dover, connives at the movements of Royalists, iii. 279

Deane, Richard, appointed one of the Generals at Sea, i. 23; sent as Commissioner to Scotland, ii. 132; left in command in Scotland, 138; makes an agreement with Argyle, 139; again appointed one of the Generals at Sea, 210; in the battle off Portland, 215; joins Monk in an invitation to the fleet to accept Cromwell's temporary dictatorship, 270; misses Tromp, iii. 32; puts out with Monk from Yarmouth, 33; killed in the battle off the Gabbard, 34

Deans and Chapters, Act for the abolition of, i. 49; 'doubling' on the lands of, 85; attempt to raise money by the sale of the estates of, 251

Debentures, orders given for issuing to the soldiers, i. 85

Decimation tax, the, imposed on Royalists, iii. 322, 323; defended by the Protector, 328–330; process of exacting, 342; proposal to lower the limit of, iv. 249; proposal for extension to others than Royalists, 254

Declaration, a royal, drafted by Hyde, i. 61; dropped, 62

Defence of the People of England, published by Milton, ii. 17

Delinquents, delay in exacting compositions of, i. 41; excepted from pardon, *ib.*; expelled from London, 247; proposed sale of the lands of, 251; Acts for the confiscation of the estates of, ii. 22, 200; sale of the lands of, 187; attempt to sell the lands of, 211; disqualified from office, 277

Dell, William, thinks University teaching useless for ministers, ii. 322, note 2

Denbigh, the Royalists hope to seize, iii. 271

Denbigh, Earl of, 1643 (Basil Feilding), chosen a member of the first Council of State, i. 5; refuses to take the Engagement in its original form, 6; re-elected to the second Council of State, 244, note 2

Denham, Sir John, verses by, iii. 337, note 4

Denmark, Montrose seeks aid in, i. 190; Newcastle sent to, 241; her relations with Sweden, iv. 197, 198

Denn, Henry, Cornet, condemned to death and pardoned, i. 54

Derby, Countess of, holds the Isle of Man for her husband, ii. 61

Derby, Earl of, 1642 (James Stanley), appointed to command in Lancashire, Cheshire, and the neighbouring counties, i. 240; holds the Isle of Man, 298; concerts measures for a rising in Lancashire, ii. 12; lands in Wyre Water and holds a conference with Charles, 37; urges Cavaliers and Presbyterians to rise for the king, 38; levies forces in Lancashire, 39; is defeated at Wigan, *ib.*; arrives at Worcester, 43; captured, 46, 59; selected for trial, 59; sentenced to death, 61; executed, 62

Derbyshire, placed under Whalley, iii. 340

Desborough, John, Colonel, join Cromwell at Warwick, ii. 41; appointed a commissioner on law reform, 82; supports Cromwell in restraining the officers from dissolving Parliament by force, 245; invited to sit in the Nominated Parliament, 288; member of the Council of State of the Protectorate, iii. 2; appointed General at Sea, 63; supports the Protector in Parliament, 204; sent to quiet the crews of Penn's fleet, 215; appointed Major-General of the West, 288; pursues the Royalist insurgents, *ib.*; commissioned to command the militia in the West, 297; confirmed in the Major-Generalship of the West, 340; reproved by Fox, iv. 7; refuses to

of the Parliamentary constituencies, iii. 171; the franchise settled by, 172; indenture required by, 173; omits to provide for the registration of voters, 174; does not empower the Council to require an affirmation of the indenture from members of Parliament, 177; the Protector asks Parliament to examine, 181; referred to a committee of the whole House, 184; Oliver's account of the formation of, 189; national approval claimed for, 190; Oliver declares himself content with four fundamentals in, 192; Oliver holds provisionally by, 193; laid before Parliament, 196; Parliament goes into committee on, *ib.*; its provisions for the power of war and peace objected to, 200; the officers declare in favour of, 218; Oliver attempts to govern, so far as possible, in accordance with, 255; questioned by the arguments in Cony's case, 301; the judges hesitate to accept as a basis of authority, 302; suggestions for the modification of, 304–308; article of, referring to summoning Parliament, iv. 255, note 2; interpreted by the Protector and Council in their own favour, 256; articles of, referring to elections, *ib.* note 2

Intercursus Magnus, the, proposed as a basis of negotiation by the Dutch, i. 327

International arbitration, *see* Arbitration

Inverkeithing, Lambert defeats Brown at, ii. 26

Inverness, seized by Royalists, i. 63; Montrose reproached by a woman at, 221

Ireland, expectations of the English Royalists from, i. 12; signature of peace between Ormond and the confederates in, *ib.*; discussion on Charles's policy towards, 18; Charles receives Ormond's invitation, to, 22; Charles resolves to go to, *ib.*; Ayscue appointed admiral on the coast of, 23; Cromwell appointed to command in, 24; Cromwell's fear of danger from, 25; Whalley's advice against the eradication of the natives of, 27; Cromwell accepts the command in,

ib.; policy of Cromwell in, *ib.*; lots cast to select regiments for, 44; want of cohesion amongst the Royalists of, 70; Michael Jones insists on the preservation of the English interest in, 72; testimony of an Irish bard to the bad effect of the quarrels of his countrymen on the independence of, 73; Monk's position in, *ib.*; antagonism between O'Neill and the Scottish Presbyterians in, 74; Cromwell Lord Lieutenant of, 86; advantage of the mastery of the sea to the Commonwealth forces in, 87; advance of Ormond's army in, *ib.*; parliamentary officers surrender to Ormond in, 89; operations of Ormond and Inchiquin in, 90; Ormond's prospects of an invasion of England from, *ib.*; Ormond's view of the situation in, *ib.*; Ormond invites Charles to, 92; Ormond fears a breach between his Protestant and his Catholic supporters, *ib.*; Cromwell has to meet the danger of an invasion of England from, *ib.*; Cromwell's plans for landing in, 94; success of Inchiquin in, 98, 99; turning of the tide by Jones's victory in, 102; landing of Cromwell in, 105; union between O'Neill and the Royalists in, 118; effect of the massacre at Drogheda on the defence of, 125; English Royalists suspected in, 136, 137; Ormond desires to rally to his cause the Celtic element in, 138; new policy forced on Ormond in, 139; failure of Ormond's policy in, 145; the resistance to Cromwell falls increasingly into the hands of the priesthood, *ib.*; views of the Irish prelates on the English invasion of, 145, 146; Cromwell justifies his invasion of, 147; explanation of Cromwell's conduct in, 148; growing preponderance of the Celtic element in, 154; Cromwell leaves, and appoints Ireton Lord Deputy of, 157; conditions of Cromwell's success in, 158; proposal to send Montrose to, 199; Ireton confirmed as Lord Deputy of, 265; appointment of commissioners to assist Ireton in, *ib.*; appointment of Ludlow as Lieutenant-

General in, *ib.* ; English prisoners sent to, ii. 65; after Cromwell's departure, 106; no field army left for the defence of, 107; Ireton's plans for the conquest of, 108, 109; opposition to Ormond in, 110; movements of Ireton in, 110, 111; success of Axtell in, 111, 112; Clanricarde appointed Lord Deputy by Ormond in, 112; proposal of the Duke of Lorraine to assist, 113; mission of the Abbot of St. Catharine to, 114; failure of the Duke of Lorraine's proposals in, 115; ground gained by the English in, 116; desolation of, *ib.* ; arrival of the Parliamentary Commissioners in, 117; proclamations for the benefit of the inhabitants of, *ib.* ; its defence hopeless after the fall of Limerick, 125; Ludlow provisional commander of the Parliamentary army in, 126; military position in, *ib.* ; submission of, 127, 128; desolate condition of, 129; rise of a national spirit in, *ib.* ; Lambert appointed Lord Deputy of, 221; arrangements for the government of, 222; Lambert refuses to serve in, *ib.* ; represented by six members in the Nominated Parliament, 282; opposition to the Protectorate in the army in, iii. 8; the Protectorate proclaimed in, *ib.* ; Henry Cromwell's visit to, 10; Parliamentary representation of, 178; a plantation policy for, iv. 79; consistency of English policy in, 80; grant of land to the Adventurers in, *ib.* ; emigration of soldiers from, 81; governed by commissioners, *ib.* ; Act of Settlement passed for, 82; the so-called pardon for the poor and landless in, 84 ; a meeting of officers asks for justice on murderers in, 86; a High Court of Justice established in, 87; arrival of Fleetwood in, *ib.* ; order for transplanting Scots in, 88; rise of the idea of transplantation of Irishmen in, *ib.* ; cost of the conquest of, 89; desolation of, *ib.* ; Cromwell resolves to colonise with Englishmen, 91; lands assigned to the Adventurers in, *ib.* ; instruction to the commissioners to survey lands in, 92; the Act of Satisfaction for, 93;

declaration by the commissioners of their intention to carry out the Acts in, 94; a general transplantation feared by the natives of, 96; delay of transplantation in, *ib.* ; temporary dispensations granted in, 97; Henry Cromwell's mission to, 98; Fleetwood lord deputy of, *ib.* ; Fleetwood receives power to dispense from transplantation in, *ib.* ; proprietors of land transplanted in, 99; petition asking for a general clearance of the natives of, 100; controversy between Gookin and Lawrence on transplantation in, 101; financial difficulties in, 104; survey of lands in, 105; commencement of the settlement of soldiers in, 106; Petty's survey of lands in, *ib.* ; demands of the soldiers in, 107; concessions to the soldiers in, 108; ravages by the tories in, 109; murders in, *ib.* ; transportation of vagrants from, 110; expulsion of natives from the towns of, 113; concessions to Protestants in, 114; Henry Cromwell to command the army in, 116; arrival of Henry Cromwell in, 117; Fleetwood enlarges the scope of the transplantation, *ib.* ; Fleetwood returns to England from, 118; failure of the scheme for a general transplantation in, *ib.* ; proposed transportation to Jamaica of boys and girls from, 218

Ireton, Bridget, marries Fleetwood, ii. 222; story of his courtship of her, 223, note 1

Ireton, Clement, attends a meeting of Commonwealth's men, iv. 259

Ireton, Henry, proposes a form of engagement, i. 4; nominated a member of the first Council of State, but rejected by Parliament, 5; accused of ruling the State with Cromwell and Harrison, 33; named Lieutenant-General of the army for Ireland, 86; sent to Munster, but lands in Dublin, 118, 119; is made Major-General, 126; joins Jones in operations near Ross, 141; left by Cromwell in Ireland as Lord Deputy, 157; is teller against a resolution against political sermons, 171, 172; confirmed in the Lord Deputyship, 265; left in Ireland as Lord Deputy,

claim of England to exercise influence in, 307 ; dependence of Penn on Spanish ports in, *ib.* ; Blake sent by the Protector in, iv. 146. *See also* Blake.

Meelick Island, Axtell defeats the Irish in, ii. 111, 112

Memel, Charles X. desires to occupy, iv. 208 ; half its tolls abandoned to Charles X., 211

Mercurius Democritus, coarseness of, ii. 83

Mercurius Elencticus, discontinuance of, i. 174

Mercurius Politicus, issued as a Government organ, i. 255 ; part taken by Needham and Milton in writing, ii. 17–19

Mercurius Pragmaticus, defies the Press Act, i. 174 ; Needham imprisoned for his writings in, 253

Mervyn, Audley, Colonel, sent to O'Neill by Ormond, i. 111 ; deserts to Coote, *ib.*

Meynell, Robert, sent by Charles to Rome to ask aid from the Pope, i. 70 ; applies to Innocent X. for help, 196 ; publication of his address to the Pope, 268

Middelburg, visit of Charles II. to, iii. 280

Middlesex, placed under Barkstead, iii. 340 ; severe measures of the justices of, iv. 39

Middle Temple, the dancing at, ii. 84

Middleton, John, Lieutenant-General, escapes from England and joins Mackenzie's force in Scotland, i. 63 ; professes ability to bring over Leslie's horse to Montrose, 210 ; to command a rising, 335 ; excommunicated, 338 ; signs a bond to unite Royalists and Engagers, *ib.* ; does penance and is released from excommunication, 347 ; Charles persuades the ministers to allow the levies of, 350 ; captured near Rochdale, ii. 46 ; escape of, 63 ; appointed the king's lieutenant-general in Scotland, iii. 84 ; his instructions, *ib.* ; expectations formed of the help to be given by, 91 ; lands at Tarbatness, 99 ; quarrels amongst the officers of, 100 ; his attitude towards the clergy, 101 ; younger sons flock to, 105 ;

his plan of campaign, 106 ; his communications with the Lowlands interrupted, *ib.* ; escapes from Monk, 107, 108 ; is defeated at Dalnaspidal, 109 ; pursuit of, 110

Middleton, Sir Thomas, receives an invitation from Charles to join him, ii. 37 ; sends the letter to Parliament, *ib.* ; is warned of danger to Chirk Castle, iii. 284

Mildmay, Captain Anthony, directed to take the children of Charles I. to Carisbrooke, ii. 4 ; obtains medical advice for the Lady Elizabeth, 5

Milford Haven, Cromwell sends the bulk of his army to, i. 94 ; Monk visits Cromwell at, 103

Militia, the, constitution of, i. 267 ; warned to be in readiness, ii. 10, 13 ; importance of, 13 ; readiness of, to join Cromwell against the Scots, 43 ; part taken in the battle of Worcester by, 47 ; proposal to supplement the army with, iii. 210 ; scheme of replacing regular troops by, 223 ; Parliament claims to control, 245 ; a commission issued for raising in London, 278 ; muster of the London, 296 ; informed that they will not be called out, *ib.* ; Order of Council for the creation of a reserve force out of, 297 ; reorganisation of, 318 ; numbers and pay of, *ib.* ; placed under Major-Generals, *ib.* ; not quartered in London, iv. 30 ; insufficiency of means to pay, 249, 250 ; number of men in each troop reduced, 250 ; saving effected by reduction of, 251 ; discontent of, *ib.* ; payment of, transferred to Army Committee of the Council, *ib.*

Milton, John, publishes *The Tenure of Kings and Magistrates*, i. 36 ; is appointed Latin secretary, *ib.* ; disobeys an order to answer *The Second Part of England's New Chains*, 37 ; publishes *Eikonoklastes*, 175 ; writes to the King of Spain to demand justice for Ascham's murder, 310 ; publishes a *Defence of the People of England* and writes in *Mercurius Politicus*, ii. 17 ; failure of his sight, *ib.* ; his 'Ishbosheth' article, 18 ; cries for justice on Presbyterian plotters, 19 ;

his sonnet to Cromwell, 103 ; his sonnet to Vane, 104 ; remains at the disposition of the Council, iii. 4 ; his *Second Defence of the English People*, 167 ; his advice to the Protector, 168 ; his opinion of the Parliamentary system, 169 ; his political views, *ib.* ; his sonnet on the Vaudois, iv. 193

Mitchell, Stephen, villainy of, iv. 151

Model of a New Representative, A, publication of, ii. 71

Moderate, The, the organ of the Levellers, i. 56

Modyford, Thomas, Colonel, comes to terms with Ayscue, ii. 141, 142 ; recommends an attack on Guiana, iv. 123, 124

Mompesson, John, joins Royalist insurgents, iii. 287

Monk, George, his position in Dundalk and the neighbouring country, i. 73 ; is staunch to the English interest, *ib.* ; asked to renew the Covenant, 74 ; negotiates with the Ulster Scots, to spin out time, 75 ; prepares to make overtures to O'Neill, 76 ; agrees to a cessation of hostilities with O'Neill, 77 ; his probable motives, *ib.* ; sends his convention with O'Neill to Westminster, and accompanies it with a letter to Cromwell, 78 ; refusal of the Council of State to ratify his convention with O'Neill, 83 ; Inchiquin despatched against, 90 ; rumoured conjunction with O'Neill, 92 ; his correspondence and treaty with O'Neill published, 93 ; applies for assistance to O'Neill, 98 ; is forced to surrender Dundalk, 99 ; goes to London, 103 ; visits Cromwell at Milford Haven, *ib.* ; censured and excused by Parliament, 104 ; gains Cromwell's good will, 105 ; Bright's regiment refuses to accept as Colonel, 269 ; a newly formed regiment placed under the command of, *ib.* ; agrees with Cromwell and Lambert on the effect of Leslie's descent from Doon Hill, 290 ; left by Cromwell in command in Scotland, ii. 30 ; reduces Stirling Castle, 66 ; storms Dundee, *ib.* ; sent as Commissioner to Scotland, 132 ; returns to England, 138 ; appointed one of the Generals at

Sea, 210 ; joins Deane in inviting the fleet to accept Cromwell's temporary dictatorship, 270 ; misses Tromp, iii. 32 ; puts out with Deane from Yarmouth, 33 ; fights the battle off the Gabbard, 33–37 ; continues the fight off the Flemish coast, 38 ; in sole command at the Battle of the Texel, 45 ; orders that no ships· shall be captured, 46 ; takes part in suppressing a mutiny of sailors, 58 ; grant of Scottish lands to, 87 ; Lilburne wishes to be superseded by, 98 ; arrives in Scotland, 102 ; issues a proclamation announcing the Protectorate and the Union, 103 ; offers pardon and grace, 104 ; sets a price on the heads of Middleton and others, *ib.* ; prepares for war, 105 ; takes the field, 106 ; devastates the Highlands, 107 ; pursues Middleton, 108 ; follows up the insurgents with fire and sword, 110 ; reports that the army in Scotland is favourable to the actions of the Protector, 227 ; is not informed of Overton's proceedings, 230 ; sends Overton to London, 231 ; receives information of a design to seize him, *ib.*

Monro, Andrew, advises Strachan to form an ambuscade, i. 216

Monro, Sir George, sent to besiege Londonderry, i. 78 ; movements of, 98 ; is joined by Montgomery of Ards, *ib.* ; forced to abandon the siege of Londonderry, 108 ; surrenders Inniskillen, 154 ; signs a bond uniting Royalists and Engagers, 338 ; his quarrel with Glencairn, iii. 100

Monroes, doubtful whether adherents or enemies of Montrose, i. 215

Montague, Edward, Colonel, a member of the Council of the Protectorate, iii. 2 ; attacks Birch's financial scheme, 238 ; is appointed a commissioner of the Treasury, 303 ; in joint command with Blake, iv. 229 ; wishes to disavow Meadowe, 239. *See also* Blake and Montague, the fleet under

Montague, Walter, banished, i. 172 ; is expected to tamper with the Duke of Gloucester's religion, iii. 274

Montgomery of Ards, third Viscount, 1642 (Hugh Montgomery), wishes

OLI

Coyet by, 198; desires an alliance with Sweden, 199; distracted between two Baltic policies, 201; explains his policy to Bonde, *ib.*; hopes that Charles X. will carry out the design of Gustavus Adolphus, 202; believes that the Pope and the Catholic powers are planning an attack on Protestants, 203; his ignorance of German opinion, 204; hesitates to make an alliance with Sweden against the Dutch, 205; is pleased at the Swedish victories in Poland, *ib.*; allows the levy of a thousand men for Sweden, 206; proposes a quadruple alliance, *ib.*; welcomes a mission from the Elector of Brandenburg, 207; opens his mind to Schlezer, *ib.*; urges Sweden to attack the Emperor, *ib.*; congratulates Charles X. on the birth of an heir, 211; fails to come to an agreement with Sweden, 212; invites New Englanders and West Indian colonists to settle in Jamaica, 220; attempts to conciliate the Fifth Monarchists, 232; a new lifeguard for, 234; sends Meadowe to Lisbon, 237; orders the fleet to Lisbon, 238; supports Blake against Montague, 240; desires to occupy Dunkirk, 241; dissatisfied that France does not offer a closer alliance, *ib.*; proposes to support the Swiss Protestant cantons, and sends Lockhart to France, 242; his claim to be the champion of the Protestant interest displeases Louis XIV., 248; agrees to reduce number of militia, 250; financial embarrassments of, 252; without means of carrying on wars abroad, 253; refuses to resign generalship in favour of Lambert, 254; unwilling to summon a Parliament, *ib.*; wishes to extend decimation to others than Royalists, *ib.*; illegal action of, 255; interprets Instrument of Government in his own favour, *ib.*; requires the Council should have power of excluding members from Parliament, 256; does not intend interference with elections, 257; learns from Wildman of intrigues of Anabaptists and Levellers, 259; orders stay of

ONE

proceedings against Wildman's estates, *ib.*; argues with Ludlow, 263; allows Ludlow to retire to Essex, 264; unconstitutional treatment of Vane by, 266; will not interfere at Norwich, 267. *See also* Cromwell, Oliver

O'Neill, Daniel, brings overtures from his uncle Owen O'Neill to Ormond, i. 76; sent by Ormond to Owen O'Neill, 112; reports well of his uncle's disposition to help Ormond, 138; accompanies the Scottish army invading England, ii. 34; sent to England by Charles II., iii. 277; his movements connived at by the officials at Dover, 279; expects the insurrection to succeed, 281; escape of, 294

O'Neill, Henry, commended to Ormond by his father, i. 140; defeated at Scarriffhollis and executed, ii. 107

O'Neill, Hugh, defends Clonmel, i. 155; drives back the enemy and carries his followers off, 156; appointed governor of Limerick, ii. 109; selected for execution, 123; pardoned, 124

O'Neill, Owen Roe, ill feeling between him and the Confederates, i. 70; hostile to the Scottish Presbyterians, 74; avows his detestation of both English parties, 76; condition of the army of, *ib.*; holds communication with Jones, *ib.*; negotiates with Ormond, 77; agrees to a cessation of hostilities with Monk, *ib.*; signs an agreement with Coote, 78; proposals made by Crelly on behalf of, 82; refusal of the Council of State to ratify Monk's convention with, 83; alleged relations of Cromwell with, 83, note 4; rumoured conjunction with Monk, 92; his treaty with Monk published, 93; fails to obtain powder from Monk, 98; makes overtures to Ormond, 107; relieves Coote in Londonderry, 108; determines to ally himself with Ormond, *ib.*; Ormond seeks help from, 109; excuses himself from receiving Ormond's envoy, and is suspected of waiting till he had received money from Coote, 111; Daniel O'Neill sent to, 112; illness of, *ib.*; makes an agreement with

three peers elected to seats in, 55 ; passes a Treason Act, *ib.* ; prohibits unauthorised reports, *ib.* ; orders the suppression of the *Eikon Basiliké*, 56 ; requests the Council of State to prepare an Act to restrain the liberty of the press, *ib.* ; appoints a committee to report on elections and the duration of the existing Parliament, 57 ; invited to dine in the City, 58 ; postponement of the dissolution of, 59 ; excepts Sir John Winter from pardon, 82 ; attempts to satisfy the soldiers, 85 ; prepares for an adjournment, 86 ; receives a report on Monk's convention with O'Neill, 104 ; censures and excuses Monk, *ib.* ; permits Lilburne to leave the Tower on bail, 161 ; orders the prosecution of the contrivers of *The Outcry of the Young Men*, 164 ; attempts to win the masses and passes an Act for the relief of poor prisoners, 170 ; attempts to suppress political sermons, 171 ; considers a declaration on the government of the Church, 172 ; refuses to declare the payment of tithe compulsory, *ib.* ; orders the arrest of Winter and the banishment of Digby and Montague, *ib.* ; allows the Act for relief of tender consciences to sleep, and issues a declaration against unlimited toleration, 173 ; restricts the liberty of the press, 173, 174 ; orders the committee on elections to meet daily, 176 ; orders that members of Parliament shall take the Engagement, *ib.* ; extends the obligation to officials, *ib.* ; passes an Act limiting elections in London, 177 ; sequesters the estates of Willoughby, Massey, and Bunce, 193 ; considers an Act for forcing the Engagement on the whole population, *ib.* ; excludes women from the operation of the Act, *ib.* ; adopts four hundred as the number of members in future Parliaments, and remits other questions about elections to a Committee of the whole House, 243 ; dislikes a dissolution, *ib.* ; elects a second Council of State, 244 ; attempts to conciliate the Presbyterians, 246 ; excuses Fairfax from taking the Engage-

ment, and passes an Act suspending its enforcement on officials, *ib.* ; expels delinquents from London, and erects a new High Court of Justice, 247 ; directs the Council of State to provide against invasion and tumults, 250 ; orders forces to be raised to keep down London and the West, *ib.* ; thanks Cromwell for his services in Ireland, and carries out his recommendations, 257 ; votes that Fairfax and Cromwell shall go against the Scots, *ib.* ; appoints Skippon to command London, 261 ; issues a declaration maintaining the justice of the invasion of Scotland, *ib.* ; appoints Cromwell General, *ib.* ; makes arrangements for the civil and military government of Ireland, 265 ; resolves to make reprisals for Ascham's murder, 309 ; demands prompt justice from Spain, *ib.* ; prohibits commerce with the Royalist colonies, and sends Ayscue to reduce Barbados, 317 ; orders a thanksgiving and a medal for the victory at Dunbar, ii. 1 ; passes a Blasphemy Act, *ib.* ; repeals the Recusancy Acts, 3 ; appoints a committee on courts of justice, 4 ; resolves that law proceedings shall be conducted in English, *ib.* ; hears of a Royalist outbreak in Norfolk, 8 ; resolves Lichfield Cathedral be pulled down, 23 ; invites Cromwell to Westminster, 58 ; thanks Cromwell, *ib.*; resolves that nine prisoners shall be tried, 59 ; orders that Charles's supporters shall be tried by a court-martial, 60 ; refuses to pardon Derby and his two officers, 61 ; pardons Love's accomplices, and shows leniency to the captured officers, 62 ; question of its dissolution raised, 69 ; difficulties in the way of a dissolution of, 71 ; pamphlets on the subject of elections to, *ib.* ; a day fixed for the dissolution of, 72 ; its chance of gaining popularity, 73 ; the fourth Council of State elected by, 74 ; fines Primate, and fines and banishes Lilburne, 80 ; passes an Act of Oblivion, 81 ; appoints commissioners on law reform, 82 ; neglects their recommendations, *ib.* ; Com-

THE END.